DATE

891.73
B113f
I

**Fallen**
    Isaac Babel

# ISAAC BABEL

## RUSSIAN MASTER OF THE SHORT STORY

# RUSSIAN MASTE

*10⁰⁰*

# ISAAC BABEL

# F THE SHORT STORY

### By JAMES E. FALEN

*1935.*

*PG*
*3476*
*B2*
*266*

**THE UNIVERSITY OF TENNESSEE PRESS: Knoxville**

DISCARDED

EL CAMINO COLLEGE
LIBRARY

Copyright © 1974 by The University of Tennessee Press, Knoxville.
All rights reserved. Manufactured in the United States of America.

*Library of Congress Cataloging in Publication Data*

Falen, James E          1935–
  Isaac Babel, Russian master of the short story.
  Bibliography: p. 239– 266.
  1.  Babel', Isaak Emmanuilovich, 1894–1941.
I.  Title.
PG3476.B2Z66          891.7'3'42          74-7169
ISBN 0-87049-156-3

Frontispiece sketch by an unknown artist in *Literaturnoe nasledstvo*
(Moscow, 1965), LXXIV, 497.

Certain excerpts in this volume are included with permission from
the following:

*Isaac Babel—The Collected Stories,* ed. and trans. by Walter Morison.
Reprinted by permission of S. G. Phillips, Inc. from THE COL-
LECTED STORIES by Isaac Babel
Copyright © 1955 by S. G. Phillips, Inc.

*Isaac Babel: The Lonely Years 1925–1939, Unpublished Stories and
Private Correspondence,* ed. by Nathalie Babel and trans. by Andrew
R. MacAndrew. Copyright © 1964 by Farrar, Straus & Giroux, Inc.

*Dissonant Voices in Soviet Literature,* ed. by Patricia Blake and Max
Hayward. Copyright © 1962 by Pantheon Books/ A Division of Random House, Inc.

*Isaac Babel: Lyubka the Cossack and Other Stories,* trans. by Andrew
R. MacAndrew. Copyright © 1963 by Andrew R. MacAndrew. Reprinted by permission of The New American Library.

*To Eve*

# PREFACE

In the first half of the 1920s, there appeared a new and original voice in Russian literature. It belonged to Isaac Babel, a Jew from Odessa, whose war stories and other miniatures—appearing first in provincial newspapers and subsequently in the leading Soviet periodicals of the day—created a sensation and made their author a literary star of the first magnitude. Babel is now recognized, some half a century later, as one of this century's masters of the short story. His fame rests mainly on three early cycles of stories: *The Odessa Tales,* which portrays a band of Jewish gangsters in half-serious, half-comic epic colors; a small group of "autobiographical" stories based loosely on Babel's childhood; and *Red Cavalry,* a collection of thirty-five impressionistic pieces reflecting the author's experiences as a correspondent attached to the Soviet Cavalry during the 1920 Polish campaign. Babel subsequently wrote two plays, several films, and a number of additional stories—a few of the last among his best work.

Quite early in his career he enjoyed the reputation of a master stylist and teacher of young writers. During the thirties, however, as the Soviet political and cultural atmosphere worsened, Babel practically ceased writing. Although he never relinquished his faith in the future and steadfastly refused to join his wife and other members of his family who had emigrated to western Europe, Babel's position became increasingly difficult. Periodically under attack for the ideological shortcomings of his earlier work and constantly under pressure to justify his existence by supplying appropriate works for the new Soviet era, he played a dangerous but apparently successful waiting game. Then suddenly, in May 1939, he was arrested. His name was erased from the history of Soviet literature, and not until he was posthumously rehabilitated during the post-Stalin "thaw" were any of his works republished.

In this study I have found it both impossible and undesirable to separate the account of Babel's life from that of his works. He is an intensely personal, even autobiographical writer, for whom questions of private identity play a central role. Although facts and events in his work have been imaginatively distorted in their transmutation into art, I have thought it best to examine the life and the work together in the hope that a fuller sense of both the man and his art might thus emerge. Since the significance of Babel's Jewish heritage is especially important, I have sought to place him within the context of a cultural as well as a more specifically literary tradition.

The first several chapters examine those aspects of Babel's background and personality which seem important in defining his central concerns as an artist. His early formative work is analyzed in terms of his developing aesthetic and some of the influences which helped shape that aesthetic are examined in detail. I have tried also to describe Babel's place within the tradition of the early Soviet period in particular and within the modernist movement in general.

The central chapters, the core of the study, deal with *The Odessa Tales* and *Red Cavalry*, those two major cycles on which Babel's fame largely rests. The latter remains his masterpiece. Its stories are not easy to describe, but they are difficult to forget. A unique combination of epic, lyric, and dramatic modes, intensely concentrated and brilliant stylistically, dealing with violence in an atmosphere of ironic tension and moral ambiguity, they are both powerfully moving and deeply disturbing. Because of Babel's unique compositional techniques, his stories often demand an actual motif-by-motif analysis, and I have accordingly given rather detailed readings of several stories, paying particular attention to the writer's use of mythic symbolism.

The final chapter deals with Babel's efforts, in the years after *Red Cavalry*, to find both new material and new forms. In a personal as well as a national sense, the thirties were a time of crisis and frustration, and Babel's struggle to remain an artist was pursued against formidable odds. His experiments in the last decade of his life included attempts to develop a new type of story, to write in longer fictional forms, and, most promisingly, to turn to the drama. By the mid-thirties, however, Babel, like other serious writers in the Soviet Union, was fast becoming unpublishable. In the epilogue I have suggested that his unexplained arrest may have been occasioned by the screenplay that was his last completed work.

Finally, I must express my indebtedness to the work of many people, both in and outside the Soviet Union, who have contributed much to whatever understanding I may have of a fascinating writer and most attractive man.

# A NOTE ON
# TRANSLITERATION

The standard international scholarly system for the transliteration of Russian has been used for all citations of bibliographical material and for the rendering of words as words. Within the text proper, however, personal and place names have been rendered in accordance with accepted English usage. Although this has necessarily resulted in some inconsistency in the treatment accorded specific letters, it does avoid an even worse grotesquerie (e.g., presenting the reader with the formation of "Trockij" in place of the more familiar "Trotsky").

# CONTENTS

# ISAAC BABEL
## RUSSIAN MASTER OF THE SHORT STORY

*"I have spent my life in struggle with this man."*

Isaac Babel, on autographing a photograph of
himself for a friend, quoted by L. Livšic, in
"Materialy k tvorčeskoj biografii I. Babelja,"
*Voprosy literatury*, VIII, No. 4 (1964), p. 135.

# I

# EARLY YEARS

*I am aging rapidly . . . from an incomprehensible ailment, implanted within my frail body in childhood.*[1]

The origins and history of Isaac Babel's family are relatively obscure. The writer's mother and father both came from Jewish families who had been living in the Ukraine for at least several generations. Their forebears were probably peddlers and tradesmen from various small towns where Jews had settled and established communities. As their circumstances improved, these people moved to larger cities where the opportunities for trade and commerce were greater, but always within the limits of southern Russia, to which the Jews were confined by Czarist edict.

By the time Isaac Babel was born, on July 13, 1894, both the Babels and the Shvevels, his mother's family, had been established for some while in Odessa, where Emmanuel Babel, his father, was a sporadically successful middle-class merchant. Success of any lasting sort seems to have eluded Babel's father, who was never able to make his way into the ranks of the upper middle-class.

Shortly after their son's birth the Babels moved to Nikolayev,

---

1 A remark by Isaac Babel reported by Konstantin Paustovsky in *Vremja bol'- šix ožidanij* (Odessa, 1961), 133.

a small port not far from Odessa, where, in 1899, their second and last child, a girl, was born. The family spent some ten years in Nikolayev, living in a house that boasted a garden, a dovecote, and a courtyard. During these years in Nikolayev, Babel's mother taught her son to read, and it was here that he first attended school and began the study of languages, in which he excelled. In addition to studying Russian and Hebrew, the boy undertook very early to master English, French, and German.

There is little direct evidence concerning the relations between Babel and his parents. Babel's mother, the "amiable Fenya" of his letters, was evidently an affectionate and indulgent parent, strong in her feelings of family solidarity and always loyal to her son, if somewhat bewildered by his career. For his part, Babel honored his mother with lifelong love and devotion. His letters give eloquent testimony to the special tenderness of his feelings for her, and in his art the figure of the mother occupies a dominant place as a leading motif and symbol.

Babel's father is a more elusive figure. Described as volatile and impetuous in personality, a man of legendary rages,[2] Emmanuel Babel was the owner of a small warehouse, a business which he had established only after working for several years as a salesman of agricultural machinery. The only available description depicts him as a melancholy man with little talent for commercial affairs and a bent for literary-philosophical pursuits:

> Returning home after a depressing sojourn at his long unsuccessful business, he would turn to writing satirical observations. He wouldn't show them to anybody, these notes in which he ridiculed the worldly vanity of his neighbors. They were kept in his office account book.[3]

It is not uncommon, of course, for a man to mock the standards by which he is judged a failure. And yet, if he himself concurs in this judgment his values and aspirations are apt, in some measure, to remain conditioned by the very standards which he

---

[2] Nathalie Babel, "Introduction," *Isaac Babel: The Lonely Years 1925–1939* (New York, 1964), xvi.

[3] S. Gext, "U steny strastnogo monastyrja," *Naš sovremennik*, No. 4 (1959), 230.

4

condemns. Emmanuel Babel was never able to discover a satisfying alternative to the business career in which he failed to excel. Embittered and unhappy, he lavished upon his only son those ambitions that were denied him in his own life. His son was to succeed where he had failed—if not in the commercial world, then through the attainment of intellectual eminence or through cultural achievement. The field of endeavor might vary, but success itself remained essential. "My father could have reconciled himself to poverty," wrote Babel later, "but fame he had to have."[4]

It seems obvious that Babel's relationship with his father is central to his inmost drives and motivation. He accepts the challenge to succeed and looks upon it as an almost sacred mission: "When I go through moments of despair, I think of Papa. What he expected and wanted from us was success, not moaning. Remembering him, I feel a surge of strength, and I urge myself forward. Everything I promised him, not in words but in thought, I shall carry out, because I have a sacred respect for his memory."[5]

But such a legacy is often a burden as well as a gift. It imposes upon a man obligations which he may not consider his own, duties that may threaten his private sense of self. It is evident that Babel's attitude toward his father was ambivalent. As a result of the aura of failure surrounding his father's life, he had both an urgent need to prove himself and at the same time a strong compulsion to resist the kind of traditional, middle-class Jewish values which his father had never abandoned. One of the major themes running through Babel's work is the revolt against paternal (or, as he sometimes calls it, "ancestral") pressure. This hostility and bitterness are directed not only against the commercial traditions of his father's class, but against its higher intellectual and cultural values as well, and at times his animus is specifically aimed at the pattern of Jewish life.

Like many parents who wish their children greater success

---

[4] "Probuždenie," in *I. Babel': Izbrannoe* (Moscow, 1957), 242. Hereinafter, except as otherwise noted, references are to this printing.

[5] Nathalie Babel, *Isaac Babel: The Lonely Years*, 87.

than they have enjoyed, Babel's father placed great faith in education. Success to him meant that his son must speak several foreign languages and that he must excel in the study of Hebrew and music. Although the younger Babel had a gift and a liking for languages, he nonetheless resented the scholastic regimen that prevailed in his home. The Hebrew lessons, as well as study of the Bible and the Talmud, lasted until he was sixteen years old, according to Babel's own account,[6] but the compulsory violin lessons faded away much earlier under the bright sun of the harbor to which Babel fled from his career as a virtuoso.

It was impossible, of course, for education to take place entirely at home, and Babel was expected to distinguish himself in his school work as well as at his private lessons. For Jews, however, the road to educational success in prerevolutionary Russia had some special obstacles. In "The Story of My Dovecote," Babel recalls in a characteristic blend of humor and bitterness the trials of applying for secondary school:

> I was only nine years old, and I was scared about my exams. I couldn't afford less than an A in both Russian and Math, because the Jewish quota at our school was very low—only five percent. Out of forty boys only two Jews could get into the preparatory class. The teachers used to question us very slyly, and they never asked anyone else such complicated questions. So when father promised to buy me the pigeons he demanded A-pluses in both subjects. He absolutely tortured me, and I fell into a state of endless daydreaming, into a long despairing childish daydream. I went to the exam in this state and still somehow came out better than everyone else. I was a good student and received my two A's. But then everything went wrong. Khariton Effrusi, the merchant who exported wheat to Marseille, slipped someone a five hundred ruble bribe. They gave me A-minuses instead of A's, and young Effrusi got my place in school. It was a terrible blow to my father.[7]

The only alternative to resignation and defeat was to work even harder to prepare for the next year's examinations. Babel

6 "Avtobiografija," *I. Babel': Izbrannoe*, 11.
7 "Istorija moej golubjatni," *I. Babel': Izbrannoe*, 186–87.

persevered and at the beginning of 1905 he was duly enrolled in the Commercial School of Odessa.

This was also the year in which Babel's parents returned to Odessa to live. The move was undertaken partly because young Isaac was to attend secondary school in Odessa, but it was also precipitated by an event that would leave a profound impression on the future writer. In the widespread disturbances following the Revolution of 1905, Nikolayev was the scene of one of those nightmarish pogroms which were periodically inflicted on the Jews of Russia. In two largely autobiographical stories, "The Story of My Dovecote" and "First Love," Babel has given stark and yet surprisingly lyrical descriptions of the brutal event as comprehended by a ten-year-old boy. The eruption of hatred and violence which the boy encounters for the first time becomes, rather strangely, not only a discovery of despair, but a promise of exultation. His world grows "tiny and terrible," but it is replaced almost immediately by a vision of great beauty and serenity. Unafraid now, the boy weeps "as bitterly, fully, and happily as I never wept again in all my life." What Babel is describing in these stories is a kind of awakening, the emergence through contact with violence of a sense of spiritual and sexual power. The loss of the child's innocent world is balanced by the gain of something terrible and beautiful. The stories are not, in all their details, an accurate account of Babel's own childhood experiences, but the images they evoke, awful and awesome, do represent an inner experience. As the purified recollection of the grown man, they possess a truth that is beyond mere factual accuracy.

Babel's family was not physically harmed during the pogrom, and life in Odessa soon resumed its normal course: lessons and more lessons. Forced to study constantly at home, Babel found the hours at his new school relaxing. The Nicholas I Commercial School of Odessa was gay, rowdy, noisy, and multilingual. His fellow students were a mixed lot: sons of foreign merchants, children of Jewish brokers, Poles from distinguished families,

7

and Old Believers.[8] Between classes at this school of all nations, the young scholars would run off to the jetty at the port or to the Greek coffeehouses in the town to play billiards, or sometimes they ventured to the Moldavanka to drink cheap Bessarabian wine in the seamy taverns.

Babel mentions only one of his teachers from this period, a Frenchman from Brittany who had a gift for literature. He introduced the boy to Odessa's French colony and to the French classics. Attracted by Rabelais and especially by the style and method of Flaubert and Maupassant, Babel began at the age of fifteen a two-year apprenticeship in composition, writing his schoolboy stories in French. Of these early stories he says: "I wrote them for two years but then gave them up; my peasant characters and other reflections as an author turned out colorless. Only the dialogue was successful."[9]

None of these French stories appears to have survived, but the devotion to French masters was to be a lasting influence and the search for "color" a continuing preoccupation.

The Odessa in which Babel spent his youth was in many ways unique among Russian cities. A settlement since at least the fourteenth century, the city had belonged in turn to Lithuania, the Crimean Tartars, and the Turks. Russia had annexed the growing town in 1791, and by the middle of the next century it had become the second largest foreign trade port in the country. Its population, which in 1914 numbered more than 600,000, included large numbers of Russians, Ukrainians, Jews (almost one third), Greeks, Tartars, Bulgarians, and Rumanians. Because of its heterogeneous population and its far-flung trading contacts, the city became a cosmopolitan center with an especially European flavor, characteristics noted by Pushkin as early as the first half of the nineteenth century:

> I lived then in dusty Odessa . . .
> There for a long time skies are clear.

[8] The Old Believers was a schismatic sect which broke off from the main body of the Russian Orthodox Church in the 17th century.
[9] "Avtobiografija," *I. Babel': Izbrannoe*, 11.

There, stirring, an abundant trade
sets up its sails.
There all exhales, diffuses Europe,
all glitters with the South, and brindles
with live variety.
The tongue of golden Italy
resounds along the gay street where
walks the proud Slav,
Frenchman, Spaniard, Armenian,
and Greek, and the heavy Moldavian,
and the son of Egyptian soil,
the retired Corsair, Morali.[10]

Often called the Paris or Marseilles of Russia, Odessa—with its university, its libraries and museums, its opera, theater, and ballet—offered its citizens a vigorous and stimulating cultural life. As a major center of Jewish culture in particular, the city gave its Jewish community a necessary sense of place and identity. The early years of this century were hard ones for Russia's Jews— a time of officially sponsored anti-Semitism, of planned pogroms, and of limited educational opportunity. Yet in Odessa, the Jews flourished in a sense. Intellectual life was especially energetic, and Hebrew poetry may be said to have had its modern rebirth there. True, the city impressed some observers as showing signs of incipient decline, but it is nonetheless at this very stage in its history that Odessa produced an unusual number of writers, scholars, and journalists. The Soviet writers born or raised in Odessa during the first quarter of this century include not only Isaac Babel, but Vera Inber (born 1890), Eduard Bagritsky (born 1895), Ilya Ilf (born 1897), Yury Olesha (who moved to Odessa in 1902 at the age of three), and the two Kataevs, Valentin and Evgeny (born 1897 and 1903).[11]

Nor was Odessa preeminent only in culture and commerce.

10 Stanza XX from "Fragments of Onegin's Journey." In *Eugene Onegin: A Novel in Verse by Aleksandr Pushkin*, trans. from the Russian, with a commentary by Vladimir Nabokov, Bollingen Series LXXII (New York, 1964), I, 340.
11 The critic Viktor Shklovsky found enough homogeneity in the literary flowering of the South to even argue the existence of a "southern school." (V. Šklovskij, "Jugo-Zapad," *Literaturnaja gazeta*, Jan. 14, 1933.)

Long considered a headquarters of the country's criminal underworld, the city's Moldavanka district was home to thieves, smugglers, pirates, fences, extortionists, and other generally disreputable and eccentric characters. For Isaac Babel these people and the life they led, dangerous and primitive, were especially fascinating. Their repudiation of middle-class respectability posed an attractive challenge and provided an exciting contrast to Babel's world of books and study. Babel himself, on the eve of the Revolution, commented on the atmosphere of his native city:

> Odessa has a very poor, crowded and suffering Jewish ghetto, a very self-satisfied bourgeoisie and a very reactionary and anti-Semitic city duma. In Odessa the spring evenings are sweet and oppressive, with the heady scent of the acacia and the unimaginable and even light of the full moon over the dark sea. . . . Odessa has a port, and in it—ships, from Newcastle, Cardiff, Marseilles and Port Said. There are Negroes, Englishmen, Frenchmen and Americans. Odessa has known both times of bloom and times of decay; of poetic, almost lighthearted and very helpless decay.[12]

Young Isaac was eager to participate in the variety of experience offered by this environment. The color and vitality of life in the port city developed and nourished his appetite for the sounds, smells, and tastes that beckoned all around him. As a child, however, he was sickly and frail. Stunted and physically inept because of excessive study and lack of exercise, he was subject to chronic asthmatic and nervous disorders and at an early age already suffered from weak eyesight. The spectacles that he had to wear became for Babel a symbol of his estrangement from a life of direct physical involvement in experience.

The desire for success had been implanted in Babel by his father, but he needed to satisfy this desire in his own way and not, as his father might have wished, by pursuing a respectable academic or professional career. Unathletic and bookish, aesthetic and intellectual, Babel nevertheless sensed and responded to another, more physical principle of existence, to the way of the

[12] From Babel's essay "Odessa," quoted in *Sovetskie Pisateli, Avtobiografii v dvux tomax* (Moscow, 1959), I, 102.

body as well as the way of the mind. This conflict was to be fundamental in his development as man and artist. The themes of initiation into experience, the test of courage, and other rites of manhood are a running thread through much of Babel's writing, and often such trials are seen as particularly important and difficult for the intellectual. Testimony from sources outside Babel's own writing corroborates the importance he attached to this need for experience. S. Gekht, reminiscing about Babel, speaks of how passionately the writer craved the excitement of the streets and of how he gently ridiculed his friend, the poet Bagritsky, for his inveterate fondness for books: "I have already escaped my bookishness and it is time, my friend, for you to do the same."[13]

One of his autobiographical stories, "In the Basement," describes Babel's own childhood obsession with books and the vivid sense of loss that accompanied his concentration upon these "objects of mind":

> I was an untruthful child. It came from reading. My imagination was always on fire. I read during class, at recess, on my way home, at night under the table, hidden by the tablecloth that hung down all the way to the floor. Because of books I missed all the important things of this world—running away from class to the harbor, the beginning of billiard games in the coffee houses on Greek Street, going swimming at Langeron.[14]

Although the Jews of Odessa had a sense of belonging to the community and were able to participate in its energetic life, the stigma of the ghetto remained, and Babel is often bitter in speaking of his youth. Raymond Rosenthal, who has written an impressive appreciation of Babel, comments on Babel's reaction to ghetto life:

> Most accounts of his youth contain as a running theme this urge to escape from the ghetto. But this wish was hardly unique with Babel. Under the buffeting of the great social storms of the late 19th and early 20th centuries in Russia, the ghetto stood in a

13 S. Gext, "Providat' by sprosit'," *Naš sovremennik*, No. 4 (1959), 235.
14 *I. Babel': Izbrannoe,* 233.

particularly exposed position. All the fury of aroused reaction was directed at its inhabitants, as though to warn them against the social transformation for which they longed. Yet in Babel, the impulse to escape took a contradictory form. While trying to throw off the hermetic restraints of the ghetto, he was still unable to rid himself of its molding influences. Throughout his writings it is this conflict between the ineradicable imprint of his Jewish heritage and his passionate wish to rise out of its circumscribed environment that imparts a lyrical tension to his prose. . . . For him, the cultural walls of Jewish life had become an obstacle to his most poignant aims.[15]

And what were these most poignant aims whose promise seemed to lie outside the ghetto walls, outside the limits of Jewish experience? In "The Awakening," a story that is central to an understanding of his life and art, Babel tells of some of his frustrated aspirations at thirteen: his desire to escape from the Jewish destiny implied by his father's wish to make him a child prodigy on the violin and his longing instead to learn to swim, to understand nature, and to write. The story is a metaphorical picture of two worlds: the closed Jewish life of his forebears, of "freaks" and "dwarfs" as he calls the musical prodigies, and the world of Efim Nikitich Smolich, proofreader of the *Odessa News*, suntanned athlete and idol of the local children. When Babel escapes from his music lessons to the port, it is to Nikitich that he runs, to the man who, like a father, can teach him to swim, who will criticize his youthful writings and encourage him to develop a feeling for nature. The yearnings attributed here to his childhood are reenacted by Babel in various guises throughout his maturity, and their expression becomes a recurring motif throughout his writing.

But "The Awakening" suggests an even deeper and more unattainable desire, one hidden from Babel himself. At times he seems to wish that art and nature become one. The lack of experience that so torments him is invariably expressed in intellectual and aesthetic terms. The boy discovers that he lacks

15 Raymond Rosenthal, "The Fate of Isaac Babel," *Commentary* (Feb. 1947), 127–28.

knowledge of nature, that he does not know the names for plants and birds. The implication is not that he will give up writing in order to experience nature, but that he will learn to put nature into art. Insofar as this means endowing the word with the weight of experience, it is no more than that essential ingredient of art sought by all writers. But Babel seems to make no distinction between the living of an experience and its aesthetic reincarnation. He desires simultaneously both to express and to possess, and this effort at making art itself into experience, this attempt to conjoin the aesthetic and the sensual, is one of Babel's most lasting struggles.

In 1910, Babel finished his studies at the Nicholas I Commercial School. Unable to attend the university because of the Jewish quota, he was sent by his father, in 1911, to Kiev to continue his education at the Institute of Financial and Business Studies. In Kiev, Babel met his future wife, Evgenia Gronfein, daughter of a friend and business associate of his father's, and here, too, his ambition to become a writer began to take definite shape.

At the outbreak of World War I, the Institute was moved from Kiev to Saratov. There, in addition to receiving his degree, Babel wrote what is probably the earliest of his surviving writings. The piece, entitled "Childhood at Grandmother's" and dated "Saratov, November 12, 1915,"[16] is a reminiscence of a Saturday spent at his grandmother's in the years when he was a gymnasium student. The narrative demonstrates, in spite of its brevity, the author's ability to develop a picture of considerable social and psychological complexity.

On a day in early spring, the young narrator is walking along the main street of his city on the way to his grandmother's. During his walk he lingers at shop windows, seems almost to study their contents, reads the signs and theater advertisements along the way, notices the stones of the houses he passes as well as the look of people and the quality of the atmosphere. From such

16 "Detstvo u Babuški," published for the first time in *Literaturnoe nasledstvo*, (Moscow, 1965), LXXIV, 483–88.

13

casual manifestations of the city he tries to extract some secret knowledge of "the essence of things." An adolescent dreamer, the youth finds the world mysterious and exciting. While standing before a ladies' wear shop and gazing at the lingerie displayed in its window, he collides with a university student. Jostled harshly back into reality, the boy is intimidated by the older man, by his large black mustache, his condescending laughter, and superior knowledge. Embarrassed and confused, he hurries on to the security of his grandmother's, where domestic warmth, supervised study, and plentiful Jewish food await him. For a moment he has retreated from adolescence into childhood: "I was a dreamer, that's true, but with a big appetite."[17]

But even at grandmother's not everything is reassuring. In contrast to the streets—open, bustling, alive, full of people and things—his grandmother's room is small and close, the door locked, the boy a prisoner at his desk. Where the streets had been cool and bracing, the room is hot and stifling. The wrinkled old lady's world consists of her son, her grandson, her dog, and her flowers. It is a Jewish world in which only study, diligence, and knowledge are counted as valuable. His grandmother is a despotic, bitter old woman whom life has made cynical and untrusting: "Study and you will achieve everything—wealth and fame. You must know everything. Everybody will fall at your feet and humble himself before you. Everyone must envy you. Do not trust people. Have no friends. Don't give them money. Don't give them your heart."[18]

His grandmother's precepts and her harsh treatment of the timid maid frighten and depress the boy. Under her watchful eye he is reading the scene in Turgenev's "First Love" where Vladimir's father strikes Ludmila with his whip. The surroundings and the story combine to produce a peculiarly powerful moment:

> At this point I had to stop reading and walk around the room. But Grandmother just sat motionless, and even the hot, stifling

17 *Ibid.*, 483.　　　　　　　18 *Ibid.*, 486.

air didn't stir, as if it sensed that I was studying and couldn't be disturbed. The heat in the room kept increasing. . . . Everything seemed so odd to me at that moment, and I wanted with all my strength to run and yet to stay forever. The darkening room, Grandmother's yellow eyes, her small figure wrapped in a shawl and all huddled and silent in the corner, the hot air, the closed door, and the crack of the whip, its penetrating whistle—only now do I understand how strange it all was and how much it affected me.[19]

As on the street before the shop window, the moment is broken by an outsider. The music teacher arrives and the hated violin lessons begin. Then the teacher of Hebrew comes and goes, and with evening come Grandmother's stories and reminiscences and her frightening commandments. To the boy the day's contrasts become overpowering: "Her stern precepts pressed heavily—and forever—on my weak and untried shoulders. . . . I felt stifled, I couldn't breathe, I needed to run out into the air, to escape. . . ."[20]

Readers familiar with Babel's work will recognize much in this early, though recently published, piece. There is that sense of two worlds: a narrow, closed Jewish world and the larger, open world outside. With their different languages, it is almost as if the boy were moving back and forth between two different countries. While there is uncertainty and ambiguity in the boy's attitude toward Grandmother and home, the dominant reaction is the need for flight, for air, for escape. Other recognizably Babelian elements are the sensitivity and impressionability of the narrator and the lyric-romantic tone that occasionally forces its way through the factual narrative sections. There is also an intimation of the adolescent's awakening sensuality, a theme which is introduced initially by the shop-window episode and then expanded through reference to Turgenev's story. In the latter instance Babel's method is to combine naturalistic detail with an intensely felt literary association. Since the literary reference, however, also involves juxtaposing the sexual motif with an

19 *Ibid.*, 484.     20 *Ibid.*, 486.

image of violence, the boy's withdrawal into art produces no sense of resolution or harmony. Instead, his inner turmoil is intensified.

Finally one must remark the use of a first-person narrative with strong autobiographical overtones; and since the narrator stands at a distance in time from the events described, there is even a tone of ironic detachment in his attitude toward himself and his romanticism: "I . . . was certain that I could see in them what mattered most, the inner secret—what we adults call the 'essence of things.' . . . I was just a kid at the time and I didn't understand anything, but I was affected by the spring anyway and I blossomed and grew rosy-cheeked under the light cool air."[21] There are many hints of the later Babel in this early story, and if it does not exhibit the mature writer's tightness and control, if it lacks the quality of thematic depth within its impressionistic framework, it nonetheless seems the work of a writer already well aware of his powers.

In a recent article, I. A. Smirin, a Soviet scholar who has performed valuable research on Babel, refers to another Babel story from the same period. The manuscript, untitled and with the final pages missing, has never been published, and Smirin's discussion of it is the only information available:

> These pages preserved in the writers' archive are written in a confident hand and show us Babel's searches for a dynamic short story form as well as his first close contact with the element of humor. A rich priest, Father Ivan, accompanied by his tenant Yankel, goes into town to rescue his son from an unpleasant situation. The humorous conflict at the base of the story is obvious from the very first lines: " 'Exploitation,' said Father Ivan, 'We moan and sigh, but still we're enmeshed by blood-sucking spiders. . . . Just take note of how things are—The medical doctor is a Jew, the merchant, captain of trade or industry—a Jew, my young son's science tutor— a Jew. . . .' " Later it develops—and in this lies the story's humor— that Father Ivan's "exploiter" turns out to be the frail Jew Yankel, who drags along behind with his master's heavy suitcases, fawns over him humbly, consoles him in his adversities, inter-

21 *Ibid.*, 483.

cedes for him with the investigator and finally emerges as the priest's benefactor and saviour. Although the end of the story is missing, it is not difficult to guess that Yankel will save the priest's son who is under trial and thus bring to a culmination the comic incongruity between "exploited" and "exploiter."[22]

Smirin also notes in this story a tendency toward the grotesque and toward concentrated aphoristic formulas, especially in Babel's use of dialogue. In Yankel's remark about the priest's heavy baggage ("Oh my god . . . these aren't suitcases, they're tigers") he hears a hint of the intonation of the later *Odessa Tales*.

These early stories give a picture of how Babel's individual manner was developing. We see him mastering the devices of a type of plotless lyric narrative set against a background of precise psychological details, as in "Childhood at Grandmother's," and we see him developing a more plotted or anecdotal story with heavy emphasis on dialogue, as in the Yankel fragment. The two stories thus belong to an experimental stage in which Babel was seeking various ways to discover his personal medium, his unique voice. He was not yet fully capable of effectively combining those lyric and comic modes of expression to which he was equally drawn. In his later work Babel's effort to integrate these differing components of his artistic personality will be seen to move increasingly toward irony, that tonal range in which the lyric and the comic find at least a tentative, if uneasy, place of meeting.

[22] "Na puti k Konarmii," *Literaturnoe nasledstvo*, LXXIV, 471–72.

# II

# LITERARY APPRENTICESHIP

*A phrase is born into the world both good and bad at the same time. The secret consists in a twist, barely perceptible. The lever must lie in the hand and grow warm, and you may turn it only once, not twice.*[1]

At the end of 1915, taking with him a growing confidence in his ability, Babel moved to St. Petersburg, the northern capital of Imperial Russia and symbolic home of her nineteenth-century literary masters. Babel had finished with formal schooling, although his parents were under the impression that he was to continue his studies.[2] Free at last of the family, its restraints and pressures, he was determined to be a writer. St. Petersburg was not immediately receptive to the aspiring author, and more than a year passed before he succeeded in getting anything published. When he did, it was in a journal edited by Maxim Gorky. Babel has described the occasion in a reminiscence entitled "The Beginning":

> Twenty years ago, when I was of a quite tender age, I was roaming around Saint Petersburg with false papers in my pocket and—severe winter that it was—without an overcoat. I must admit I had an overcoat, but I didn't wear it as a matter of principle. My only possessions at the time were a few stories—as risqué as they were short. I took these stories around the editorial offices; but no

[1] From Babel's story "Gjui de Mopassan," in *I. Babel': Izbrannoe,* 250.
[2] He did enroll briefly in an institute for psychoneurology. See "Iz pisem k druz' jam," *Znamja,* No. 8 (Aug. 1964), 147n.

one thought of reading them; and if anyone accidentally chanced to glance at them, they produced the opposite of the desired effect. The editor of one journal sent me out a ruble through the porter; another editor said my manuscripts were utter nonsense, but that his father-in-law was a flour dealer and I might find work with him as a shop assistant. I declined and realized there was nothing left for me to do but go to Gorky. . . . I went to see him on Bolshaya Monetnaya Street. My heart kept pounding, then stopping dead.[3]

Gorky agreed to read Babel's manuscripts and told him to come back in three days. When he returned, Gorky disposed of his other callers before turning to Babel.

Everyone left. We were alone—Maxim Gorky and I, who had fallen from another planet, from our own Russian Marseilles (must I explain that I mean Odessa). Gorky called me into his office, and what he said to me there decided my fate. "There are small nails," he said "—and there are nails as large as my finger," and he brought his long, powerful, delicately chiseled finger up to my eyes. "A writer's path, dear dreamer, . . . is strewn with nails, mostly of the larger sort. You will have to walk upon them barefoot and they'll make you bleed. And with each year the blood will flow more freely. . . . If you are a weak man, they'll buy and sell you, harass you and lull you to sleep, and you will wilt while pretending to be a tree in bloom. . . . But for an honest man, an honest writer and revolutionary, to travel this path is a great honor; and it is for this arduous journey, my friend, that I give you my blessings. . . ."

I can think of no more important hours in my life than those I spent in the editorial office of *The Chronicle*. When I came out, I had lost all physical sense of my existence. In the 30-degree, blue, burning frost I ran in delirium through the huge, majestic corridors of the capital, open to the remote dark sky. I came to my senses only when I had left the Black River and the New Village behind me.

Half the night was gone before I returned to the Petersburg side, to the room I had rented the day before from a young and inexperienced woman, the wife of an engineer.[4]

Another picture of Babel's meeting with Gorky is given by

3 "Načalo," in *I. Babel': Izbrannoe*, 282.
4 *Ibid.*, 283–84. The young woman Babel mentions, Anna G. Slonim, became a lifelong friend. Babel maintained his ties with the Slonim family and in the late twenties even did some of his writing in their Moscow apartment.

the Hungarian writer Ervin Sinkó, who lived for several months of 1936–37 in the same house with Babel and had occasion to hear many of his reminiscences. "He had prepared for this visit for a long time but postponed it again and again. Each time he wanted to set out for Gorky's or was already on the way he discovered new failings in his story. He rewrote it innumerable times, filed and polished it and finally did look up Gorky."[5]

The lavish attention and care which Babel devoted to a story, his way of rewriting the whole thing several times and then further polishing it, were a permanent part of his method. Konstantin Paustovsky, in his well-known reminiscences of Babel, speaks of a later story ("Ljubka the Cossack") that went through twenty-two separate revisions.[6] Not infrequently the author's dating of a story, covering an eight- or ten-year span, indicates an extremely long period of composition.

This first meeting with Gorky was the beginning of a friendship between the two men that lasted until Gorky's death in 1936. In all that time Gorky encouraged, defended, and protected Babel through all the vicissitudes of his literary career. For Babel, Gorky was "my conscience, judge and example. I am linked to him by twenty years of unclouded friendship and love."[7] At the time of their initial meeting in 1916, Gorky decided to publish two of Babel's stories in his journal *The Chronicle.*

The stories were "Ilya Isaakovich and Margarita Prokofievna" and "Mama, Rimma and Alla." In some respects they seem less characteristic of the later Babel than the two pieces previously discussed. They give a picture of bleak, lower middle-class existence beset with personal worries, financial problems, and the loss of human dignity. In the first story a Jewish merchant has ventured into the city illegally and has to hide from the police in order to finish his business in town. He spends his

5 E. Sinkó, *Roman eines Romans, Moskauer Tagebuch* (Cologne, 1962), 296.

6 K. Paustovsky, *Vremja bol'šix ožidanij,* 134.

7 From a letter dated June 19, 1936, written to his mother just after Gorky's death ("Vyderžki iz pisem I. È. Babelja k materi i sestre," *Vozdušnye puti* [New York, 1963], No. 3, p. 112).

nights with a prostitute whose initial hostility is worn away by the almost domestic companionship of their two days together. When he leaves for Odessa she appears at the station with the gift of a greasy bag of food for him to take on his journey.

In the second story a woman is unable to cope with either the rude, vulgar students who rent rooms in her house or with her two rebellious teen-age daughters who succumb to a dreary pattern of seduction. The petulant Polish student who assaults her daughter Rimma is capable of neither warmth nor affection; Rimma herself, who craves some touch of poetry to redeem the sordidness of their affair, is nonetheless unable to rebuff his crude advances. A kind of inarticulate compassion for each other finally seems to unite the three women. When the mother writes to her absent husband in distant Kamchatka a tired and dismal recital of everyday worries—the girls are thin, her liver is acting up—there is no hint that their younger daughter Alla has had an abortion.

The construction of these stories is less tightly concentrated than in Babel's later work; the narrative in "Mama, Rimma and Alla" is fuller, its sentences are longer, and its attention to detail is more like that of the nineteenth-century realist. Indirect speech is used more often than dialogue. In both stories the narrative tone is subdued and the style almost dull, with none of that romantic or lyrical quality which Babel later learned to use so effectively. Semihumorous and detached, he achieves a dry, rather than striking, objectivity. With their grim depiction of the everyday life of average people, these stories resemble the kind of humanitarian literature associated with Gorky. In lines that could almost have been written by Gorky, the merchant of the first story tells the prostitute: "People are good. They've been taught to think they're bad and they believed it."[8]

Still, there are a few intimations of the mature Babel, particularly in his tendency to exploit grotesque and incongruous situations. The pairing of the Jewish merchant and the Russian prostitute, for example, achieves a comic effect reminiscent of *The*

8 *I. Babel': Izbrannoe* (Kemerovo, 1966), 253.

*Odessa Tales*, while the frankness with which sexual matters are described foreshadows many later stories. Babel's interest in sex was a feature of his work that brought him into conflict with the authorities, as he relates in his reminiscence, "The Beginning":

> The shortness of my stories was matched by their disregard for all decent conventions. Most of them, luckily for well-intentioned people, were never published. The others, clipped out of magazines that had carried them, were used as evidence to drag me into court for two offenses: subversion of the existing order and pornography. I was going to be tried in March of 1917, but was saved by the people: they rose in February, and the indictment was burned and along with it the building of the Circuit Court itself.[9]

Babel himself has referred to these early stories as "tolerable attempts"[10] and he did not include them in later editions of his works.

Throughout 1916 and 1917, Babel continued to show his work to Gorky, who, though he read everything and encouraged the younger writer, accepted nothing more for publication. According to Babel,

> Finally, we both got tired and he said to me in his muffled bass voice: "It is clear by now, my friend, that you don't really know anything, but you guess at much. . . ."[11]
> . . . and since it was clear that my two or three tolerable attempts as a youth were but an accidental success, that I wasn't getting anywhere with literature, and that I wrote amazingly badly,— Alexei Maximovich sent me out into the world.[12]

Once more the call to experience was to dominate the writer's imagination, and for the next several years he became an almost homeless wanderer. Concrete information on this period is difficult to obtain. In his two-page "Autobiography"[13] Babel devotes

---

9 "Načalo," *I. Babel': Izbrannoe*, 284–85. The translation with slight changes belongs to Andrew MacAndrew (*Lyubka the Cossack and Other Stories*, New York, 1963, 99). Babel was spared prosecution then, but the charge of "naturalism" was to be a constant refrain to his literary career throughout the Soviet period also.

10 "Avtobiografija," *I. Babel': Izbrannoe*, 12.

11 "Načalo," *I. Babel': Izbrannoe*, 285.

12 "Avtobiografija," *I. Babel': Izbrannoe*, 12.

13 See L. Livšic, "Materialy k tvorčeskoj biografii I. Babelja," *Voprosy litera-*

but one short paragraph to the seven years of his life between 1917 and 1924, and information from other sources does little to complete the picture of this important stage in his development as a writer. Ilya Ehrenburg has said that Babel loved to play hide-and-seek,[14] and Babel's daughter Nathalie that he delighted in mystifying people.[15]

The years from 1916 to 1920 in particular were a time of wandering, of learning life, of absorbing the experience of a country in the midst of revolution, civil war, and unprecedented social transformations. Though he had been exempted from military service at the outbreak of war in 1914, Babel volunteered for the army in October 1917 and was immediately sent to join the army fighting on the Romanian front. He soon contracted malaria, however, and in early 1918 was evacuated home. There is no record of Babel's reaction to his first experience of war, but that most terrible of human activities was to exercise an attraction that would bring him back more than once to study the behavior of men in battle and, most importantly, to test and observe himself.

Russian participation in World War I had come to an end with the Brest-Litovsk Treaty of March 1918. After a stint as a reporter in St. Petersburg, Babel, in the summer of that year, was off to participate in grain collecting expeditions in the Volga region.[16] Back in St. Petersburg, toward the end of 1918, he worked for a time in the Peoples' Commissariat of Education. A letter of December 7, 1918, to his friend Anna Slonim, apologizing for having been out of touch, mentions some of the activities in which he had been immersing himself.

During the time of my disappearance life twisted me in all directions. I've been coming and going, I was sick, I was called up for

---

tury, VIII, No. 4 (1964), 110–35, for a discussion of some interesting contradictions between variants of the author's "Autobiography."

14 I. Ehrenburg, *People and Life, 1891–1921*, trans. Anna Bostock and Yvonne Kapp (New York, 1962), 123.

15 Nathalie Babel, "Introduction," *Isaac Babel: The Lonely Years*, xiv.

16 *Znamja*, No. 8 (Aug. 1964), 146n. See Babel's story "Ivan-da-Mar'ja" for a reflection of his experiences at the time.

service.[17] I found myself in the position of being ashamed to turn up and then became ashamed that I hadn't. That's the way it usually is. But in spite of oppressive circumstances I've managed to come through all right. Today I am leaving for Jamburg to open a peasants' university[18] and I will return next Wednesday. ... I'll come see you. ... An intolerable trait of fanaticism and an unrealistic attitude toward reality are in my character, and this in spite of a certain amount of worldly adaptability. All my conscious and unconscious sins proceed from this. I must eradicate it; from the distance "fanaticism" has the look of disrespect for people. Lord have pity on us. Anna Grigorievna, forgive a vagrant, pensive soul. There—that's all.[19]

At some point in these early postrevolutionary years Babel seems to have served with the Cheka (the Soviet Secret Police), beginning, according to one account, in December 1917.[20] Although Nathalie Babel reports her mother's assertion that this was pure fabrication on Babel's part, that seems unlikely. Not only does Babel mention his Cheka affiliation in his official "Autobiography," but some of his semiautobiographical stories (especially "The Road" and "Sulak") offer additional evidence to support his statement. More than once Babel spoke to Dmitry Furmanov and others of his intention to write a book about the Cheka,[21] and it may well be that, as usual with him, personal experiences were to serve as a basis for the work. Babel's wife may have had little knowledge of his activities before their marriage, or perhaps, more understandably, she was reluctant to discuss the question. For how long and in what capacity Babel served is not known; he may have held only a minor clerical position, or perhaps served as a translator or interrogator. But in any case there was, according to Babel himself, sharp reaction outside the Soviet Union as early as his first trip abroad: "My

---

[17] Probably a reference to his service on the requisitioning expeditions.
[18] Probably connected with his work for the Commissariat of Education.
[19] *Znamja*, No. 8 (Aug. 1964), 146.
[20] L. Livšic, "Materialy k tvorčeskoj biografii," 110.
[21] See, for example, D. M. Furmanov, *Sobranie sočinenij v četyrex tomax* (Moscow, 1961), IV, 377.

stories of former service in the Cheka caused a scandal abroad and I was more or less ostracized."[22]

Whatever Babel's Cheka service involved, it was not long before he was back in military uniform, this time fighting in the Northern Army against Yudenich, presumably in October 1919, during the assault on Petrograd. Whether by chance or design, it was almost as if fate were making him by stages an expert on violence and war, leading him toward that profound and lasting shock that would eventually give birth to *Red Cavalry (Konarmija)*.

But not everything in those years consisted of battles; there was time for other confrontations and experiences as well. In 1919, Babel married his childhood friend, the beautiful and artistic Evgenia Gronfein, and settled in Odessa, where he worked in the editorial department of the State Publishing House of the Ukraine. Neither had he neglected his writing during the time he followed Gorky's advice to go "out into the world"; although Babel himself claims that only in 1923 did he once again begin to write,[23] there are a number of pieces he actually published much earlier.

In 1916 and 1917, in a magazine called *Journal of Journals*, several miniatures signed Bab-Èl' were published under the general heading "My Notebook" ("Moi listki"). With the exception of two pieces separately republished in 1965, only excerpts quoted in critical articles are readily available in Russian. But there is enough to enable us to picture something of Babel's development. For an idea of these unavailable pieces we must turn once again to I. A. Smirin:

> These early works are typical examples of minor journalism: genre and psychological studies, sketches from nature, essays reflecting the young author's Odessa and Petersburg impressions. In "The Public Library," for example, there are sketches of various types of readers; in a short, one-page essay the author recreates the

22 Quoted in L. Livšic, "Materialy k tvorčeskoj biografii," 110.
23 "Avtobiografija," *I. Babel': Izbrannoe*, 12.

particular atmosphere of that "kingdom of the book"—"a mixture of weariness, inquisitiveness and ambition...." "Martyrs of the book," or simply bored and resting visitors, fanatics possessed by an unknown idea, modest toilers or loafers—almost always they are presented as people with some special "point," distinguished by some peculiarity or flaw, some eccentricity or hypertrophy of one or another psychological trait. "Oh how Gogol would have described them," the author cries; and this exclamation shows us to some degree the fundamental direction of his writer's eye, searching for the vivid type amid the everyday and keenly observing the different absurdities of life, the petty but revealing material evidence, by means of which—in a few phrases—a man's character, biography and fate can be laid bare.[24]

One of the more revealing of these early pieces is a story entitled "Inspiration." In it Babel examines the difficult and paradoxical nature of his craft, the process of artistic creation. A young writer brings the narrator a story he has written; the latter, even before hearing it, has misgivings. The manuscript shows no trace of corrections; its author makes no reference to the labor of art but only to the happy hours of his midnight inspiration. His ecstatic mood is rather ridiculous (as when he compares his method to Dostoevsky's: "Dostoevsky always wrote at night and drank a lot of tea while working; with me it's cigarettes.... You should see the smoke in my room").[25] And of course, rather than the masterpiece the young man thinks, the story is hackneyed and mediocre ("The words in his story were boring, stale, and smooth, like pieces of polished wood").[26]

Babel's attitude is clear: exhausting, unsparing, concentrated work is what art demands; the seizures of inspiration are likely to be a beautiful but deceptive illusion. Still, there is a sadness in all this too, in an art that seems to promise so much and gives so little, in the disparity between a man's desires and his talents. In tone, this early story with its unsuccessful, self-deluded hero and its gentle, sad, skeptical narrator has an openly expressed ten-

[24] I. Smirin, *Literaturnoe nasledstvo*, LXXIV, 470.
[25] *Znamja*, No. 8 (Aug. 1964), 124.
[26] *Ibid.*, 123.

derness that is uncommon for the author of *Red Cavalry*.[27]

Babel's early attitude toward the Revolution is most clearly seen in the articles he wrote in 1918 for the newspaper *New Life*, of which Gorky was the leading spirit. Gorky himself at this period began to express severe doubts about some of the revolutionary excesses, and his young protégé was also far from being an immediate enthusiast of the cause.

At the time he met Gorky, he was, Babel says, "a red-faced, puffy-cheeked unfermented mixture of Tolstoyan and Social Democrat."[28] In one of his 1917 sketches he writes in passing that "far from the deep sea the factories give off their smoke and Karl Marx goes about his usual business."[29] Clearly, political commitment did not occupy the forefront of his thought at the time. But by the next year the events that had taken place made it necessary to try to define his attitude to the Revolution more sharply. Babel's mixed reaction of horror and hope can be seen in his 1918 newspaper pieces, which are, as might be expected, impressionistic studies rather than conventional newspaper reports.

In "The Beaten" ("Bitye"), Babel gives a gloomy portrait of revolutionary St. Petersburg as a city of death and starvation. The bodies of the executed and the murdered are dumped at the morgue in growing numbers; they lie unburied for weeks on end, a symbol of the decay in civilized behavior. The quality of life in the immediate postrevolutionary period, like the battles of the Civil War era, made a profound impression on Babel, and he returned to the theme more than once in later years. From the very first he evinces that morbid, outwardly passionless curiosity about death which marks his effort to come to some kind of understanding of violence. Here is his description of a visit to the morgue:

27 Several of Babel's early studies, in their detached tone, are reminiscent of Chekhov. The deeper one penetrates into Babel's art the more one finds links with the great names of Russian literature—links that are often at first surprising. As Ehrenburg says: "There is something that connects Babel with all the great Russian writers from Gogol to Gorky . . . ." (Introduction, *I. Babel': Izbrannoe*, 10.)

28 "Načalo," in *I. Babel': Izbrannoe*, 283.

29 Quoted by I. Smirin, in *Literaturnoe nasledstvo*, LXXIV, 472.

Accompanied by the attendant, I enter the morgue. He lifts the coverings and shows me the faces of people who died three weeks ago, covered with black blood. The people are all young with strong bodies. Their feet stick out, some in boots, some wrapped in cloth, some naked and waxen. Yellow bellies are exposed, hair plastered with blood. One of the bodies has a tag on it: "Prince Konstantin Eboli de Trikoli." The attendant jerks back the sheet. I see a well-formed, lean body; a small, insolent and terrible face, its teeth bared. The prince is wearing an English suit and patent leather shoes with black suede tops. He is the only aristocrat within the silent walls.

On another table I find his friend—the lady Francesca Britti. After being shot, she had lived for two hours. She had been taken to the hospital, and her slender, crimson body is wrapped in bandages. Her mouth is open and her head slightly raised—as if in a savage effort to move. Her long white teeth glisten rapaciously. In death she preserves the imprint of beauty and insolence. She seems to be sobbing, to be cackling scornfully at her killers.[30]

Babel's only directly expressed reaction to all of this horror is the one word, "terrible" (tjažko), with which he ends the article. His nerves appear to flinch at nothing and his eye takes in the most sinister details (the prince's shoes, for example). The physical description abounds in color (black blood, waxen feet, yellow stomachs, crimson body, white teeth). Although the authorial tone is coldly impersonal, the effect of the article is to repudiate the wanton killing. In spite of the fact that the only bodies described are those of two haughty and privileged members of the nobility, the sense of outrage is unmistakable. It is as if Babel were saying to his readers: Here they are, our enemies and persecutors, dead and unrelenting, but the scene is no less terrible than if these were our brothers stretched out and exposed before our eyes.

Comparing the youthful impressionist of this piece with the mature writer we note several important distinctions. Babel's tendency as he developed was to conceal more and more his personal attitudes to the thing described. "I will draw no conclu-

---

30 *Novaja žizn'*, March 29, 1918.

sions,"[31] he declares, and like Chekhov disclaims the role of problem-solver. His later method becomes increasingly ambiguous with regard to his personal attitudes, and his technique becomes an ever more direct assault upon the reader's sensibility. He strives to pare things down to bare essentials, to eliminate excess verbiage. Words, he finds, can get in the way. Babel told the writer Lydia Sejfullina of how he learned this lesson: "I once was horrified when, after I had sent a manuscript to the printer describing a body as bluish, crimson, terrifying, sinister and so on, I came upon a book of Anatol France's in which I read the phrase 'pious and fat prelates.' I was horrified at what I had written, it would have no effect on the reader and so I changed it to: 'a long body lay upon the table.' Immediately the phrase became expressive and sinister."[32]

One might even think that Babel is referring here to parts of the passage quoted above. His quest for immediacy of effect, for involving his readers, led him even in his early work toward an ever more objective authorial tone. At the same time, however, he employs such striking verbal effects that his pursuit of the laconic is partially undermined. Throughout his writing career Babel struggled with this paradox and had to guard in particular against an excessive reliance upon adjectives. His constant reference, in discussions of style, to the need for pruning shows how assiduously he strove to avoid what he regarded as verbal excess:

> When I write down the first version of a story, the manuscript looks disgusting, absolutely horrible. It's a conglomeration of more or less successful bits, joined together by the dreariest connecting links, what are called "transitions," but which are really like dirty ropes. . . . It's at this point that you have to get down to work. This is where it begins. I check sentence after sentence, and not once but many times. First I throw out the useless words. You need a sharp eye for that, because language is very good at concealing its garbage of repetitions, synonyms, and outright absurdities; it seems to be trying to outwit you all the time.

31 *Novaja žizn'*, April 13, 1918, quoted in Livšic, "Materialy k tvorčeskoj biografii," 112.
32 Lidija Sejfullina, *O Literature* (Moscow, 1958), 93.

After this, I retype the manuscript to see the text better, and put it aside for two or three days—that is, if my impatience doesn't get the better of me—and then I check it again, sentence by sentence, word by word. And again I'm certain to find a number of weeds and nettles I've missed. . . .

. . . I think that a noun needs only one adjective and it must be very carefully chosen. Only a genius can afford to use two adjectives.[33]

Many years later Babel's conviction and his sense of struggle would remain unchanged: "My relationship to the adjective is the story of my life. If I were to write my autobiography, I would call it 'The Story of a Certain Adjective.' "[34]

In 1918 Babel had not yet found his own literary voice. The newspaper work of that period is interesting less as a foretaste of his later style than as an indication of his human reactions to the events of the day. The *New Life* articles have in common a deep sense of commiseration for the sufferings of the Russian people and a humanitarian concern for social justice.[35] In a piece entitled "First Aid," Babel ridicules the ineffectiveness of a medical aid station that can manage to answer but two or three calls a day.[36] Formerly operated by the Red Cross but now under city administration, the station simply ceases, in the bureaucratic atmosphere, to function. Babel's humorous tone in the essay is tempered by his conviction that underneath it is not a joke for "there is much blood flowing in the streets and in the houses."

But the Revolution offers hope for life, too, amid all the killing. In another newspaper piece Babel rejoices in the transformation of a former nobleman's palace into a maternity hospital, and his pleasure is the keener because the building might have been used for less human purposes:

[33] Quoted by K. Paustovsky in *Vremja bol'šix ožidanij*, 136–37. The translation is by Andrew MacAndrew (in *Dissonant Voices in Soviet Literature*, ed. Patricia Blake and Max Hayward, New York, 1962, 49–50).

[34] From a 1937 interview in *Naš sovremennik*, No. 4 (1964), 100.

[35] I have located three of these articles; brief quotations from others have appeared in recent Soviet articles on Babel.

[36] "Pervaja pomošč'," *Novaja žizn'*, March 9, 1918.

It is good that the building was not assigned to the committees of confiscation and requisition. It is good that the white tables are not awash with watery soup and that there is none of the all too common talk about arrests. . . . It may not be a bad idea sometimes to grab a rifle and start shooting at each other. But that's not all there is to revolution. Who knows, perhaps that's not revolution at all. To see that children are born properly—that is real revolution. Of this I am sure.[37]

Babel elects for the humane rather than the violent revolution, but he does not seem to have fully appreciated yet that the two might be horribly and inextricably intertwined. Within less than two years his experience of the Civil War was to impress this paradox deeply and ineradicably into his consciousness and his art, but for the next few years he ceases to write about the Revolution at all.

In all of Babel's 1918 newspaper work one can easily picture in the background, as model and inspiration, the influential presence of Maxim Gorky. At precisely the same time these impressionistic newspaper articles were appearing, however, Babel also published in a St. Petersburg newspaper a short story that in theme and inspiration comes from a quite different source.

"Shabos Nahamu," though written in Russian, belongs to that great body of Yiddish *shtetl* tales whose acknowledged master is Sholom Aleichem. The hero of Babel's anecdote is the poor starving Jew Hershele,[38] a warmhearted eccentric whose resourcefulness and patience help him to survive in a harsh world. Hershele, whose fame "has spread through all Ostropol, all Berdichev, and all Viliusk,"[39] is, like Sholom Aleichem's Tevye, a lover of words, a man who talks to his faithful horse as well as to himself, and who answers his complaining wife in verse.

37 "Dvorec materinstva," *Novaja žizn'*, March 31, 1918.
38 Hershele of Ostropol, the Jewish folk hero of many disguises. The story is based on an old anecdote, used for instance by the German Meistersinger Hans Sachs in the 16th century. In giving a familiar tale a new twist or setting, Babel was following a tradition well established in Yiddish literature.
39 *I. Babel': Izbrannoe* (Moscow, 1966), 195. Subsequent citations from this story will be indicated in the text by page numbers referring to this edition.

Babel's language in this story is a supple instrument that already exhibits some of the features to be found later in *The Odessa Tales*. There is a characteristic blend of styles to be seen in the way the story opens in biblical overtones only to slide toward the humorous:

> First the morning and then the evening passes—it is the fifth day. Another morning goes, evening comes—it is the sixth day. On the sixth day, on Friday evening, you have to pray. After prayers you take a walk through the *shtetl* in your best hat and then go home in time for supper. At home a good Jew drinks a glass of vodka—neither God nor the Talmud forbids him to have two (195).

Even the narrative passages exhibit the accents and rhythms of speech. In a few lines describing why Hershele refuses to argue with his wife, the vocal inflections actually hint at the physical gestures accompanying the words: "Why throw logs on the fire when it's burning so brightly as it is! That's number one. And what can you answer a cantankerous wife when she's right? That's number two" (196).

The imagery in the story, striking in itself and tending toward comically grotesque exaggeration, already carries the stamp of Babel's later style:

> With a belly as empty as a wind instrument... (196).
> Her voice was like thunder in the hills (196).
> In every other house the candles burn as if oak trees were on fire. In my house the candles are as thin as matches... (196).
> The orchestra playing in his belly was as big as the one that played at Count Potocki's parties (197).
> His nostrils swelled like a blacksmith's bellows (197).
> More plans were born in his head in that minute than King Solomon had wives (197).
> Her high breasts looked like two tightly stuffed bags of grain (198).[40]

---

[40] A variation on this last image is to be found in the later *Red Cavalry* tale, "Story of a Horse": "She went up to the Commander, carrying her high heels, a breast that stirred like an animal in a sack." (*I. Babel': Izbrannoe*, 73). In the latter story the image has moved from a vegetable to an animal frame of reference and has acquired a sensuality that is appropriate to the new context. More important stylistically, the image now permeates the structure of the sen-

The rhythmic alliteration of the phrase "her voice was like thunder in the hills" (golos ee gremél, kak gróm v goráx) is not the only example of "poetically" rhythmical phrasing. The effect, as again in the following example, is often faintly comic: "The green leaves bent toward one another, caressed one another with their flat hands, and whispering softly in the treetops, rustling and quivering, they nudged themselves back to their places" (197).[41]

According to the subtitle Babel gave to this story, this was one of a projected cycle of tales that was to have Hershele as its hero. Apparently this is the only segment that has survived. It may well be that in the meantime events were causing his writer's eye to move in other directions. Between 1917 and 1919, Babel had twice been a soldier as well as a member of grain-requisitioning expeditions and a functionary in the Cheka. In such circumstances it cannot be considered surprising that the saga of Hershele may have ceased to occupy the forefront of his mind. In fact, his next stories to appear in print are very different in both subject and form.

In 1920, when he was a married man living in Odessa, Babel's reflections were directed once more to themes of violence. In June of that year he published in a forgotten local journal (Lava) four stories about war which, more directly than anything else in his early work, foreshadow the Red Cavalry stories.[42] The author tells us that the content of his stories is adapted from the memoirs of French soldiers and officers who participated in World War I. This claim for authenticity sets the tone of his

---

tence and has become active and direct rather than merely statically descriptive. The inert verb "looked like" disappears, to be replaced by the forms "carrying" and "stirring," which themselves help to form the image and contribute to its immediacy of effect.

41 The English here fails to reproduce the alliterative and onomatopoetic effects of the Russian.

42 The four stories, "On the Field of Honor," "The Deserter," "Old Man Marescot's Family," and "The Quaker," were published in the Odessa magazine Lava. Once again the material is difficult to find. Only one of the stories is readily available in Russian, "On the Field of Honor"—republished in the émigré magazine Vozdušnye puti (1963), No. 3, pp. 52–53. For descriptions of and quotations from the others I am indebted to brief discussions by Soviet scholars.

narration as well. Here, in his first battle miniatures, Babel has already developed to a considerable degree that detached authorial stance for which he was apparently searching in so much of his earlier work. His impassivity is brutally effective as he lets the shocking and dramatic events speak for themselves.

A captain executes a young soldier who has grown tired of the fighting and wants to go home to his mother and bride. A peasant carries in a sack the war-shattered remains of his wife and children, hoping to bury them in the family plot, but finds that the war has destroyed it as well. War is grim and horrible, not only in its physical destructiveness, but also in the degraded morality it brings, setting loose all man's repressed violence and awakening his worst instincts. The author's method of comment is never direct, but rather built into the texture of his stories through the devices of irony, dissonance, and shock. The captain who shoots the young soldier has "a quiet, cordial voice"; he "loves France with a heart-devouring tenderness" and "is capable in private life of forgiving small offenses."[43] The Quaker in the story of that name perishes because of his noble and quixotic love for horses, but the deaths of countless human beings seem to pass unnoticed.

It will be illuminating to examine in greater detail the one story for which the full Russian text is available. Its very title, "On the Field of Honor," strikes an ironic note. A captain is making rounds in the trenches as the regiment prepares for a counterattack. In a shell hole he comes across the enlisted man Bidoux, an idiot:

> The soldier was doing what lewd old men in villages do to give themselves pleasure—or dirty little boys in public lavatories. The less said about it the better.
>
> "Button your fly, Bidoux," said the captain with disgust. "What are you doing here?"

---

[43] Quoted by I. A. Smirin, in "Na puti k *Konarmii*," *Literaturnoe nasledstvo*, LXXIV, 473. This problem of the conflict between public and private moralities has, of course, intrigued many writers. Herman Melville devoted to it his whole short novel *Billy Budd*. Though Babel only hints at the problem, it is remarkable that in a two-page miniature he manages to suggest such larger issues.

"I . . . I can't tell you . . . I'm afraid, Captain! . . ."

"Some wife you've found yourself, you swine! And you even dare to tell me to my face that you're a coward, Bidoux. You've left your comrades at this moment, when the regiment is ready to attack. . . ."[44]

Bidoux collapses from fear:

The idiot put his head on his knees, covered it with his arms and began to cry. Then he looked up at the captain. In the slits of his pig-like eyes glimmered a timid and fragile hope.

Ratin had an explosive temper. He had lost two brothers in the war, and he had a wound on his neck that hadn't healed. A flood of blasphemous abuse fell upon the soldier, a hail of those loathsome words that make the blood throb in the temples and after which one man kills another.[45]

But nothing can make the soldier leave his sheltered hole:

Then the captain went up to the edge of the hole and hissed very quietly:

"Get up, Bidoux, or I'll wet you from head to foot."

He did as he had said. Captain Ratin didn't joke. A foulsmelling stream spattered the soldier full in the face.[46]

The scene, besides being the center of this short story, shows clearly an aspect of Babel's art that, while later handled with greater restraint, is nevertheless characteristic.[47] Babel uses such physiological scenes to shock his reader; if the scene verges on bad taste, it also works. It brings home to the reader something true about war. A pathetic reaction to fear in an idiot has brought forth an even more appalling act from his captain. These are the results of the chaos that comes when "one man kills another." But if Babel maintains such dispassionate objectivity in his description, may we not still accuse him of mere sensationalism— or worse? Isn't some personal comment necessary? The rest of the story clearly refutes any such charge:

Bidoux was an idiot, a village idiot, but he couldn't bear this insult. He screamed, a prolonged, inhuman shriek. This desolate,

44 *Vozdušnye puti* (1963), No. 3, p. 52.    45 *Ibid.*, 53.    46 *Ibid.*

47 The *Red Cavalry* story "Two Ivans," for example, has a similar but more subtly exploited episode, a distant echo of the one described here.

forlorn, despairing wail went out over the plowed-up field; the soldier rushed from his hole, threw up his arms, and ran across the field toward the German trenches. An enemy bullet went right through his chest. Ratin finished him off with two shots from his revolver. The soldier's body didn't even twitch. It stayed where it was, halfway between the opposing lines.[48]

There is a very definite authorial comment here, but notice how it is given—concealed in the narrative with no abrupt change of key, no personal interjection by the author. Bidoux is an idiot, but he has, after all, the dignity of a man, and it is the insult to this dignity that wrenches forth his "inhuman shriek." The author's comment is heard in that wild howl that hangs at the end of five adjectives. But to linger over the moment too long is to shatter the starkness of the picture, and the author at once returns to staccato sentences of cold narration that, in contrast to the preceding lines, have no emotional coloring. The story is brought to a conclusion:

Thus died Célestin Bidoux, a Norman peasant from Aury, at the age of twenty-one—on the blood-stained fields of France.

All that I have related here is true. It is described in a book by Captain Gaston Vidal, *Figures et anecdotes de la Grande Guerre*. He was a witness to this. He also defended France, Captain Vidal.[49]

In these first war stories Babel is perhaps somewhat obvious in his intention to shock the reader, but he already shows an impressive mastery of many of the devices and techniques he employed later in *Red Cavalry*.[50] The *Red Cavalry* stories will have

48 *Vozdušnye puti* (1963), No. 3, 53.

49 *Ibid.* The book Babel refers to actually exists. It was published in Paris in 1918 and is described by Nathalie Babel in her notes to *Isaac Babel: You Must Know Everything, Stories 1915–1937* (New York, 1969), 77–80. She characterizes the original book as "garrulous, romantic, ... padded with clichés"; Babel's adaptations she calls "an exercise in compression and precision."

50 A summary of these characteristics would include: the marked tendency toward dramatic, episodic content; the miniaturelike form of his narrative and its "photographic" quality; the bold use of the psychological and grotesque; the linking of death and war with sexuality; the description of war in a peculiar blend of the heroic and the nonheroic; the ironic tone and the use of paradoxical contrasts; the authorial restraint and apparently cold objectivity which contribute to the desired effect of "documentary" authenticity; and the effort to shock the reader into the experience.

a harder aesthetic surface that will give their brutality a less shocking, more ambiguous effect, but the most striking difference between the two collections of war stories is the absence, in these first four, of the lyrical "I," the participating narrator who dominates the later stories. Before this "I" could come into being, Babel had need of something that the battle memoirs of other people could not supply. And so at the very time the *Lava* stories were appearing in print, Babel himself had already departed to see more of war at first hand. With the help of friends, he had been appointed a war correspondent in the Soviet-Polish conflict of 1920. But fate was arranging things with an eye to the ironic when Isaac Babel—writer, intellectual, and Jew, former ghetto inhabitant with a desire to experience the world—was sent into battle at the side of the Cossacks of Budyonny's First Cavalry.

# III

# LITERARY BACKGROUND

*In Russian literature there has not yet been a genuine, clear, and joyous description of the sun. . . . The Literary Messiah who has been awaited so long and so hopelessly will come from there —from the sunny steppes washed by the sea.*[1]

Babel's return to civilian life toward the end of 1920 found him on the eve of the most fruitful years of his creative life. During the relatively brief period from 1921 to 1925 he completed, in addition to a number of excellent stories, the two major collections on which his fame rests: *The Odessa Tales* and the *Red Cavalry* cycle. Although some of his finest stories were written somewhat later, Babel was never again to enjoy a period of comparable productivity; his later falling off is indeed so marked that he seems, in retrospect, almost completely a writer of the twenties.

Throughout the world, the twenties were years of radical change, politically and culturally. In the arts it was a period that witnessed an exceptional flowering of genius. In American literature these years saw the emergence of Faulkner, Fitzgerald, Hemingway, and Dos Passos. Eliot, Pound, and Frost were remaking the English poetic vocabulary, while James Joyce in *Ulysses* was changing the shape of the novel. The same decade saw the publication of major works by Yeats, Lawrence, and Shaw; by Kafka, Mann, Rilke, and Brecht.

[1] From Babel's 1917 sketch "Odessa," in *I. Babel': Konarmija, Odesskie rasskazy, P'esy* (Chicago, 1965), 157, 158.

In the Soviet Union the twenties experienced a similar artistic ferment, and this seminal decade of Soviet literature was also its most interesting and creative period. With the end of the fighting in 1921 came both a resumption of the nation's cultural life and the inauguration of the New Economic Policy (NEP), which meant a retreat from the rigors and dogmas that had prevailed during the period of war communism. The economic relaxation was accompanied by a correspondingly liberal climate in social and cultural matters, and although debate in the arts was characterized by a lively polemical style the government generally refrained from interceding. Under the aegis of the NEP, which lasted until 1928, literature enjoyed a freedom that has not since been equaled in Soviet cultural life. It was a good climate for a new literature, and with the atmosphere conducive to boldness of experiment the early twenties gave promise of an exciting future. In order to see the period in perspective, however, we shall have to look at the whole complex of influences, trends, traditions, and innovations out of which it arose. Only then will we have an understanding of how, in the earliest years of a new literature, so sophisticated an artist as Isaac Babel could appear.

Russian fiction had inherited from Pushkin, Lermontov, and its other nineteenth-century masters a prose whose ideal values included simplicity and unobtrusiveness. In their overt commitment to social and moral questions, the Russian realists had developed forms appropriate to their content, styles that would carry detailed observation but would neither impede the reader's understanding nor attract especial attention. Concerned with the human being, with character, they were not inclined to explore the structural possibilities of new styles or narrative techniques. Essentially, and with important exceptions, the language of Russian realism was functional and descriptive.

By the last decade of the nineteenth century, however, the very achievements of Russian realism had brought it to an impasse. Both the natural discontent of a younger generation of writers as well as the stimulus of modernist movements in the

West encouraged a reaction against this dominant strain of Russian fiction. Sparked by the *fin de siècle* mood and exhausted by the apparent failure of Russian radicalism in its effort to change a decaying social structure, a cause with which Russian realism had been closely involved, Russian intellectuals and writers questioned the tradition's achievements, its basic assumptions about the nature and function of art. There was a sense of liberation in the discovery that art need not be tied to a socially utilitarian ethic. Russian realism had had a place in its aesthetic for truth and goodness, but it had sadly neglected—or so the modernists held—the claims of beauty. A new wave of aestheticism encouraged Russian writers to turn to the West; they were ready to accept, and make their own contributions to, symbolism and other imported movements.

The new century brought to all the arts in Russia a wave of experimentation that lasted for more than two decades. In literature, the old values of an unobtrusive style were no longer held sacred, and the younger generation of writers and critics took a renewed interest in questions of structure and technique. Like their counterparts elsewhere, the Russian modernists sought to bring literature closer in form to painting and music, to the pictorial immediacy of the one and the abstract structure of the other. In their view language was less a functional instrument for conveying information than it was the expressive material of literature, analogous to paint and musical sound in the other arts.

In their reforming mission the Russian innovators even found allies in the very past they sought to repudiate. They discovered in two great nineteenth-century predecessors, Nikolai Leskov and Nikolai Gogol, writers who were preeminently stylists and whose language contrasted markedly with the prose of the major realists. Leskov had had to await this reaction against the dominant nineteenth-century tradition to be accorded sympathetic attention. Gogol, who had been appropriated in his own day by the Belinsky school of criticism as the father of Russian realism, was given a new reading and claimed by the modernists as their own. In an era of heightened aestheticism and antiutilitarianism, Gogol was admired for the strikingly unrealistic quality of his imagination, for the grotesque and surrealistic elements in his work, and especially for the rich and unusual texture of his language. Along with Leskov he was recognized and admired as a master in the use of *skaz*, oral narrative devices, and these were analyzed, classified, and copied. Taken together, these nineteenth-century masters of the *skaz* suggested new avenues for exploring narrative technique. They demonstrated that manner was as significant as matter, and by their influence they brought the Russian modernist schools closer to contemporary Western literature, which, after Flaubert and James, had been similarly involved in a self-conscious investigation of the artistic medium itself.

Another factor contributing to modernist experimentation was the vigorous development of twentieth-century Russian poetry. After Pushkin, most of the names prominent in nineteenth-century Russian literature had been writers of prose. The traditional concerns of Russia's liberal intelligentsia and the fierceness of their social and political struggles had perhaps made this inevitable, but as the century dragged on writers grew tired of participating in an apparently endless battle. They demanded that literature be freed of its extraliterary obligations; as a result, poetry emerged from the relative decline of half a century to assume once more an honored place in Russian letters. The new schools—symbolism, futurism, and acmeism—heralded a second great poetic age for Russian literature and helped initiate the trend toward linguistic and literary experimentation. None of the modernist schools was particularly long lived, but they made permanent contributions to Russia's poetic vocabulary and broadened the poetic sources of all literary language, in prose as well as verse. In the twenties, when it again became necessary for literature to confront contemporary reality, prose in the Soviet Union was once more in the ascendancy. It was no longer the restrained prose of classical realism, however, but one that showed the effects of a poetic renascence.

Thus several varying but mutually supporting tendencies and influences converged: a reaction against the popular traditions of realism and a turn to different but equally strong native literary traditions; a new receptiveness to Western influences that complemented the growing interest in technique, especially in narrative and poetic devices; and a revived aestheticism stimulated by the sense of political frustration and despair. All these elements gave rise in the early twentieth century to an artistic climate in which the rigid distinctions between poetry and prose tended to be blurred. As a result of this new cross-fertilization, the innovative Russian prose styles of the early twentieth century, for all their variety, have been accorded the general appellation of "poetic" or "ornamental prose."

The term is perhaps too broad to denote anything so well defined as a literary school, but the major features of the phenomenon are clear. It was first, and most importantly, an extension of that literary tradition which considers language and speech not merely as *instruments* of depiction, but as its *objects.* This interest in the very fabric or substance of language resulted in a conscious striving for unusual stylistic effects, a striving manifest in the widespread predilection for highly figurative, metaphor-laden styles, for complex and unusual syntactical constructions, and for musical qualities more common to poetry than prose, such as phonetic instrumentation and rhythmical syntactic constructions. Like poets, too, in their feel for the sound and shape of words, the prose writers of this generation sought out the rare and special, enriching their vocabulary with archaisms and neologisms, exploiting the linguistically rich sources in folklore, dialects, jargons, and slang. Their literary language was strongly oriented toward spoken speech, and their literary style was dominated by the *skaz* manner of colloquial narration.[2]

---

[2] In the twenties the predilection for "poetic" styles was to become the most striking feature of prose. For some the influence was transitory. Leonov and Fedin, for example, later adopted more conventional styles; others, like A. Tolstoy, were only briefly affected—more in response to a vogue than through natural inclination. But for several writers (including Babel, Zamjatin, Pilnjak, and

Two of the prerevolutionary writers associated with these modernist tendencies had a particularly significant influence on writers of the succeeding generation. Andrej Bely and Alexej Remizov, both of whom were shaped by the symbolist era of Russian literature, share in the period's philosophical attitudes as well as its literary flavor. As "writer's writers," their influence is predominantly in the sphere of style. Inheritors of the native Gogolian-Leskovian tradition and counterparts of avant-garde experimenters in the West, Remizov and Bely were the foremost representatives of the modern Russian "ornamental prose" movement. The importance of their linguistic example, like that of Joyce in English, lay in their encouragement of word play. They coined new words, they distorted traditional grammatical categories to create new linguistic formations, and they revived the Russian of ancient manuscripts. Always in search of the intricate, the mannered, and the obscure, they borrowed freely from the exotic language of proverbs, legends, and fairy tales; they sought out all manner of dialectisms and archaisms and all forms of colloquial and folk Russian.

Remizov and Bely also express certain themes that reappear often in early Soviet literature. The mood of disillusion so common to writers in the twilight of Old Russia is reflected in their work by a sense of life as a series of grotesques and by a belief in the cosmic rule of madness and disorder. They have a deeply ambivalent and typically Russian attitude toward the West, but their conviction that Western man is caught in the throes of a spiritual crisis is partially relieved by a Dostoevskian affirmation of Russia's potential moral superiority. Like many Russian intellectuals, Bely and Remizov found an antidote to pessimism in a mystical, messianic interpretation of the Bolshevik Revolution. Each of them embraced it, if only for a time, out of the fervent hope that it would lead to a spiritual rebirth for Russia and perhaps to a new order for all mankind.

This preoccupation with the Revolution was, if anything, even

---

Zoshchenko) the poetic prose movement, though it did not survive the twenties, remained a major force in their work.

43

more pronounced among the younger writers. Many of those who became the first cultural luminaries of the Soviet regime had been participants in the fighting, and all, whether active combatants or not, had been profoundly affected by the years of upheaval. There was a natural if obsessive need, shared by all writers, to describe the nation's recent experiences and to bring some kind of perspective into the precipitate rush of historical events, events that seemed unprecedented in scale and significance. This sense of the vastness of the common experience gave rise to interpretations of the Revolution as a cosmic but inchoate phenomenon, full of the qualities that produce epic and myth, but too immense and too close to be rationally understood. Since writers were usually participants in the events they described, a natural if exaggerated belief in the value of personal experience dominated the artistic consciousness of the day.[3] Writers of the younger generation saw communism and the Revolution as a heroic effort to create a new epoch, and their visions, augmented by the shock of experience, were colored by romantic dreams of personal participation in a great historic enterprise.

The symbolist poet Alexander Blok and the futurist Vladimir Majakovsky were among the first who tried to describe the meaning of contemporary events. They view the Revolution, in imagery of fire and ice, as an elemental force, destructive yet cleansing; they picture as its instrument the wild and drunken mob, as much the victim as the agent of chaos. Most intellectuals, of course, could only regard with distaste the prospect of replacing man-as-individual with the abstraction man-as-mass; but so great was the disgust with contemporary Western culture and the indictment of its social injustices so harsh that such personal qualms were cast aside. The Revolutionary cause inspired new hope, and if it was a hope that could be sustained only through violence many were prepared to smother their doubts in affirma-

---

3 The poet Eduard Bagritsky (1895–1934) spoke in a sense for the whole era: "All works of literature are nothing in comparison with the biographies of those who witnessed the Revolution and took part in it." Quoted by M. Slonim in *Soviet Russian Literature* (New York, 1964), 129.

44

tion of that violence. Those writers who accepted the Revolution as the forward thrust of history were often mesmerized by the vision of its destructive power. Longing for the defeat of Western rationalism and the annihilation of bourgeois values, they sought release from their own spiritual despair and welcomed the storm as much from hatred of the past as from belief in the future.

Blok and Majakovsky—and after them such writers as Pilnyak, Ivanov, and Babel—were united in proclaiming a new liberation of the imagination and of instinct; in the Revolution's duality, in its paradoxical possibilities as both destroyer and purifier, they saw a hidden potential for joy. For some of them, however, a tormenting dilemma remained: whether they, as men devoted to the life of the mind, could put into actual practice the violent Revolutionary beliefs which they accepted in principle. Consequently the writing of the period often pictures the uneducated masses as performing the bloody but necessary tasks from which intellectuals shrank. Writers saw the unsophisticated soldier or peasant as the inarticulate but mighty architect of a new order. Caught between a world *in extremis* and a world *in ovo*, writers sought sharp, shocking material to convey their impressions: the Civil War, especially in its Blokian "storm" aspect, became the dominant subject; rebellions, partisan activity, and peasant unrest became favorite themes. Violence in all forms was the raw material and the desired effect was shock. Plot lines and situations tended to become confused and blurred, full of stark contrasts and broken rhythms; the reader was often assaulted through his senses; and there was a widespread penchant for naturalistic and sensational detail—all in an effort to reflect the rawness of events.

Perhaps, as a corollary to these features, a special importance adheres to the personality of the author or his narrator. He is often not only the necessary human focal point of a story, but its nerve center, reflecting all of the confusion of events. Generally he is a witness-participant whose comments are ambiguous and ironic. The narrators in Soviet prose of the twenties tend to fall

45

into two categories. One is the uneducated man, coarse and inarticulate, the actor in a drama that he himself barely comprehends. In such stories a major structural device is characterization by speech, or *skaz*. The other kind of narrator is the intellectual, who often merges in the reader's mind with the author himself. A passive figure, more acted upon than acting, usually he alone, in his fictional world, possesses a highly developed consciousness. Sensitive and articulate, he analyzes both himself and events in a language and style uniquely lyrical.

Many of the characteristics of writing in the twenties have their origin, as we have seen, in prerevolutionary trends. So closely indeed are the two periods interwoven that the term "Soviet literature," at least as it applies to the first decade of Communist rule, is something of a puzzle. Certainly the effects of the Revolution on literature were profound and far reaching, but it is misleading to think of October 1917 as an abrupt dividing line between two distinct literary traditions. Not only do many of the prominent literary schools span both eras, but the careers of a number of leading writers overlap as well. Some, like Remizov, eventually left Soviet Russia for permanent exile in western Europe, but many remained or, like Bely, made their reconciliation with the new regime and returned. The continuing prevalence of prerevolutionary trends and their influence on early Soviet literature is therefore hardly surprising. In fact, in so far as the innovating tendencies of the modernist movement are concerned, the Revolution at first actually expanded upon them. The great upheaval in political and social life could hardly fail to nourish an art that would reflect innovating tendencies of its own.[4]

4 By the thirties a more solidly entrenched and less youthfully idealistic regime, concerned with the preservation and consolidation of its power rather than with encouraging attacks on authority, found literary freedom and stylistic experimentation intolerable. With the promulgation in 1934 of the doctrine of socialist realism, an attempt was made to impose not only ideological conformity, but a style closer to those of the 19th-century classics. Only recently have many of the earlier Soviet literary trends and writers been officially rehabilitated and allowed a measure of respectability and belated influence.

Because the antitraditionalism of the immediate postrevolutionary years had favored all sorts of experimentation with language and style, the era was abundant in works that defied generic classification. The effort to embellish prose fiction by an infusion of "poetic" devices and the somewhat contradictory attempt to invigorate it by introducing the "raw material" of life had resulted in a sometimes bewildering mixture of literary forms. The effect of the poetic renascence brought on a plethora of impressionistic "poems in prose," while the kaleidoscope of daily events, wilder even than the literary imagination, gave rise to such nonfictional forms as memoirs, letters, and especially journalism. When narrative prose of a more recognizable sort did return—and the short story was the first prose genre to be revived—it not surprisingly continued to exhibit the characteristics of poetic prose, as well as to evince the pervasive influence of documentary writing.

That the short story should be the first prose genre to revive is likewise no surprise. Given the hectic pace of events, the absence of extended leisure time, and the acute shortage of such amenities as paper, the climate was not conducive to the production of longer works. The shorter form, with its capacity for impressionistic illumination and its evasion of the larger, more comprehensive patterns demanded by the novel, was perhaps best suited to the turbulence of the period.

To be sure, the novel was to reassert its traditional dominance soon enough. Before the end of the twenties the need for a more comprehensive statement on the meaning of recent experiences called for the larger perspectives of the longer narrative. When the passage of time and the amelioration of conditions made the production of the novel possible once more, Konstantin Fedin and Leonid Leonov emerged as major practitioners; Mikhail Sholokhov left off his *Tales of the Don* to undertake the monumental canvas of his Don novels. By the thirties the novel was well entrenched, and socialist construction had replaced the Revolution and Civil War as the major themes of literature. But for

47

a brief period the episodic structure and the affective immediacy of the short story served Soviet literature well—largely because, in Isaac Babel, the form had found a master. Amid the general run of loosely constructed writing and the motley conglomeration of bastard genres, Babel's work stands out as the product of a highly sophisticated literary mind. Although he does exhibit a heterogeneous mixture of stylistic devices (for example, his combination of a profusely metaphorical style contrasted with a sharp documentary directness, and his blend of lyric, epic, and dramatic qualities), these components are always subordinated to his keen sense of construction, to a tightly controlled and highly original conception of form.[5]

Babel's mastery of the short story contributed much to the popularity of that form in the mid-twenties. He himself, despite repeated forays into other genres and despite the short story's decline in popularity during the thirties, remained loyal to it all of his artistic life. As late as 1937 he was still a proud advocate of the virtues of the short story and a critic of what he considered its neglect in Russian literary tradition:

> I think it would be a good idea to talk about the technique of the short story, because the genre is not very popular with us right now. One has to admit that the form has never really enjoyed particular success in Russian literature; the French have always been far ahead of us here. Actually, the only real short story writer we have is Chekhov. Most of Gorky's stories are actually shortened novels; the same is true with Tolstoy—except for "After the Ball," which is a real story. Generally speaking we write stories badly, we tend more toward the novel.[6]

Throughout his life, Babel defended his preference for the condensed form and pressed its claims against those of the novel:

> In one of Goethe's letters to Eckermann I read a definition of the novella or short story, the genre in which I feel more comfortable

[5] The documentary note that Babel occasionally strikes, particularly in *Red Cavalry*, is a good demonstration of his ability to use a given stylistic device for specific artistic effect.

[6] From a transcript of Babel's remarks during a discussion of his work at the Union of Soviet Writers on Sept. 28, 1937. First published in *Naš sovremennik*, No. 4 (1964), 99.

than in any other. Goethe's definition was very simple: it is the
account of an unusual incident. Perhaps this is incorrect, I don't
know, but that's what Goethe thought.

I have neither the power, nor the knowledge, nor the interest
to write of the typical in the torrential manner of Lev Tolstoy. I
am interested in reading him, not in writing in his manner.
. . . Let me tell you a secret. I wasted several years in an attempt
to write long, detailed and philosophical things. . . . I didn't succeed. And so, although I remain an admirer of Tolstoy, in order
to produce anything at all, I have to proceed in my work by a contrary path. . . . The point is this. Whereas Tolstoy, remembering
all that had happened to him, had temperament enough to describe the entire twenty-four hours in a day, I have only temperament enough to describe the most interesting five minutes that I
have experienced. And this, it must be, is what gives rise to the
genre of the short story. . . . [B]ut in order to forestall any suggestion
of self-abasement, I should add that the majority of my comrades,
although they have at their disposal no greater number of interesting facts and observations than I, write about them in the
"Tolstoyan" manner. The result is well known to the suffering
reader.[7]

Despite continued study of other forms of fiction, Babel's principal and life-long artistic concern was with the theory and practice of the short story. His preference for the form is closely tied
to an acute awareness of his own proclivities as a writer, an awareness that came with long experience in his craft and with the
hard lessons of fruitless experiments. He was, it is true, definitely
attracted to the epic mode. When we consider that his two major
early works, *The Odessa Tales* and *Red Cavalry*, as well as his
final projected but unfinished series on collectivization, are not
merely collections of stories, but thematically integrated cycles,
we can recognize that this tendency in his work was both inherent and lasting.[8] One might say that the stories in these collections, without ceasing to be stories, also aspire to be parts of
a larger canvas. The critic Renato Poggioli, in a brief essay on

---

[7] *Ibid.*, 98, 99.
[8] Even the story "Šabos-naxmu," to judge from its subtitle (A Story from the
Cycle "Hershele"), was originally conceived as part of a larger work.

Babel, has remarked that his "epic breath is genuine, but, as in all moderns, rather short."[9]

But if the connected cycle was the somewhat hybrid solution that best answered Babel's needs, his basic unit of narrative construction always remained the story.[10] In this regard he considered himself unique in Russian letters, acknowledging only one other true short-story writer, Anton Chekhov. Babel's conception of the story, however, is quite different from Chekhov's; his language is far removed from the latter's nonpoetic prose, and as a rule neither the atmosphere nor the structure of his stories is in any sense Chekhovian. If Babel's remarkably original stories have any counterpart at all, it is to be found in the Western literary tradition, in the short story as developed by Maupassant in France, by Kipling in England, and by Poe, Crane, and Hemingway in America.[11]

Like the Western masters of the genre, Babel believed the short story's virtues to be economy of form and intensity of effect. His method of construction, however, is unique and does not follow the lines of the classical novella. Neither plot nor unity of theme plays a role in his stories, and many of them seem more like lyrical poems than traditional narratives. In *Red Cavalry* especially, Babel is a master of the miniature, a form in which he employs sharply contrasting, extreme effects. Often such miniatures deal with scenes of violence, but their harshness

9 R. Poggioli, "Isaac Babel in Retrospect," in *The Phoenix and the Spider* (Cambridge, Mass., 157), 235.

10 Although Babel tried longer forms, he never published any narratives other than stories. He had greater success in dramatic fiction, publishing two plays and a number of scenarios.

11 Ilya Ehrenburg has spoken of an affinity between Babel and American writers of the twenties and thirties. Like Hemingway, Caldwell, and Steinbeck, Babel "strove not to tell about man, but to show him, and like them, he shunned authorial discourse and attached great importance to dialogue." Ehrenburg adds, however, that as far as he knows Babel was indifferent toward American literature (*I. Babel': Izbrannoe*, 7). Babel constantly suggests comparisons with other artists, both Russian and Western; but the question of his affinities with American writers, especially in light of his pronounced interest in violence, is particularly intriguing. Several commentators have compared Babel to Hemingway, and some striking correspondences in theme and style may also be noted between Babel and Stephen Crane.

is sometimes partially subdued through a process of aesthetic distancing. At their best these tales are capable of evoking the immediacy and fluidity of direct experience, while at the same time transfixing the moment or the action in indelible imagery. In depicting character Babel's use of authorial narrative is extremely truncated. He shuns lengthy introductions or probing psychological analyses in favor of dramatic and symbolic presentation. Short dialogues or monologues, full of slang, jargon, or dialect, reveal characters through their speech. Perhaps even more important is Babel's use of "symbolic depiction." He builds clusters of images and themes into symbolic leitmotifs, and often the reader's reception not only of a given character but of an entire story is governed by this use of a network of internal symbols.

Babel's commitment to his conception of the story has another important aspect. He believed that the form offered an opportunity to express a poetic, affirmative vision of life, something which in his view had been denied by the Russian novelistic tradition. In a literary manifesto written the very year of the Revolution, when he was twenty-three, Babel declared that Russian literature had been dominated for too long by the gloomy symbol of St. Petersburg.[12] Bewitched by the grim northern capital, the nineteenth-century novelists had developed a vision of life as stifling and bleak and of man as dull and pathetic. Only once in Russian literature, according to Babel, had a joyous, sun-filled, romantic note been struck—in the southern or Ukrainian tales of Gogol. Taking his inspiration from these "southern" works of Gogol's (he refers specifically to the stories from *Evenings on a Farm Near Dikanka* and to the historical romance *Taras Bulba*), Babel proposed an alternative literary ideal, one whose symbol would be his own Odessa, city of sun, sea, and light.

At first glance it seems peculiar that Babel should cite Gogol

12 See Babel's sketch "Odessa." The image of St. Petersburg in Russian literature (exemplified in Pushkin's *Bronze Horseman*, in Gogol's "Northern" or Petersburg stories, and in Dostoevsky's novels) is that of the modern city, dehumanizing and demonic.

as an inspiration for his new literature, for Gogol was one of the creators of the very "Petersburg myth" that Babel was rejecting. Gogol himself, however, as a young man of twenty-four, had expressed a similar view, suggesting a southern city as symbolic antithesis to the northern "Petersburg" principle of Russian culture. The capital, with its "heap of houses . . . roaring streets . . . commercialism . . . ugly fashions . . . civil servants, wild northern nights, glitter and low colorlessness," is contrasted with his "beautiful, ancient, chosen Kiev, wreathed with populous gardens, girdled by my southern, beautiful, wonderful sky, by ravishing nights . . . and washing it, my clean and swift one, my Dnieper." Elsewhere in Gogol's work it is Rome that is contrasted to St. Petersburg, but again the vision of a shining southern city should "rouse the world, in order that the dweller of the North, as through a dream, might sometimes visualize this South, so that the dream of it might tear him out of his milieu of cold life, given over to pursuits that dry up the soul. . . ."[13]

There are a number of suggestive parallels between the two writers. Gogol's indictment of philistine complacency, of life's frequent triviality, is echoed in Babel's protest against urban materialism and in his general rejection of bourgeois values.[14] Both writers express a similar sense of frustration at the enormous gap between the ideal and the real.[15] Like Gogol, too, Babel cannot repress a strong feeling of identification with the milieu he detests. His alienation from contemporary Western

[13] Quoted by Donald Fanger, in *Dostoevsky and Romantic Realism* (Cambridge, Mass., 1965), 107, 109.

[14] Despite his condemnation of the modern city, Babel himself remained an inveterate city dweller. Although he constantly reviled cities in his private correspondence and sought frequent personal relief through periodic retreat into the country, the themes of his art deal with the problems of urban man. Significantly, in his early artistic manifesto, his alternative to St. Petersburg is Odessa, another city; and the sea which figures so prominently in Babel's Odessa is not the elemental, primeval sea, but an avenue of commerce. The rural setting in Babel's art is primarily a mysterious backdrop for the feverish condition of modern man, evoking nostalgia for the time when he was an integral part of nature.

[15] One recalls, in connection with Babel's Gogolian themes, that the author's speech to the 1934 Writer's Congress was entitled "Pošlost'—vot vrag" (Trite vulgarity is our enemy). See Bibliography.

culture (including his own specifically Jewish tradition) alternates with a strong sense of identification with that heritage. Konstantin Paustovsky has reported in this connection some revealing remarks Babel made during a conversation in the early twenties:

> "Do you remember Blok's 'I see an enchanted shore and an enchanted horizon'? [From "The Unknown Lady"(Neznakomka).] Blok reached that shore, but I shall not. I see it from an unbearable distance. My mind is too sober. But I am thankful that at least fate has put into my heart a longing for that enchanted horizon. I work to the limit of my strength, I do my utmost, because I want to be at the feast of the gods and am afraid I may be driven away."
>
> A tear gleamed behind the convex lenses of his glasses. He took them off and wiped his eyes with the sleeve of his drab, patched jacket. "I didn't choose my race," he said suddenly in a broken voice. "I'm a Jew, a kike. Sometimes I think there's nothing I can't understand, but one thing I'll never understand: the reason for that black vileness which goes by the humdrum name of anti-Semitism." He fell silent. I too was silent and waited for him to calm down and for his hands to stop trembling.[16]

Here the sense of alienation and the longing for some distant and unobtainable ideal are linked by Babel himself to his Jewishness. These remarks also reveal that partially stifled but intense lyrical quality of Babel's temperament. He is a poet whose vision is anchored in prosaic reality; and if he does not, as Gogol often does, label his prose works "poems," they are nevertheless full of the same kind of lyrical impulse. For Babel, the objective world, with all of its palpable and prosaic reality, cannot smother the poetic longing.

Both Gogol and Babel are alienated from the banality of the modern economic and social order; each proceeds from a rejection of the dead souls of bourgeois mediocrity. Most significant of all, perhaps, this similarity of *Weltanschauung* is reflected in a similarity of technique, in a number of stylistic characteristics

---

16 K. Paustovsky, *Vremja bol'šix ožidanij*, 135. Trans. Andrew MacAndrew, in *Dissonant Voices in Soviet Literature*, 48–49; I have made some slight changes in his translation.

which they share. Both men have a penchant for hyperbole and for the grotesque or absurd; they each employ abrupt transitions —from prosaic reality to fantasy, from the crudely naturalistic detail to the lyrical digression. There is a similar vacillation in both writers between the comic and the serious and a common reliance on anecdotal structure, frequently involving the interweaving of several disparate strands into a single story. Significantly, they both have a predilection for the *skaz* style of narration, and as a result their work exhibits a similar confusion of voices between characters, narrators, and author. In both the various voices speak in a bewildering variety of intonational patterns: bombastic, pathetic, rhetorical, biblical, and prosaic. Substandard oral speech contrasts with the polished and literary. And in both writers the tension of clashing verbal styles is paralleled by the uneasy union throughout their work of epic, lyric, and dramatic impulses. In light of these stylistic similarities, there seems hardly any doubt that Gogol was a key figure in Babel's development. His example was important in suggesting a number of ways in which a modernist aesthetic might repudiate both the temper and the style of realism.

In other respects, however, Gogol proved an inadequate guide. He found it difficult in his work to express a sustained and sustaining positive vision, and his few attempts at creating the idyllic are only with difficulty distinguished from his portrayals of hell. The galloping troikas of Gogol's art lack the governing sense of a real if unknown destination, and his restless wandering through life never found him a home. In the end Gogol tended to withdraw into an idealization of a fanciful and patriarchal Russia, or, succumbing to "Petersburg," forsook his art in a self-defeating religious obscurantism. Babel, on the other hand, felt a strong attraction for the concrete, objective world, felt a need, that is, to immerse himself in, rather than withdraw from, experience. An optimist who still dreamed of reaching his "enchanted shore," Babel had to recognize that Gogol's was an incongruous name with which to conjure up a literature of joy. He finally had to look elsewhere for a model and guide.

In his 1917 manifesto, Babel turned next to his early mentor Maxim Gorky, whom he calls "the first in Russian letters to have spoken of the sun, to have spoken with ecstasy and passion." Babel admired Gorky's interest in life's oddities, his romantic sympathy for the socially wayward and outcast. He was, furthermore, considerably indebted to the older man for aiding his career and regarded him with genuine affection and respect. But at the same time something keeps Babel from expressing an unqualified enthusiasm. Gorky is not really "a singer of the sun, but a herald of truth; . . . he knows why he loves the sun and he knows why he should," but for Babel his love is too rational and willed. The Russia that Gorky actually depicts in his work is dreary and depressing, and since Babel espouses a literature of passionate joy Gorky remains only a forerunner, "the most powerful of our time—splendid and mighty, but still a forerunner." Because of these reservations Babel turns to yet another model, this time in France.

"I can guarantee you Maupassants," exclaimed Babel to Konstantin Paustovsky, "and that is because here in Odessa we have plenty of sea, sun, beautiful women, and food for thought."[17] Much has been said of Babel's indebtedness to the French master of the short story. His search for *le mot juste*, inspired by a desire to subject vivid impressions to a tight formal control, is almost French in its dedication. Like Maupassant, Babel sought a detached and ironic tone in his art; both in his themes and in their expression—especially early in his career—he, too, was something of a naturalist. But other affinities are more significant. Babel is attracted to the French writer who "perhaps knows nothing and perhaps knows everything" because he sees in him an appetite for experience akin to his own. He responds in particular to Maupassant's unquenchable curiosity about sensual experience, to his exploration of the sexual life. "There is no greater joy for me," confessed Babel, "than to follow impassively the play of passions on human faces,"—and of all the passions, especially

---

17 K. Paustovsky, *Vremja bol'šix ožidanij*, 114.

those of the brothel client.[18] In Maupassant, Babel thought he had found his singer of sun and passion, and only in Odessa, he believed, might a Russian equivalent appear. That he had hopes of supplying that need himself we can scarcely doubt.[19]

Both of Babel's chosen figures, standing, as it were, on either side of realism, suggested to him possibilities for expressing the disordered modern sensibility. In certain respects they complement one another well. Through his stylistic exuberance Gogol speaks to a deeply romantic quality in Babel's temperament, one which French naturalism failed to address. His use of the grotesque and of *skaz* narration was especially influential, and his attack upon prosaic reality through fantastic language already contains the characteristic modern blend of naturalism and symbolism toward which Babel was moving. What Babel sought from Maupassant was a certain open profanity of subject matter and a laconicism of tone, as well as liberation from the sort of moral conscience that attended Gogol. But if Babel's ambition was to become a Russian Maupassant, he was destined to be something of a French Gogol as well—especially in his first major work, *The Odessa Tales.*

18 L. Livšic, "Materialy k tvorčeskoj biografii," 110. Viktor Shklovsky (in *Lef* No. 2 [1924], 152–55) recalls that in 1919 Babel was "forever writing one and the same story—about two Chinamen in a brothel." The interest in brothel themes is reflected in several published stories—"Ilya Isaakovich and Margarita Prokofievna," already discussed, "Answer to an Inquiry," "Through the Fanlight," and "My First Fee." A favorable view of prostitution or of nonmarital sex is of course not uncommon in Maupassant. In his 1917 manifesto Babel refers with admiration to Maupassant's tale "L'aveu," in which the "fat and cunning youth Polyte" makes love in a moving carriage to a strapping and clumsy peasant girl.

19 There is no hint here of the pessimism found in the French author, and Babel would seem to have chosen still another peculiar figure to epitomize his new literature of joy. To be sure, in a late story that bears the title "Guy de Maupassant" (pub. 1932), Babel's affinity with the Frenchman has acquired a somber, almost morbid, coloring. The practice of art itself has become inextricably mixed with the dangers of eroticism, and an aura of guilt and doom hangs over the hero. In Maupassant's madness and death at the age of 42 he feels "the foreboding touch of some essential truth." Strangely enough, these late themes of madness, artistic crippling, and moral guilt are reminiscent of Babel's other early favorite, Gogol.

# IV

## The Odessa Tales:
# AN INTRODUCTION

*Odessa is a miserable town. Everyone knows what they do to the Russian language there. . . . but all the same,* quand même et malgré tout, *[the place] is extraordinarily, quite extraordinarily, interesting.*[1]

Upon his demobilization in 1920 Babel had to find a means of supporting himself and his wife; accordingly, rather than embark immediately upon the uncertain path of a writing career, for a short time he took a job with a government printing house in Odessa. The settled routine and the duties that kept him from his own work were not to his liking, however, and he soon abandoned Odessa to work toward a happier destiny as a reporter in Tiflis.[2]

During the years 1921–23, Babel, in order to supplement his income, published an occasional short story in addition to his newspaper pieces, but for the most part he resisted the temptation to rush prematurely into print. With the greatest care and the highest sense of purpose, he was carefully planning, executing, and reworking the two ambitious cycles of stories that were to be his real occupation for the next several years. Following

---

1 From Babel's sketch "Odessa," in *I. Babel': Konarmija, Odesskie rasskazy, P'esy*, 155, 157.
2 Babel's newspaper articles from Tiflis, all dated 1922, are not accessible; there is, however, one extant piece of journalism from this period, an article entitled "Her Day" (first published in *Red Cavalryman*, the political organ of the cavalry), which impressionistically describes the work of a front-line nurse. The article may also be found in *Literaturnoe nasledstvo*, LXXIV, 488.

Gorky's advice, Babel had served his apprenticeship to life as well as art and now felt himself ready to undertake their imaginative fusion. The years of revolution and war just behind him had left him with a wealth of confused but startling impressions, and he was determined to explore to the utmost the ambiguities and paradoxes in which they were clothed.

Babel's service with Budyonny's Cossack Cavalry had been one of those profound experiences to which he responded, in a sense, for the rest of his life. The war was the catalyst that set Babel on the path to self-discovery, and it helped to shape the patterns of the art through which he would express and combat his personal alienation. The depiction of violence and conflict, far more than a mere device or technique, becomes a controlling feature of his fiction, and it clearly lies at the heart of both of his famous collections, *The Odessa Tales* and *Red Cavalry*. The artistic relationship between these two cycles of stories and the role that the war played in the genesis of each are somewhat clarified by an understanding of the time and sequence of their composition.

Both in the Soviet Union and abroad, the prevailing view has been that *The Odessa Tales* were written later than *Red Cavalry* and that they represent a decline in the author's powers. Actually Babel had written at least three of the four stories collected in *The Odessa Tales* by the spring of 1923; two of them had even been published, one as early as 1921. The first appearance in print of any of the *Red Cavalry* stories, however, was in February 1923, when Babel published five stories in the Odessa *Izvestija*. Furthermore, Babel published these latter stories to alleviate financial worries and only reluctantly did he release what he called "excerpts." The remainder of the *Red Cavalry* stories, on which Babel was apparently still working in 1923, appeared separately over the next two years, while the first collected edition was not issued until 1926. The date of 1920 which accompanies many of the cavalry stories and which has misled the critics must consequently be understood to refer not to the time of composition, as has been assumed, but to the time of the action described. It seems clear now that many of the *Red Cavalry* stories were only finished in 1924 and 1925, at a time, that is, when *The Odessa Tales* were already complete.[3] The proper sequence of composition thus established, the actual path that Babel's creative development took and the peculiar relationship these two cycles of stories bear to one another become clearer.

Written almost simultaneously, the two sets of stories share certain themes and attitudes and have as a common setting a background of passion and chaos. Though the Odessa stories possess a surface of broad comic intent, they, like those of *Red Cavalry*, have conflict and violence at the heart of their world. While *Red Cavalry* portrays soldiers engaged in actual combat, in legally sanctioned war, the Odessa characters are criminals, men at war with the society and their fate. The life of the Jewish underworld depicted in *The Odessa Tales* shows traditional moral and cultural values as fully under assault, and in much the same way, as they are in *Red Cavalry*. Furthermore, in both cycles the moral questioning of violence is linked to certain common attitudes toward Jewish identity. Thus, in spite of differences in style, tone, and point of view, these two sets of stories are like two contrasting but complementary expressions of a single creative impulse, two interrelated versions of a dichotomous, perhaps flawed, but nevertheless single artistic vision which informs all of Babel's art. Let us examine first *The Odessa Tales* since these are the earlier and more properly introductory pieces to Babel's mature work.

As far back as 1918, Babel had treated of Jewish lore and anecdote in his story "Šabos-naxmu." In *The Odessa Tales*, as in that story, there is much to remind us of older Yiddish literature; though he wrote in Russian, Babel owes much to such Yiddish writers as Sholom Aleichem. Obviously there is the theme of Jewish culture, both as a complex, self-contained phenomenon

---

[3] The fullest discussion of when both groups of stories were written is in Livšic, "Materialy," 118–24. Nathalie Babel corroborates the relatively later provenance of the *Red Cavalry* stories when she says that her father began work on the stories during a stay in the Caucasus in 1923 (*Isaac Babel: The Lonely Years,* xix).

and as a tradition surrounded and beleaguered, but not sub-
merged, by a very different and largely hostile culture. But it is
not only through his interest in the closed world of the Jewish
community that Babel is related to the Yiddish literary tradition:
the very texture of his language and the quality of his humor,
with its peculiar mixture of the sardonic and the highly emotional, are best understood in the light of that tradition.

At the same time, *The Odessa Tales* are strikingly different
in tone from the work of other Jewish writers. Babel does not
share the basic attitudes toward ghetto life which are common
to Yiddish literature and which are still implicit in his 1918 pre-
war story "Šabos-naxmu." The war seems to have confirmed in
Babel a less indulgent attitude toward Jewish experience, and
when he turned once again to Jewish themes and characters he
did so in the light of his anomalous position as a Jew who had
lived and fought side by side with the Cossacks. Hershele, the
folk hero of "Šabos-naxmu," is a recognizable stereotype: the
comic, pathetic, but resourceful misfit frequently encountered
in prerevolutionary caricatures by both Russian and Yiddish writers. Hershele's world, though a ghetto, is essentially the self-
congratulatory milieu of Jewish folklore, and in this sense
"Šabos-naxmu" may be said to belong to the older tradition.

Yiddish literature, associated with a people who everywhere
in Europe constituted a minority, understandably reflected the
efforts of Jews to preserve both their traditional values and a
sense of community. Their attempt to maintain a distinct religious identity was met with especially hostile opposition not only
from the differing religious traditions of the larger culture, but
also from the largely secularized atmosphere of contemporary
Western society. Both internal and external pressures, therefore, resulted in the closing off to Jewish experience of many
of the main currents of Western life, of the opportunity to share
fully in the broader social and political milieu in which Jews
were a cohesive but isolated minority. As a result of this insulation the literature that concerned itself with Jewish fate in the
Diaspora was liable at its worst to accept all of its traditions un-

critically and to succumb to nostalgic self-indulgence or to eulogies to the obscure or picturesque. At its best, as in Sholom Aleichem, such literature was capable of both skepticism and sympathy, of irony as well as affection, and it was able without sentimentality or idealization to affirm the values of Jewish life and to revere its culture, learning, and humanism.

For Babel, however, insulation from the mainstream was a deprivation. As a man of preeminently modern sensibilities he found the cultural walls of Jewish life yet another aspect of the ghetto. Returning from war and revolution, after participating in a great historical event, he views the backwater of Jewish life with new distaste, with a conviction that the ghetto had paid too great a price for its production of saints, scholars, and artists. In these years of upheaval Babel welcomes the destructive winds of change which he hopes will topple not only the physical ghettos created by the old decayed society, but the spiritual and emotional ghettos of Jewish life as well, those shackles which have deprived human beings of the experience of joy.

The hope of chaos is a desperate hope and indicates a profound sense of social alienation in the man who holds it. In Isaac Babel the estrangement from traditional cultural values in general, and from the milieu of his birth in particular, is dramatically underlined by his admiration for the Cossack soldiers of the Revolutionary army in which he had served. There is a striking anomaly and no small paradox in this reaction on the part of a Jew to men whose way of life seems so antithetical to his own deepest traditions; but for Babel those who wield the cleansing sword of destruction are figures of heroic significance. He minimizes neither their violent instincts nor their primitive morality, but at the same time he delights in the animal grace and beauty of their bearing and in the spontaneity and directness of their physical passions. In the conflict between these virtues and the values of Jewish tradition, Babel often seems ready to forego the latter. His experience outside the ghetto had touched the deepest places of his being, and for the moments of wild and exultant freedom that he craved he was prepared at times to abandon traditional Jewish ideals such as intellectual eminence or moral dignity as irrelevant and incongruous, as marks of the imprisoned and deprived Jews of the ghetto. He sought instead to extract from within the Jewish experience something to compare with his vision of the Cossack ethos, something that would permit him, as a Jew, to participate in that same primitive celebration of life.

As a new ideal Babel creates a Jewish version of the Cossack: a man schooled in violence, immune to the vacillations of the intellectual or the moralist, and reveling in all the physical pleasures and challenges of life.[4] In his *Odessa Tales*, Babel sought to portray a Jewish hero who was *in* but not *of* the ghetto. The gangster Benja Krik and his cohorts represent an antitraditional image of the Jew; they are aggressive and powerful fighters who challenge authority and answer violence with violence: if they are outcasts at all it is only in the sense that they have elected to cast themselves out into the world and accept no external limitations on their right to experience. Although the deprived and suffering Jew of the ghetto is still present in Babel's stories, he is placed in the shadow of this physically towering, resplendent, outrageous new folk hero.

*The Odessa Tales* is a collection of four stories interrelated as to characters, themes, milieu, and narrative tone. In the first, "The King," we make the acquaintance of Benja Krik (Benny the Yell), leader of the exotic underworld of the Moldavanka. We learn how he came to be married to the rich Eichbaum's daughter, and we see how he and his men forestall a police raid (planned to catch the gang while celebrating the wedding of Benja's forty-year-old sister) by setting fire to the police station. In "How It Was Done in Odessa" we are told the story of Benja's rise to fame and power, how he robbed the rich and clever Jewish merchant Tartakovsky, how he meted out punishment to the overzealous member of his band who killed Tartakovsky's clerk,

---

4 This provocative idea of the Jewish Cossack seems to have been first suggested by R. Rosenthal in his article in *Commentary* (Feb. 1947), 126–31.

and, finally, how the murdered clerk was accorded the most sumptuous funeral Odessa had ever seen. In "The Father" we learn of Benja's marriage to Basja, the gigantic daughter of the red-headed, one-eyed gangster Froim Grach, and of how these two great bandit families are united by ties of blood and marriage. And in the last story, "Ljubka the Cossack," we meet a kind of female counterpart to Benja, the formidable Ljubka Schneeweiss, whose family name is incongruously embellished with the awesome nickname "the Cossack" and whose inn is the rowdy home of Odessa's smugglers and gangsters when they relax.

But a bare plot synopsis of these tales is less than useless because they are primarily phenomena of style and tone, experiments in narrative composition, and masterpieces in the use of colorful language. Babel once declared that his main interest as a writer was the "how" and "why" of things rather than the "what."[5] His *Odessa Tales*, above all, require a proper understanding of this aspect of his imagination.

The stories are an intricate blend of many rich ingredients, and although these ingredients are words they are so visually and palpably effective that they make an almost physical impression upon the senses. Part of the problem in trying to describe the secret of these tales lies in the inimitable quality of Babel's version of the Odessa speech, a jargon that defies translation or paraphrase and that cannot be adequately described by an analysis of its grammar. Odessa had been famous long before the Revolution as the home of a characteristic brand of regional anecdotal humor. Its unique and colorful local idiom, strongly influenced by Yiddish and Ukrainian folklore, had developed a characteristic accent and rhythm as well as its own special way with a word or turn of phrase. In one of several essays on Odessa written early in his career Babel spoke of the great literary potential in the rich Odessa speech. He predicted that the city would experience a cultural renascence, that it would bloom

5 *Naš sovremennik*, No. 4 (1964), 97.

again with its own "bright and self-made word."[6] Because of his own fascination with this Odessa "word" and his intimacy with it from childhood, Babel himself was in no small measure responsible for the eventual truth of his prediction.

Odessa did indeed give to Soviet literature in its earliest period a number of prominent writers, including Eduard Bagritsky, Vera Inber, Valentin Kataev, and the team of Ilf and Petrov. The work of these writers, while by no means of a piece, shared a sufficient number of traits to give rise to the notion of a "southern school." Their lack of respect for classical rules, as well as their richly metaphorical language, was not exclusive to any particular school, of course, but in their penchant for the picaresque and for the use of exotic speech and local color, as well as in their peculiar union of romanticism with humor and ironic modes of narration, all of these writers shared something of a common aesthetic.[7]

Babel reveals something of the Odessa flavor in a short piece he wrote as introduction to a projected collection of stories by seven young Odessans (including Ilf, Bagritsky, and the immigrant Odessan Konstantin Paustovsky): "In Odessa every youth—until he marries—wants to be a cabin-boy on an ocean-going ship. The steamships putting into our port enflame our Odessan hearts with a thirst for beautiful new lands."[8] Then after a brief word about each of the seven young authors and the "melancholic," the "mellifluous," and the "miraculous" things they have to tell, Babel closes with a typically ironic and self-mocking variation on his opening: "The whole point of

[6] "Listki ob Odesse," *Večernjaja zvezda* (Petrograd), No. 38, March 25, 1918. Letters to his relatives over a 24-year-period show that Babel always retained his love for the Odessa idiom. He frequently prefaces a humorous remark with a statement like "as they say in Odessa," and when he describes a visit to that city in 1935, after long years in Moscow, he notices with nostalgia that "the Odessa talk is still as colorful as before."

[7] A particularly noticeable feature of early Soviet prose is the attraction of the rogue or outlaw as a type. Babel's *Odessa Tales* and Kataev's *Embezzlers*, as well as Ilf's and Petrov's *Twelve Chairs*, are a few examples; even Leonid Leonov's *The Thief* (1927) would seem, though on a different level, to point to a similar preoccupation.

[8] *I. Babel': Izbrannoe* (Moscow, 1966), 401.

this book is that in Odessa every youth—until he marries—wants to be a cabin-boy on an ocean-going ship. There's only one trouble with us—in Odessa we are extraordinarily insistent on marrying."[9]

In the four stories that collectively bear the name of his native city, Babel has reproduced the intonations of the Odessa speech. He is extremely careful to make his literary version of this salty jargon both representative and comprehensible to the general reader. He avoids an excessive dosage of dialect and relies instead on the judicious use of characteristically distorted syntax and morphology, or on other slight deviations from the norms of standard speech. Part of his success in capturing the flavor of speech is accounted for by his creation of a diction and speech rhythm for his heroes. They speak in proverbs and formulas, they mix levels of discourse, and they misuse clichés, thereby making them newly vivid. Dialogue at times has a kind of comic brevity, a clipped staccato quality which is heightened by the use of truncated repetitions. Often it proceeds in the sort of circuitous question-and-answer style that is typical of much Jewish humor. Through his mastery of speech patterns Babel achieves both comedy and characterization, and he conveys with precision the milieu to which his speakers belong.

The language of Benja Krik, the King himself, is a spicy verbal counterpart to his wildly improbable career. Never at a loss for a phrase, Benja will laconically toss off an aphorism or invent a graphic image as vivid as a line of comic verse: "My brains stood on end along with my hair when I heard this news." Again, this time pleading with the wealthy dairyman Eichbaum for the hand of his daughter, Benja is carried away by the enthusiasm of his suit to heights of impassioned rhetoric:

> "Listen, Eichbaum," said the King. "When you die I will bury you in the First Jewish Cemetery, right by the entrance. I will raise you, Eichbaum, a monument of pink marble. I will make you an Elder of the Brody Synagogue. I will give up my own business [Benja's business is robbery and extortion!] and enter yours as a

9 *Ibid.*, 402.

partner. Two hundred cows we will have, Eichbaum. I will kill all the other cow-keepers except you. No thief will walk the street you live in. I will build you a villa where the streetcar line ends. Remember, Eichbaum, *you* were no Rabbi in your young days, either. Who was it that forged that will, but we won't talk too loud about that. And your son-in-law will be the King—no snotnose, but the King, Eichbaum."[10]

The speech is effective both as comedy and as characterization. Benja's supralogical, rapid-fire sequence of thoughts has Eichbaum dead and magnificiently buried before making him owner of two hundred mythical cows, and the offer to kill off the competition (with an obliging "except you" for a prospective father-in-law) is hardly calculated to instill confidence in a man whose own funeral has just been painted in such glowing colors. Without pausing for either breath or logic, Benja next promises to protect Eichbaum from thieves in the district (a bitter pill under the circumstances); then to build him a dacha on the outskirts of town; and, finally, he ends the entire peroration with a thinly veiled threat neatly and irresistibly sandwiched between a humble admission of human frailty and a proud boast of superhuman power. It is no doubt shrewd not to be a saint if one intends to indulge in blackmail, and being a "King" instead of a "snotnose" lends credence to the threat while at the same time appealing to Eichbaum's vanity.

Benja's ever-present aplomb is conveyed through his language. When Manja, the sixty-year-old "progenitress" of the bandits, lets out with a piercing whistle to celebrate the burning of the police station, Benja is quick with a typical reproof, one that contains a neat "Krikism" in its translation of the French term *sang-froid*: " 'You're not on the job, Manja,' observed Benja, 'a little more cool-bloodedly, Manja!' "

Another example of Odessa bandit palaver can be seen in this excerpt from a conversation (from "How It Was Done in Odes-

10 Trans. Walter Morison in *Isaac Babel: The Collected Stories* (New York, 1955), 207. Subsequent citations from this translation will be indicated in the text by page numbers referring to this edition. I have occasionally made slight changes.

sa") between Benja and Froim Grach (Ephraim Rook). Benja
is applying for membership in Grach's band:

> "Take me on. I want to moor to your bollard. The bollard I moor
> to will be the winning one."
> Rook asked him:
> "Who are you, where do you come from, and what do you use
> for breath?"
> "Give me a try, Ephraim," replied Benja, "and let us stop
> smearing gruel over a clean table."
> "Let us stop smearing gruel," assented Rook.
> "I'll give you a try" (212–213).

After accepting the difficult assignment of raiding the wealthy
Tartakovsky, Benja once again displays his mastery of style in
the extortion note he writes; it is similar, the author tells us,
to all letters of this type:

> "Highly respected Ruvim son of Joseph! Be kind enough to place,
> on Saturday, under the rain barrel, etc. If you refuse, as last time
> you refused, know that a great disappointment awaits you in your
> private life. Respects from the Bentzion Krik you know of" (214).

During the raid Benja as usual is a model of self-composure:

> "A little calmer, Solomon," observed Benja to one who was shout-
> ing louder than the rest. "Don't make a habit of being nervous on
> the job" (215).

One member of the gang, however, loses his head and murders
Tartakovsky's clerk, Muginstein. Tartakovsky's ensuing accusation against Benja is an example of the fusion, common to the
Odessa jargon, of humor with an underlying philosophical
seriousness:

> "You hooligan's snout," he cried, perceiving the visitor, "you ban-
> dit, may the earth cast you forth! A fine trick you've thought up,
> killing live people" (218).

Benja too displays a philosophical side when, referring to the
murder (in what must surely be termed an exaggerated under-

statement) as a "tremendous mistake," he pleads with Mugin-stein's mother for understanding:

> "—if you need my life you may have it, but all make mistakes, God included. A tremendous mistake has been made, Aunt Pesja. But wasn't it a mistake on the part of God to settle Jews in Russia, for them to be tormented worse than in Hell? How would it hurt if the Jews lived in Switzerland, where they would be surrounded by first-class lakes, mountainous air, and sheer Frenchmen? All make mistakes, God not excepted. Listen to me with all your ears, Aunt Pesja" (219).

A sardonic tone like that of Benja's lament is a characteristic feature of Jewish humor that has been well exploited in Yiddish literature. For instance, Sholom Aleichem's work, which Babel knew well, has running through it just such rueful disputes with God, and the blending of humor and seriousness peculiar to such street-corner philosophizing does much to create the special flavor of the Odessa jargon that Babel imitates so well. It will be noted also in this passage how Benja's use—or misuse—of words ("first-class lakes, mountainous air, and sheer Frenchmen") helps to delineate his personality and background.

Examples of Babel's Odessa jargon might be selected at random from any of the stories; the intonations, the syntactical and semantic patterns, and the mental styles they exhibit are common to almost all of the characters. What is of interest from a structural point of view, however, is that the narrative frame itself often echoes these speech peculiarities. The narrator will introduce dialogue by using the same inflections, the same staccato rhythms and comic repetitions, that later appear in the dialogue itself. By thus anticipating his characters' language the narrator not only contributes to comic unity; he lends a pronounced oral flavor to the entire story. As a result of this oral structure, the narrative style and tone take on significance and the narrative voice becomes a major character in its own right.

Cases where one can identify the narrating voice as that of a "disinterested author" are relatively rare. Such tonally neutral lines as do occur are kept to the minimum required for moving the plot, and they are distinguished from other narrative passages by their isolation and brevity as well as by their placement, usually at the beginning of paragraphs.

Frequently in Babel the narrative technique involves a blending of voices, an interlacing of varied speech masks into a richly textured pattern. Actual mimicry of his characters is only one of the oral devices in the narrator's bag of tricks. He may, for example, assume a philosophical or biblical pose and express himself in maxims or proverbs. The effect is often one of comic or ironic incongruity, as in this explanation (from "The King") of how the seating was arranged for Dvoira Krik's wedding: "Not according to their years did the wedding guests take their seats. Foolish old age is no less pitiable than timorous youth. Nor according to their wealth. Heavy purses are lined with tears" (205).

Sometimes the narrator's voice highlights an exaggeratedly farcical scene through the device of inappropriate matter-of-factness. By keeping the tone, if not the words, calm and brusque, he pretends to be unaware of his story's outlandish comic proportions. Here, for instance, is the narrator's description of how Benja comes to ask the man he has just robbed for his daughter's hand:

> Two days later, without warning, Benja returned to Eichbaum all the money he had taken from him, and then one evening he paid the old man a social call. He wore an orange suit, beneath his cuff gleamed a bracelet set with diamonds. He walked into the room, bowed politely, and asked Eichbaum for his daughter's hand. The old man had a slight stroke, but recovered. He was good for another twenty years (206–7).

Only in the final short sentence, a rapidly delivered aside, is the comedy of the scene permitted to break through to the narrative surface.

In "The King" the narrative voice includes still another tonal range: the poetic. Belonging neither to the Odessa dialect nor to a disinterested author, this poetic tone lies mainly beneath the narrative surface. Usually it is subdued and channeled into one of the other narrative strains, but sometimes it shows itself through other speech patterns, and occasionally it bursts into full-throated song. The timbre of this other, unidentified voice is sometimes lyric, sometimes epic, by turns ironic and solemn. It is a voice betraying a heart full of romantic longings and a mind bemused by the word-fragrance of books. Though we cannot identify it as Babel's voice, the personality it invokes is close indeed to the figure off stage. This impression is strengthened because the lyric quality we detect appears inconsistent with the more dominant tones of the narrative; as a result, the narrative voice at these times seems to belong to an outsider, to a man who admires the world he describes, but who nonetheless stands apart from it.

This implied onlooker stance of the narrator's represents both a calculated rhetorical device and an integral part of the story's thematic structure. As rhetorical device it gives to the recital of the story an authority independent of the characters. Thematically, it introduces enriching elements of contrast and irony, since the partially repressed romantic lyricism in the onlooker's voice paradoxically serves to both beautify and expose the reality it describes. The hyperbolic tone, so obviously at variance with the general features of the stories' milieu, results in an ambiguous and delicately balanced tension between encomium and parody.

Consider the poetic color, the luxuriant wordiness and the crescendolike structure of the following two passages describing the wedding feast in "The King":

> At the wedding feast they served turkey, roast chicken, goose, stuffed fish, and fish-soup in which lakes of lemon gleamed like mother-of-pearl. Over the heads of defunct geese, flowers swayed like luxuriant plumages (207).

The prose in the next passage (the quotation represents less than half of a long and elaborate single paragraph) vibrates at an exaggeratedly heightened pitch. It is a description of the exotic fare smuggled from distant places for the enjoyment of

Odessa's bandit élite and, as the narrator tells us in the declamatory last two lines, of their attendant beggars:

> All that is noblest in our smuggled goods, everything for which
> the land is famed from end to end, did, on that starry, that deep-
> blue night, its entrancing and disruptive work. Wines not from
> these parts warmed stomachs, made legs faint sweetly, bemused
> brains, evoked belches that rang out sonorous as trumpets sum-
> moning to battle. The Negro cook from the *Plutarch,* that had
> put in three days before from Port Said, bore unseen through the
> customs fat-bellied jars of Jamaica rum, oily Madeira, cigars from
> the plantations of Pierpont Morgan, and oranges from the en-
> virons of Jerusalem. That is what the foaming surge of the Odessa
> sea bears to the shore, that is what sometimes comes the way of
> Odessa beggars at Jewish weddings (207–8).

This passage produces a number of conflicting impressions.
It gives a sense of Hebrew tradition, of feasting rich in religious
symbolism. Beggars and noble bandits share wine together at
this repast, and we recall the words of the Haggadah of the
Passover: "Blessed art thou, Lord, our God, King of the Universe, who dost create the fruit of the vine," and "He lifts up
the poor from the dust, from dungheaps he raises the lowly, to
seat them with nobles, with the nobles of his people." But the
occasion is essentially nonreligious, or at least nonspiritual, and
such associations seem ambiguous and mocking. In the light of
religious suggestion, the passage inflates and distorts what it tells,
describing ceremoniously what is after all (as the ensuing description shows us) an occasion of wild drunkenness. Ultimately,
however, the effect is not to ridicule the proceedings, but rather
to separate the occasion from those religious associations which
are an incongruous and unnecessary appendage. The feasting is
after all only feasting, but its magnificence is undiminished.

If the celebratory atmosphere is not the result of religious
symbolism, neither is it the result of any alternative set of values
inherent in the meaning of the words. The effects are achieved
through the sheer phonetics of the sounds themselves, from the
heavy weight of sonorous Russian words and the rhythm of roll-
ing cadences. The goods enumerated in this passage are fit for

a king because they sound exotic; the ship *Plutarch* is not a real ship, but a legendary vessel bringing nectar for the feast of god-like men and illustrious heroes. Port Said, Jerusalem, and the plantations of Pierpont Morgan, all contribute not only their lush southern delicacies, but the splendor and melody of their names as well. The language, with its repetitions and alliteration, its profusion of adjectives and its imagery, is itself intoxicating; the prolonged, clause-laden sentences go to the reader's head like the wines and rich foods they describe.

One of the most striking qualities of the passage is the way Babel's delight in the exoticism of the setting colors his portrayal of actual things. His adjectives and modifiers tend to dominate and submerge the inert nouns they describe; the ordinary reality of things retreats before the power of his rhythmic phrasing. The lavish tone of the description subordinates actions and things to a decorative vision. As in poetry, this is accomplished through the prominence given to particular words. As ornaments on the textured surface of the style, these words become entities in their own right; their phonetic properties take on new weight and importance. Freed of their responsibilities to be merely signs for things, they become the rhythmic ingredients for a musical prose composition.

Babel intends, of course, that his word-musical view of things will invest them with a new reality, with a hard brilliance and an almost sensuous beauty. What he despises and rejects is the tyranny of things as possessions. When viewed in this way, as they typically are by the middle-class, things are gray and lifeless; paradoxically, it is they who possess their owners. The Moldavanka bandits, on the contrary, display an attitude toward things that is more "aristocratic." Here, for example, is the description of how they bestow their gifts on the newly wedded pair in "The King":

> And now the friends of the King showed what blue blood meant, and the chivalry, not yet extinct, of the Moldavanka district. On the silver trays, with ineffably nonchalant movements of the hand, they cast golden coins, rings, and threaded coral (208).

In Babel's hands language itself becomes a means of escape from life's drabness. Through his ornamental style he forces his reader to view the commonplace through a topsy-turvy kaleidoscope or, to use one of his own images, through a pair of magic spectacles. In order to convey a new and magnified reality he employs all manner of linguistic, stylistic, and thematic devices of creative distortion and exaggeration. In delineating characters he even approaches the grotesque. Here, for example, are some of the phrases describing the girl Basja in "The Father":

Rook . . . saw . . . a woman of gigantic height. She had enormous hips, and cheeks of a brick-red hue (223).
She had put on men's boots and an orange frock, and she wore a hat bedizened with dead birds (224).
She weighed five poods and a few pounds over (225).
Mounds of linen would glide across her great straddled knees (226).

Description is not only bizarre and exaggerated; it is frequently expressed, even in minor details, in boldly physical terms:

The child strained toward her, bit at her monstrous nipple, but achieved no milk ("Ljubka the Cossack," 238).
Policemen, their buttocks waggling, were rushing up smoky staircases . . . ("The King," 210).
The old crones would lave fat infants in troughs, slap their grandchildren on their shining buttocks and wrap them up in worn-out skirts ("The Father," 226).

Babel is attracted by the primitive and vital aspects in the life force. He constantly draws attention to living, functioning flesh and to bodily processes; the reader of his stories is likely to find himself assaulted by a barrage of sensuous imagery. In addition to the abundant detail which Babel devotes to actual physical attributes—to arms and legs, bosoms, buttocks, and pregnant bellies —there are the lavish descriptions given to food and drink, as well as frequent reference to blood, sweat, and spittle. Even the sense of smell is enlisted to invigorate the reader's perception of people or things, often in a context of strange or jarring juxtapositions:

From their wide hips wafted the odors of the sea and of milk ("How It Was Done in Odessa," 220).

Each ware had its own price, each figure they drank down with Bessarabian wine that smelt of sun and bugs ("Ljubka the Cossack," 240).

The old man drank some vodka from an enameled teapot and ate the hash, fragrant as a carefree childhood ("The Father," 224).

Still another device that emphasizes the primitive physicality of Babel's fictional world is the frequent attribution of animal features to its human inhabitants. Sometimes the implication is of weakness: Dvoira's husband in "The King" is likened to a mouse; the murdered clerk Muginstein, bachelor son of Aunt Pesja the poultry dealer, is described in "How It Was Done in Odessa" as having spent his life "like a bird on a bough"; and Basja's beloved in "The Father" is named Capon. More often, however, the attribution of animal features tends to magnify the human, to endow it with animal energy. Dvoira is as carnivorous as a cat; Benja is likened to a cat, a lion, and a tiger; other of the Moldavanka bandits are characterized in a similar fashion by the use of animal names: Froim Grach (rook) is a scavenger and thief like the bird whose name he bears; another of the gangsters goes by the blunt and enticing sobriquet of Levka Byk (Lefty the Bull); while Benja and Dvoira, though they lack specifically animal names, share the aggressive implications of their family surname, Krik (the Yell), which reminds us that in the beginning was not the word, but the yell—barbaric and uncivilized. In his figurative language, too, Babel frequently uses animal imagery, as in these examples:

Velvet-spread, they [tables] wound their way down the yard like so many serpents with variegated patches on their bellies ... ("The King," 203).

Sweat with the pinkness of fresh blood, sweat as pink as the slaver of a mad dog ... ("The King," 203).

They wore black frock coats with silk lapels and new shoes that squeaked like sacked sucking-pigs ("How It Was Done in Odessa," 220).

After him like sheep went all the lawyers, all the ladies with brooches ("How It was Done in Odessa," 222).

74

The pregnant women, nibbling at this and that, would fill up with juice as a cow's udder fills on the pastures with the pink milk of spring . . . ("The Father," 226).
It [the sun] climbed to the middle of the sky and hung there quivering like a fly overcome by the heat ("Ljubka the Cossack," 237).
The sun lolled from the sky like the pink tongue of a thirsty dog . . . ("Ljubka the Cossack," 238).
. . . a moon that skipped through black clouds like a stray calf ("Ljubka the Cossack," 242).

Babel's use of the intensely physical, even the erotic, is intended partly to shock the reader into new perceptions. But Babel also celebrates the erotic in its own right, as an essential ingredient of the full life. It represents a challenge to the squeamish gentility of the bourgeoisie and an antidote to the blanched dullness of their lives. Babel rejects the urban middle-class denial of the biological truth of human nature, and in his art he turns to a freer, more aggressive world, one where primitive physicality is allowed ample expression. To provide a proper setting for his celebration of this physical principle of existence, Babel creates a lush and exotic background. His fictional Moldavanka is the direct antithesis of all that is lifeless or gray; its bizarre people live in a carnival world, in an atmosphere of lurid color. Dark and light, set closely together, heighten each other like the color effects of an impressionistic painting:

> The purple eye of the sunset, groping over the earth, that evening lit on Rook as he snored beneath his cart. The impetuous ray fastened with flaming reproach on the sleeper and led him out to Dalnitskaya Street, dusty and gleaming like green rye in the breeze ("The Father," 229).
> Evening had long since turned to night, the sky had grown black, and its milky ways were filled with gold, glitter, and coolness ("The Father," 233).

In the following passage, touches of pale color help to characterize the foreign asceticism of the Tartar pilgrims who pass through Odessa on their return from Mecca; the effect of the scene is to transfer for a moment the sun-struck religious impulse of the distant, bleached, and holy desert to the urban landscape of modern Odessa: "Inflexible striped robes stood stiffly on the Tartars, flooding the pavement with the bronze sweat of the desert. White towels were wound around their fezzes, and these distinguished such as had bowed to the dust of the prophet" ("The Father," 229–30). The transfer is accomplished, however, only for a moment, and with the inevitable accompaniment of mockery. One of the pilgrims, an old Turk covered with "pearly sweat," is dying in the courtyard of Ljubka's inn, where his religious conviction in the face of death is subjected to brutal and insensitive ridicule. The descriptive language, with its stately repetitions, amplifications, and its selection of a bright color, manages to give subtle sustenance to the dying Turk by linking his death with the vibrance of growing things: "An old Turk in a green turban, an old Turk green and light as a leaf, lay on the grass" ("The Father," 230).

The color green is used frequently by Babel in conjunction with motifs of death or decay. It serves to emphasize the ultimate triumph of living processes as well as to point to the harsher truth that life must feed upon death in order to rise above it. There is a passage in "The Father" that describes old Mendel Krik, defeated and disfigured by his own sons. Despite the element of travesty on the theme of resurrection, there is a somber grandeur in the old man's struggle to deny decay.[11] The peculiar presence in the passage of the word "green" seems especially remarkable:

> Mendel Krik sat at one of the tables drinking wine from a green tumbler and relating how he had been crippled by his own sons— the elder Benja and the younger Ljovka. He yelled his tale in a hoarse and terrible voice, exhibiting his ground-down teeth and getting people to feel the wounds on his belly (231).

The linking of death with greenness and the resultant intima-

11 In a later story, "Sunset," and in the play of the same title, Babel makes Mendel Krik his central character and develops more fully and with greater sensitivity the theme of inevitable earthly decay.

tion of life's persistent vitality are made early in "How It Was Done in Odessa":

> Reb Arye-Leib was silent, sitting on the cemetery wall. Before us stretched the green stillness of the graves (212).

The story will end where it began—in the cemetery—and though there may be an ironic truth to the fact that all stories must have their final act played before the eyes of Arye-Leib, sitting atop his cemetery wall, it is a truth that Babel seeks to circumvent by subjecting even death to the distorting lens of his fantasy. The solemn stillness of the graveyard is shattered at the story's climax by a burst of noise and color as life—through Benja and his men—asserts its unconquered power. Midway through the story, when the clerk Muginstein is about to die at the hands of one of the gunmen, Babel, with a few quick strokes, changes the pallid specter of death into a living reality of color. The clerk, within the space of several short lines, is described as "white as death," "yellow as clay," and "green as green grass." The colors summarize and predict for us not only Muginstein's immediate future, but his ultimate destiny as well: he is seen, almost at once, as corpse, as body interred in the earth, and then transmogrified into the grass that will grow above his grave. At the later funeral ceremonies death is again decked out in nature's greenery.

In "The Father" the closing scene is once more set against the backdrop of a Russian cemetery. It is not a place of solemn stillness, but one where "Lads were then dragging lasses behind the fences, and kisses re-echoed above the tombstones" (234). Life has chosen an unexpected and incongruous spot to reassert its power, and death is perhaps partly subdued by being associated with vast, revivifying natural processes.

Babel's fantasy greatly depends on the striking use of color: silver, gold, blue, white, black, yellow, green, and purple all add their specific hues to the kaleidoscopic world created by the writer's imagination. But Babel's favorite color, the one most common to these stories, is red. In a great variety of shades, reds and related colors such as orange serve as a kind of prism through which people and objects are refracted and changed; it is as if the spectacles through which the narrator views the world are rose-colored, and as if the author himself were wearing similar glasses and asking the reader to do the same. So pervasive and dominant are the reds that the resultant impression is something of a cross between a garish nightmare and a child's drawing in which a single color is boldly and illogically used for everything.[12]

Babel's reds have a thematic as well as a decorative function. They stand for energy and exuberance, for passion and life:

> ... Kate, the whole-hogging Kate, was still heating up for Benja Krik her many-colored, Russian and rubicund paradise ("The Father," 233).
> Little Dave looked at him in amazement and waggled his little raspberry legs bathed in infant sweat... ("Ljubka the Cossack," 237).
> There awaited her Mr. Trottyburn, a man like a pillar of russet meat ("Ljubka the Cossack," 239).
> An orange star which had slid to the very brim of the horizon gazed wide-eyed at them ("Ljubka the Cossack," 241).
> ... the pink milk of spring ... ("The Father," 226).
> ... the sky was red like a red-letter day ("The Father," 224).
> ... on the other side, draped in orange shawls, were the honorary dairy-maids from Bugajevka ("How It Was Done in Odessa," 219–20).
> Sweat with the pinkness of fresh blood ... ("The King," 203).

The most vivid characters are also imbued with hues of red: Froim Grach has red hair; his daughter Basja has brick-colored cheeks; Benja Krik drives a red car and he promises Eichbaum a

---

12 Benja Krik himself uses the word "nightmare" ("košmar") to console the police chief when his station is on fire. The analogy with a child's drawing is particularly appropriate with regard to Babel's use of color: Lev Tolstoy has described, in *Childhood*, how he once made a drawing in which—for lack of any other available colors—people, horses, dogs, and a rabbit were all done in blue. A realist might look askance at such illogical use of a single hue, but with Babel the choice is deliberate and the intended effect much like the fantasy world of children—illogical, weird, and often uncongenial to the pragmatic adult mind.

monument of pink marble; Benja and his men wear outlandish
and colorful costumes in which red and orange play a prominent
role:

He wore an orange suit, beneath his cuff gleamed a bracelet set
with diamonds ("The King," 206).
Aristocrats of the Moldavanka, they were tightly encased in
raspberry waistcoats. Russet jackets clasped their shoulders, and
on their fleshy feet the azure leather cracked ("The King," 208–9).
Here Benja paused. He was wearing a chocolate jacket, cream
pants, and raspberry boots ("How It Was Done in Odessa," 218).[13]

Everything about the gangsters is exaggerated and fantastic.
They are the Moldavanka's élite, of a different stamp from ordinary tradesmen, and their passage through the town is a truly
incredible procession:

All the shops on Dalnitskaja had now shut, and the gangsters
were driving past to Glukhaja Street, where Jo Samuelson kept
his whorehouse. In lacquered carriages they drove, dressed up like
birds of paradise, their jackets all colors of the rainbow. Their eyes
were agoggle, each had a leg jutting out on the footboard, and
each held in an outstretched arm of steel a bouquet wrapped in
tissue paper. Their lacquered jaunting cars moved at a walking
pace. In each carriage sat one gangster with a bouquet, and the
drivers, protuberant on their high seats, were decked with bows
like best men at weddings. . . . [T]he sons of the shopkeepers and
shipwrights envied the kings of the Moldavanka.
Little Solomon Capon the grocer's son and Monja Gunner son
of the smuggler were among those who tried to turn their eyes
from the blaze of an alien glory ("The Father," 224–25).

All of this decorative color enhances and enlarges the characters depicted, makes them bigger than life, epic in stature.
The bandits have "steel shoulders" and "burning eyes," they are
bolder and stronger than ordinary men, they do everything on
a grander scale. Their attire is like the plumage of exotically

---

13 Particularly in this example, but elsewhere as well, the choice of vocabulary
(chocolate, cream, and raspberry) adds the dimension of taste as well as of color.
One observes again that on one level of these stories, Babel is indulging childlike
fantasy; on another, he is emphasizing the sensuous through a dual assault upon
the senses of his readers.

colored birds, or like the armor of famous knights; their lacquered carriages resemble fabled steeds; and in "The King" they carry long poles like spears or lances. "Aristocrats of the Moldavanka," they are a special class within the Jewish community, a warrior caste amid the clerks, tradesmen, herders, and women. Because of their physical attributes and their legendary deeds of plunder and adventure, a special glory attaches to them alone within the tribe.

The element of fable that Babel exploits in these tales lends them a curious quality of timelessness, so that in spite of the fact that the stories take place in a modern city the sense of historical reality is suspended and nebulous. Rather than the reactionary and troubled post-1905 era that constitutes the actual historical setting for these stories, the evoked atmosphere suggests a tribal or feudal past. There is no direct reflection in the tales of the two revolutions or of the contemporary reordering of social institutions. On the contrary, there is a distinct sense of ancient modes of behavior and of old, tribally limited loyalties —rather as if Babel, by appropriating elements of epic tradition, were seeking to re-create, half seriously and half satirically, a heroic tradition for the Odessa Jews.[14]

In Arye-Leib the "Moldavanka knighthood" has its court chronicler or bard; he is a Jewish Homer whose words impart the sagas of the giants to the young, and we shall see later how his use of biblical diction contributes to the aura of myth. Benja himself is a mythic figure, a knight and avenger, a king among figures as splendid and colorful as himself. When he ventures forth he is surrounded by a retinue of attendant warriors; to reflect further glory on his person his exploits are compared in epic fashion to the deeds of other illustrious heroes. He and his men are both bold and crafty; they triumph over great adversaries: the law and the power of oppressive wealth. The bandits indulge in Homeric feasts, and there is an epic quality to the fre-

---

14 The appropriation is eclectic: although the biblical epic is central to Jewish historical and cultural experience, Babel exploits as well echoes of the Homeric Greek epic and even of the medieval epic romance.

quent poetic enumeration of foods and other goods. It is significant that for the most part the lists of things are not of possessions
to be accumulated, but of things to be used and enjoyed: the fare
at the wedding feast in "The King"; the delicacies of Capon's
grocery in "The Father"; the wares found in the inn of "Ljubka
the Cossack."

At the funeral in "How It Was Done in Odessa" the mourners
are tradesmen and clerks, dairymaids and poultry dealers, but
Arye-Leib's narration makes them a stately procession passing in
salute to the illustrious dead. The narrative style idealizes the
bandits—particularly Benja, whose heroic stature is disclosed in
the Homeric simile that Arye-Leib uses to describe him: "and the
sun rose above his head like an armed sentry" (221). Situation and
psychology as well as narrative language cast Benja in an Achil-
lean mold. Like the Greek hero who felt a sense of personal guilt
in the death of his friend Patroclus and who avenged him by
killing his slayer, Benja avenges Muginstein by slaying the murderer Savka Butsis. Also like Achilles, he arranges a splendid
funeral for his departed brother, a ceremony that serves not only
to ease the deceased's passage to heaven and to console those left
behind, but to assuage Benja's personal sense of responsibility
as well.

There is a further suggestion of the Homeric epic in Arye-
Leib's recital of how the Jews outwit a hostile gang during a
pogrom by staging a mock funeral with a machine gun in the
coffin instead of a body. At the appropriate moment, after the
procession has penetrated into enemy territory, the weapon is
brought into action and the enemy routed. The situation is a
travesty of the legendary Trojan horse episode and carries the
suggestion of a bitter new adage: Beware of Jews bearing coffins.

Of course there is a comic incongruity to much of the epic tone
in these tales. The heightened pathos at times sounds distinctly
ironic and often gives rise to an impression of satire or parody.
The ironic note, however, is neither simple nor consistent, and
the author is often apparently at odds with himself. There is a
level at which the stories constitute a kind of parody of the epic

81

conventions they imitate. The various rites and ceremonies, the initiation trials (e.g., Benja's being sent in pursuit of Tartakovsky's wealth), the emphasis on sensual rather than spiritual experience, and the roguish hero himself—all suggest a satirical picaresque variant of the medieval romance, a burlesque of the religious or symbolic functions of the epic hero.

At the same time there is a strong element of mockery in the treatment of the heroic characters themselves. With their inimitable jargon and outlandish clothes, Babel's Moldavanka bandits are a decidedly urban phenomenon, more Damon Runyan in intonation than ancient warrior or medieval knight; nor are they convincing as modern Robin Hoods. The Homeric simile as applied to the bandits is at times distorted into a comic parody of itself and of them: "Wines not from these parts...evoked belches that rang out sonorous as trumpets summoning to battle" (208). For all their rejection of the ordered life of bourgeois merchants, they remain essentially the product of their milieu. Even Benja the King is not immune from mockery. He outwits the police and extorts money from the rich, but he bows to the power of tradition and custom: he would prefer to sit down with "Monsieur" Tartakovsky and discuss like a business transaction the terms of his extortionary demands; he is annoyed because he doesn't receive a prompt and civil reply to his extortion note; he argues until hoarse over the pension Tartakovsky will pay Muginstein's mother and in the end settles for a mutually agreeable compromise. There is similar bargaining between Benja and Eichbaum and between Benja and Froim Grach over the terms of marriage contracts, and Benja accepts Tartakovsky's reproach about "killing live people."

The other Moldavanka aristocrats are mock-epic figures too. In "The King," for example, the narrator explains how the gangsters fire their revolvers into the air "because if you don't fire into the air you might kill someone." In their bourgeois respect for caution and tradition, the bandits reveal that ultimately they share, for all their daring, in the same underlying attitudes toward Jewish folkways as do the bankers, tradesmen, rabbis, and

clerks. The effect is to satirize such traditional values as modera-
tion and compromise and to ridicule such homely virtues as
gentleness and concern with family and community. All four of
*The Odessa Tales* deal in a farcical way with Jewish communal
ceremonies or institutions—with weddings and arranged mar-
riages, with feasts and funerals, and with family and community
life in general. The bandits are thus, in part at least, mock-
chivalric figures, and Benja is the warrior and lover of a mock
epic. The operatic melodies of Benja's automobile (the horn of
his car plays a march from *Pagliacci*) invoke a comic-opera quality that mocks the bandit élite as much as it affronts their supposed antithesis, the staid bourgeoisie.

Yet beneath all the mockery Babel's use of the ironic voice conceals an authentic longing for heroic action, and he continues to
find the epic a viable mode for the artistic embodiment of his
most profound desires. But as the modern condition mocks the rebellious human spirit, and the unheroic fact confronts the heroic
act, Babel, like many modern writers, finds that the antiheroic
minor key is the necessary counterpoint to a contemporary epic.
Under these conditions the ironic mode is far more than a rhetorical device; it becomes literally indispensable to the preservation
of any vestige of the heroic spirit.

A useful term for the kind of treatment Babel gives to epic
themes has been provided by Victor Terras in a discussion of *Red
Cavalry*.[15] He speaks of Babel's approach to the epic as travesty,
that is, "replacing (or distorting) the form of an original without,
however, changing the content," which is to be distinguished
from parody—"replacing (or distorting) the content of an original, while retaining the form." The application of this concept
of travesty to Babel is highly suggestive for it illuminates a trait
that recurs through most of his work. In *Red Cavalry* especially,
but even in *The Odessa Tales*, Babel disguises and conceals his
epic themes, but he does not parody them. He reclothes (to use
a formulation close to the etymological meaning of the word

15 Victor Terras, "Line and Color: The Structure of I. Babel's Short Stories
in *Red Cavalry*," *Studies in Short Fiction*, III, No. 1 (Fall 1965), 141–56.

"travesty") his epic heroes in an unusual and incongruous modern garb; but despite the distortion of the outward form, they retain an epic cast.

The claim of an underlying earnestness in Babel's *Odessa Tales* may seem surprising at first, but some sort of didacticism would seem to be common to all manifestations of the epic impulse. In echoing those traditions Babel is concerned to reveal, to celebrate and proselytize, a distinctive style of life. His *Odessa Tales*, for all their seeming ahistoricity, are rooted in a specific time and place. Their setting, though only implied, is still the reactionary post-1905 era, and Odessa, for all its cosmopolitan charm and color, was then a city in which the Jew-hunting Black Hundred and the Union of the Russian People were able to thrive as well. The pogrom was a common occurrence; even the national government, immoral and opportunistic, encouraged and supported such an anti-Semitic horror as the Beilis trial of 1913. The Jews were a special target in this moment of revolutionary hiatus, as they often are in times of national crisis, self-hatred, and fear.

Babel's Odessa stories are not, however, as might be expected, aimed directly at anti-Semitism. Written after the revolutionary upheavals of 1917 and the Civil War which confirmed them, they exude a retrospectively buoyant, almost exultant sense of release; they have a brash and—as it seems now—an overly confident tone that takes the destruction of the old order for granted. They celebrate somewhat prematurely a success not yet tasted. But despite his humor and the hope engendered in him by the new vistas opened to Russia at the beginning of the twenties, the author is unsure. Babel wrote *The Odessa Tales* after his own participation in the Civil War as a comrade-in-arms of the Russian Cossack, and he is celebrating in them his own sense of liberation and enlarged experience. But he remains divided and perplexed about the meaning of his Jewish past, about the nature of the present, and also about what he wants the future to become.

Despite the surface gaiety of the tales, their inner view of contemporary man is rather dark. Violence remains the corrosive center of this world, and the dominant feature of its city landscape is the cemetery. Urban degradation is the underside of Babel's vision, and although he seems to want to smother this awareness it constantly threatens to expose the bright exterior itself as illusion.[16] The stories, as a result, are an extremely volatile mixture of uncertain attitudes and irresolvable conflicts. The multifaceted style as well as the proliferating ironies that give the stories their unique flavor reflects the author's own inner ambivalence.

The situation of the Jew, and in particular of the East European Jew, fraught with overtones of exile and estrangement, has often been taken as a paradigm for the phenomenon of contemporary alienation. As with many modern Jewish writers, Babel's rejection of the ghetto involves more than an attack upon Jewish conditions: it reflects an awareness of the urban ghetto as the modern condition of all men. In its yearning for another place Babel's work suggests an almost mythic search for the uncitified past. But at the same time there is a certain specifically Jewish quality in Babel's alienation. His *Odessa Tales* repudiate and mock many traditional features of Jewish life, and they do so with the bitterness of the apostate. The kind of joy and fulfillment that Babel sought from existence lay outside the limits of Jewish experience and seemed to demand not merely transcendence of that experience, but repudiation of it. Babel attempted, partly as a response to the war, to displace the Jewish mores of his heritage with an altogether alien ethos. It is clear that the displacement, radical though it was, meant a kind of release; he identifies his sense of liberation with a liberation of

---

16 The rather uneasy, at times macabre, fun of these stories is reminiscent in some respects of Gogol's early Ukrainian pieces. That Babel himself came to suspect the exuberance of his Odessa stories is reflected in the fact that he returns to these characters again and again in later works: in the story "Froim Grach," in the screenplay "Benja Krik," and in a story and a play both entitled "Sunset." Babel's treatment of the same milieu and characters becomes darker and more serious; the comic is increasingly crowded out by the emergence of that darker vision which is only inherent in the earlier stories.

the senses, with a new-found joy in physical life.[17] At the same time, however, this joy is inseparably bound up with a feeling of guilt. This rejection of Jewish values produces in Babel a lingering suspicion of self-betrayal, and in the end he is as unable to rid himself of his past as he is to forego his claim to a larger future. Babel's dilemma goes beyond the confines of the specifically Jewish element of his experience to that conflict, not uncommon in Russian literature, between aesthetic and worldly pleasures and the claims of any rigorous and insistent morality.

In Benja Krik, Babel tried to create a figure who would embody the liberation for which he himself was searching. Benja may not have fully emerged from the ghetto, but like his creator he has elected to do battle with life in a larger arena of experience and, so far as he is able, without the encumbrance of either Jewish morality or Jewish exclusiveness. Benja is larger than his environment, not completely defined by it; with regard to the mores of the Jewish community he is an iconoclast, and it is this that makes him unique even among his fellow "aristocrats." Only Benja is prepared to accept the onus of the tenth raid on Tartakovsky and the possibility of murdering a fellow Jew. And he alone has fully enjoyed the pleasures of the nonghetto world, partaking, for example, of the prostitute Katya's "many-colored, Russian and rubicund paradise." These two aspects of Benja's self-expression, his ready violence and his open sexuality, seem crucial. As viewed by Babel—and this is where he runs afoul of humanist criticism—these qualities are not so much the result of struggle against injustice, a reluctant election of violence as the only alternative to annihilation; they are the essentials of

17 In Babel's letters to relatives abroad this belief in some basic incompatability between Jewish destiny and the experience of joy is a not infrequent refrain. To his mother on March 26, 1927: "... live like a human being should. Now it has become quite clear to me that, for two centuries, we haven't lived properly. I would feel much better and would enjoy life more if I were sure you weren't refusing yourself any of the necessities of life...." To his sister on Dec. 15, 1928: "We must decorate our houses with gaiety not with tsores. But how can one convince people of that?" To both his mother and sister on April 27, 1930: "Apparently, of all our family, only that little Weeweeki [Babel's daughter Nathalie] and I have any talent for gaiety." (*Isaac Babel: The Lonely Years*, 92, 112, 138.)

Benja's free personal existence. Benja is not merely fighting to survive; he is demanding to live, to matter, and he chooses to define himself by taking from life what he needs. Though this does not make him attractive to the humanist tradition, it does place him securely within a major branch of modern literature. Babel makes of Benja a kind of profane messiah, an exemplar-rogue whose very knavishness demonstrates the possibility of a self-expressive joy. Benja's will to be is essentially and of necessity anarchic; to exist at all he must constantly challenge authority, whatever its source. "Where there's an emperor, there is no room for a king," is the policeman's response to Benja Krik, and the assertion is an inadvertant tribute to the force of Benja's self-proclamation, to the challenge he hurls in the face of the world.[18] But Babel appears to find this external challenge easier to meet. Benja's more serious adversary resides in the communal values that remain alive and strong within himself, in that cultural heritage that retains its authority over him even as he tries to renounce it.

It is for this reason that Benja's advent, if glorious, is also comical. Something in Babel's ambivalent attitudes, a perversely skeptical sense of reality or a finely ironic sense of truth, forces him to mock his hero as much as he does his other targets. Benja remains the product, in many respects, of the very community his actions ridicule; his kingly attributes and his exploits are travesties of its values and dreams. Even his kingly title is conferred upon him by the community, and the biblical overtones in the stories, though they mock religious values, nevertheless link Benja with ancient Hebrew prophetic and messianic traditions.[19]

18 The terms of the policeman's statement suggest other confrontations: David versus Goliath, Judea versus Rome, religion versus secularism, nation versus the monolithic, supranational state.

19 The network of religious associations permeating Babel's work is striking. Nathalie Babel has testified that her father was an atheist, and although the stories offer much that is consistent with this view, Babel's attitudes are ambiguous and complex. He exhibits a good deal of mockery, even hostility, toward religious institutions, but this very hostility is testimony to the influence that moral and religious categories exercise upon his habits of conceptualization. Synagogues and churches loom large on his fictional landscape, and he frequently, if idiosyncratically, employs a symbolic subtext heavy with religious associations.

If the sublime and the ridiculous are never far apart, Babel brings them perilously close. His reasons are not difficult to ascertain. The use of comedy and irony, like the use of crude naturalistic detail, can forestall the charge of sentimentalism; more specifically, it helps to parry any possible accusation that Babel has a too ready and uncritical acceptance of his exemplar-hero. Pure fantasy, like unadulterated didacticism (and Babel's work contains elements of both), may produce a counterreaction in the reader, turning him against what he is meant to admire. Benja Krik's story is really a fairytale, and the danger for Babel, one that he recognizes, is that fairytales are untrue. A dose of mockery is therefore a healthy corrective, an injection of reality into the realm of romantic dreams. The question remains, however, does the device work? In Babel's *Odessa Tales* it is, at best, only partly successful.

At first the elements of parody and irony are totally confusing. We are not immediately certain where the author stands in relation to his major figure and ultimately to the Jewish world of the stories. Ambiguity is almost universally regarded as a virtue by the modern sensibility, and we are prepared, almost reflexively, to grant Babel his pervasive ambiguities—especially when self-mockery plays as prominent a role as it does in his work. But Babel's mockery is one-sided; it is directed almost exclusively against values that are characteristic of Hebrew and humanist culture. Insofar as this irony is leveled against the author himself or against author-related figures such as the narrators, it seems a legitimate device; such figures are adequately representative of their cultural milieu, and we are able to infer their virtues as well as to accept the negative accusations made against them. But as applied to Benja the same mockery seems inappropriate, since the ethos that he represents is openly presented in the tales as the antithesis of that tradition which the narrative voices embody. To criticize or ridicule Benja for the bizarre surviving traces of his bourgeois upbringing is not to criticize him at all. To mock Benja in earnest would be to mock him where he is most himself, where he most diverges from his milieu and poses

88

an alternative to its central values. But Benja as a creature of brute violence and animal physicality, Benja as didactic exemplar of a new path to joy, is in fact exempted by Babel from mockery; we are allowed the approving laughter that helps to make ferocity more palatable, but we are permitted to direct the laugh of condemnation only against the gentler, more "civilized" attributes. Since we have grown to expect irony and ambiguity, the lack of it here at the central and most vulnerable point of these tales comes as both a surprise and a disappointment.

Many readers are fooled by Babel's ability to conceal the blunt purpose of his central hero. At least one American critic has reacted to these stories with extreme distaste:

> Babel respected the Jews only when they answered the violence done to them with violence of their own. . . . These stories of Odessa seem to me unpalatable. Aside from their moral dubiousness, they affect a folksy amiability and relaxation which are not appropriate to their intense violence and chicanery. Unlike the stories of *Red Cavalry* they seem to have been "gotten up" into literature, but Babel's deliberation over them was unproductive of finer and more humane judgments.[20]

Yet Babel does not espouse violence as an answer to violence. He has gone beyond this toward an understanding of the creative possibilities of the aggressive instincts. He sees how modern urban societies repress spontaneous self-expression, how they throttle the sensual and emotional life, and in the face of this frustration he reasserts the claims of "natural" man. It is true that Babel comes close at times to affirming violence itself as a positive value, but at his best he is capable of establishing the truth of primitive passions without himself becoming a barbarian.

The reader may still find this unpalatable, of course. He may feel that in exalting strength and scorning weakness Babel has obscured what would otherwise be insistent moral dilemmas. He may argue that Babel's characters are stereotypes, grotesque distortions that are unfair to the finer realities of Jewish culture.

20 Steven Marcus, "The Stories of Isaac Babel," *Partisan Review*, XXII, No. 3 (Summer 1955), 407.

But such a view, concentrating on individual characters, misses the point that none of the heroes, whether strong or weak, bandit or bourgeois, is psychologically real. Babel's Odessa heroes are essentially static figures, types rather than persons; taken individually they cannot express the kind of conflicts we look for in complex fictional portraiture. The reader who seeks a recognizably human hero in a recognizably human dilemma must look beyond the psychological implausibilities of Babel's characters to the structural center of his stories, to the narration itself. It is in the narrator (and implicit behind him, the author) that the various static and conventionalized types converge to create a portrait of considerable moral complexity. The author, not the actors, sees the irony in Eichbaum's marrying his daughter to the man who has robbed him, in Grach's search for a son-in-law in a whorehouse, and in the sumptuous funeral given by the bandits for their victim. The stories come alive, finally, in the hidden person of the author, for whom the various characters are only different masks.

We are thrust back then to the heavy burden carried by style in Babel's short stories, to the way in which the clash of opposed views permeates the very language. Narrative and authorial identities sometimes flow together, sometimes diverge; lyrical pathos contrasts with the earthy jargon of the characters; narrative and descriptive coloring clashes with its own content and sounds parodic; the cliché follows hard upon the poetic image; and vulgarity alternates with high sensitivity. Comic incongruity, however, is really only the obverse of poetic congruity, and though these apparently contradictory impulses appear irreconcilable in the tales both have their source in the author. It is he who manipulates the strings and weaves the strange patterns, and the irony and ambiguity of his art are rooted in his vision of himself. In truth, almost all the irony is self-irony, and when this is grasped it becomes clear how insistently moral are Babel's central concerns. In the end Babel's irony is probably self-defeating for it keeps him fatally estranged from both the real and the ideal; but it does exonerate him from the charge of having devised a mindless defense of violence.

If Babel's attempt to depict a new Jewish ethos ultimately fails, it nevertheless marks the beginning of his effort at self-identification, at understanding his own Jewishness. His attack upon Jewish tradition was necessary precisely because that tradition was so strong a force in his own consciousness, and beside the harshness of his attack should be placed the powerful affection for Jewish experience that exists in the very core of his work—in his language. In the verbal dimension of his art, despite the grotesqueness of his characterizations, one finds an underlying sympathy.[21] The variety and profusion of Babel's verbal energy link him directly with Jewish sources; his interweaving of history, poetic myth, and metaphysical speculation with the mundane and prosaic is true to the spirit of ordinary Yiddish conversation, and his very irony and humor reveal a belief in words that relates him to the nonviolence of the ghetto at its best.

Babel's violence, too, is a thing of words: he murders in art. For Babel art is an investigation and trial of the possibilities of life; it is a necessary surrogate for the jungle or battlefield, and he transposes the violence of existence to the relatively manageable arena of words. He has a profound personal need for the catharsis and sublimation of aesthetic creation, and as a result, his stories record the painful but always awesome and rare struggle of the human spirit against itself.

21 The specific formulation of "sympathetic grotesques" as a description of *The Odessa Tales* I have taken from Renato Poggioli, "Isaac Babel in Retrospect," in *The Phoenix and the Spider*, 237. The concept of "travesty," discussed earlier, is equally suggestive in this context, pointing to those values of Jewish culture that Babel disguises but ultimately does not mock.

V

# The Odessa Tales:
# READINGS OF THE STORIES

*Toss me a couple of ideas,... and I'll try to make you a master-piece.*[1]

Many of Babel's stories are based upon little more than a two-line anecdote. When shorn of their verbal adornment his plots seem too meager to support the weight of the finished tales. In a sense there is no plot skeleton to a Babel story; it exists almost totally in its verbal dimensions alone. Nothing else really explains how so many disparate components are so successfully united.

The highly original conception of form implied by such a structure is the subject of most of Babel's remarks about his art, and it is revealing to note that whenever he discusses his work he invariably turns to questions of craftsmanship. He speaks of language as a material to be forcibly shaped and manipulated through the agency of style, which he describes as an "army of words, an army in which all kinds of weapons may come into play." In a particularly memorable passage he describes a phrase as "born into the world both good and bad at the same time. The secret," he says "lies in a slight, an almost invisible twist. The lever should rest in your hand, getting warm, and you can

---

[1] Babel's facetious quotation of an Odessa journalist, as reported by K. Paustovsky in *Vremja bol'šix ožidanij*, 133–34.

only turn it once, not twice." With regard to timing and punctuation he informs us that "no iron can stab the heart with such force as a period put just at the right place."[2] Elsewhere he speaks eloquently on the nature of the adjective and the shape of the metaphor, the subtleties of participles, and on the proper use of the paragraph. But never does he speak of controlling themes, motifs, or ideas in themselves; nowhere does he discuss construction in the broader sense—or, indeed, in any terms other than those of a man preoccupied with the problems of style.

For Babel, style itself is the basic ingredient of structure. He takes some ephemeral impression, some slight fragment of reality, and under his hands this simple kernel is shaped, cut, and faceted with words and then endlessly polished until it reveals the unsuspected beauty of its hidden depths. Babel himself is the severest analyst of his art, and the critic would do well to listen to what he says:

> . . . it's style that does it. I can write a short story about washing underwear and it will read like Julius Caesar's prose. It's all a matter of language and style. . . .
> What I do is to get hold of some trifle, some little anecdote, a piece of market gossip, and turn it into something I cannot tear myself away from. It's alive, it plays. It's round like a pebble on the seashore. It's held together by the fusion of separate parts, and this fusion is so strong that even lightning can't split it. And people will read the story. They'll remember it, they'll laugh, not because it's funny but because one always feels like laughing in the presence of human good fortune.[3]

The first of *The Odessa Tales* ("The King") gives an excellent illustration of Babel's technique. The grain of sand around which this pearl of a story grows is a simple, mildly amusing anecdote; but through the agency of style it is transformed into an episode from some half-serious, half-comic saga, into a fairytale for grown-ups. The plot tells how Benja Krik and his men foil

---

2 From Babel's story "Guy de Maupassant." Trans. Walter Morison, *Isaac Babel: The Collected Stories,* 331, 332.

3 From Konstantin Paustovsky's memoirs, trans. Andrew MacAndrew in *Dissonant Voices in Soviet Literature,* 47–48.

an intended police raid by burning down the precinct station. But a different "plot" is hidden in the verbal fabric of the story; to hear this tale one must heed the inner logic of the imagery and attend to motifs that are buried in word associations. This underlying plot of "The King" is a celebration of the rites of flesh: all of the apparently disconnected images coalesce around this theme like patches of color in an impressionist painting.

The story opens at the wedding of Benja's sister Dvoira. The very first words invoke the theme. First a brief nod toward the sanctification traditionally demanded by society before the enjoyment of conjugal bliss may begin—"The wedding ceremony ended, the Rabbi sank into an armchair"—then, with the religious ceremony over, the actual rites can begin. A description of the tables set up in the courtyard for the wedding feast sets the scene:

> There were so many of them that those at the end *thrust their tail* right out into Hospital Street. Velvet-spread, they *wound their way* down the yard *like so many serpents* with *variegated patches* on their *bellies*, and *they sang full-throatedly*, those patches of *orange and red velvet* (203; italics added).

The italicized words all emphasize the voluptuousness of the central image, that of a serpent whose coiled entry into this garden of Eden (a garden blessed by the holy presence of the rabbi) is an insinuation of the presence of original sin. Even the apparently unmotivated reference to "Hospital Street" contributes to the underlying theme and helps to prepare for the direction of its subsequent development. The next paragraph begins with a short neutral sentence and then, in what might be called an invocation to the flesh, elaborates upon the implications of the initial image by introducing the motif of fire:

> The living quarters had been turned into kitchens. A sultry flame beat through the soot-swathed doorways, a flame drunken and puffy-lipped. The faces of the old crones broiled in its smoky rays— old women's tremulous chins and beslobbered bosoms. Sweat with the pinkness of fresh blood, sweat as pink as the slaver of a mad dog, streamed this way and that over those mounds of exorbitant and sweetly pungent flesh. (203).

It is startling to observe how virtually every word in this passage is concentrated upon a single effect. There is a sweet smell of decay about all of this sweating and abundant flesh (note the play on the words bosoms and mounds—Russian "grudi" and "grudy"), and the flames of this kitchen seem to suggest corruption and hell as much as they do the cooking of food. After this opening we are distracted by the arrival of an "unknown young man" who has news of the police for Benja. But this commencement of the outer plot does not detain us for long because the narrator almost immediately tells us he must digress to relate the interesting story of Sender Eichbaum. The supposed digression is actually a narrative ruse, a joke; it takes us right back to the original theme, for the "story of Sender Eichbaum" is a history of Benja Krik's own violent courtship.

We are told how Benja set about, through terror and extortion, to rob Sender Eichbaum of a goodly number of his cows. He threatens to kill all of Eichbaum's stock if rebuffed and gives point to his demands by putting his threat into immediate action. Benja's final prize, however, is to win Eichbaum's daughter, and the slaughtering of the cows is really a kind of ritual preliminary to the ensuing nuptials:

> They came in the night, nine men bearing long poles in their hands. The poles were wrapped about with pitch-dipped tow. Nine flaming stars flared in Eichbaum's cattle yard. Benja beat the locks from the door of the cowshed and began to lead the cows out one by one. Each was received by a lad with a knife. He would overturn the cow with one blow of the fist and plunge his knife into her heart. On the blood-flooded ground the torches bloomed like roses of fire, and shots rang out (205–6).

The scene is etched against the night like a somber pagan ritual: nine priestlike ruffians officiate beneath nine flaming "stars." The torches, reflected in the sacrificial blood of the animals, bloom like roses of fire. Then the description is abruptly halted for a brief exchange of comic dialogue during which Eichbaum quietly accedes to Benja's demands. The raid has achieved its purpose, but the narrator explicitly tells us that "the wonder came later," that the real story is elsewhere and the climax not yet reached. The awesome ceremonies are invoked once more as the language again takes on its coloring of black magic:

> During the raid, on that dreadful night when cows bellowed as they were slaughtered and heifers slipped and slithered in the blood of their dams, when the torch-flames danced like dark-visaged maidens and the milkmaids lunged back in horror from the muzzles of amiable Brownings—on that dread night there ran out into the yard, wearing nought save her V-necked shift, Tsilya the daughter of old man Eichbaum (206).

The word associations here dispel all doubt as to the nature of the ceremony: the torches and maidens performing their dance in front of the revolvers, the heifers stained with their mothers' blood, and the reference to milkmaids all point to a ritual ceremony celebrating betrothal and the sacrifice of virginity.[4]

Eichbaum is reluctant to relinquish his daughter, but Benja's powers of persuasion are sufficient and he attains his desires:

> And Benja Krik had his way, for he was passionate, and passion rules the universe. The newlyweds spent three months on the fat lands of Bessarabia, three months flooded with grapes, rich food, and the sweat of love's encounters (207).

There is a pun in the biblically resonant and expansive maxim about passion, for in context it contracts into a comically specific and literal meaning. Returning from a blissful three-month sojourn in Bessarabia (an occasion and setting slightly less legendary than a thousand and one Arabian nights, but with other advantages more attractive to the King of Odessa), Benja sets about the forcible marrying off of his forty-year-old virgin sister Dvoira, who suffers from goiter. Like Benja, Dvoira is to embark on her great adventure "amid the grape, rich food, and the

---

4 Cattle stealing has an ancient history as a marriage feat. Early Greek tribal chieftains paid for their brides with the proceeds of a cattle raid, women being valued in terms of so many cows. The Old Testament recounts such episodes too, but here Benja pays Eichbaum for his daughter with his own animals.

sweat of love's encounters."[5] The lingering description, which follows next, of the exotic wines and abundant foods at Dvoira's wedding feast has already been noted; only the third ingredient of this profane trinity, the sweat of love, remains to be fulfilled. The feast takes on a suitably fantastic air, half bacchanal, half courtly revel. Relatives, guests, and the shammashim from the synagogue all become drunk; the orchestra plays martial music as, in accordance with "ancient customs," the guests bestow gifts upon the newly wedded pair. The bandits, those "aristocrats of the Moldavanka," call upon the couple to kiss, chanting the traditional Russian cry of "bitter." The feeble little groom whom Eichbaum's money has purchased for Dvoira must find the word particularly appropriate as he glances at the forty-year-old bride sitting at his side, disfigured by disease, with swollen goiter and bulging eyes. Then, as the wedding celebration draws toward a close, there is a sudden moment of excitement. Something is burning:

> Over the courtyard there suddenly spread a faint smell of burning ... the smoke cloud grew more and more venomous. Here and there the edges of the sky were turning pink, and now there shot up, narrow as a sword blade, a tongue of flame. The guests, half rising from their seats, began to snuffle the air, and the womenfolk gave little squeaks of fear (209).

If the words of this climactic passage are compared with those of the story's opening, the cross-relationships of the two sections stand out in bold relief. The sultry flame and sweating bodies that began this tale of a wedding feast are reinvoked by the greater conflagration that serves as climax, but in a new light. The serpent, whose intimated presence at the initial celebration had contributed an ominous note of damnation, is exorcized and consumed by the devouring flames, and the "unknown young man" who had appeared earlier materializes once more to report

---

[5] The phrase in Russian ("sredi vinograda, obli'noj pišči i ljubovnogo pota"), with its alliterative repetition of the labial consonants v, b, and p and its two rounded and labialized culminating vowels, is itself sensuously suggestive.

with irrepressible delight on the fire—a further suggestion that the satanic serpent has given way to a rather merry, giggling Mephisto.

The fire is actually the burning police station that the bandits have set ablaze, but Benja's diversionary action in foiling the police is merely a corollary of the diversionary tactic of the narrative itself. The network of verbal associations and the pattern of images are what really dictate the fiery finale.[6] Climaxing the theme of flesh and damnation, the fire unites this verbally conditioned understructure with the comic narrative surface that comprises the more obvious strand of the "plot."

The hidden tale is also essentially parodic in intention. The comic aspect of the conflagration dispels the notion of a blazing inferno of damnation, and the mockery of religious associations suggests that rather than flames of hell, these are flames of passion dedicated to carnal love and to the wedding night of Dvoira Krik.[7]

The climax is not quite the end of the story. As is frequently the case in Babel's structural schemes the ending consists of a relatively short, sharp stroke that illuminates once more the general outlines of the tale. Here is the concluding paragraph in which the main dish of the wedding feast is at last served up:

> When Benja got back home the little lamps in the courtyard were flickering out, and dawn was beginning to touch the sky. The guests had departed and the musicians were dozing, leaning their heads on their double basses. Dvoira alone was not thinking of sleep. With both hands she was urging her faint-hearted husband toward the

6 An impressive array of images and words is directed to the themes of fire, flesh, and hell. Especially striking is the abundant use of color and the lavish way in which red tones (the colors of both flesh *and* fire) predominate. Babel uses a whole series of color adjectives (red, pink, orange, raspberry, ruddy) as well as other color-inducing words and images (e.g., flame, blood, flesh, blazing stars, dawn, torches, fiery roses, grape, wine, oranges, tongue, burn, shine, blaze).

7 The Bible and Haggadical writings are full of the use of fire as a symbol of the Lord's destructive power (e.g., from the Haggadah of Passover: "And I shall do wonders in the heavens and earth: Blood, and Fire, and Pillars of Smoke"). The fire here is an act of rebellion against both the chief of police and the rabbi, and thus the theme of sexual liberation is linked to the idea of political and spiritual emancipation as well.

door of their nuptial chamber, glaring at him carnivorously. Like a cat she was, that holding a mouse in her jaws tests it gently with her teeth (211).[8]

"The King" was the first of the Odessa tales to be published and probably the first to be written. A veritable tour de force, it has the stamp of being the happy issue of a first inspiration and remains unique among *The Odessa Tales.* Although the same volatile ingredients are combined in the other stories of the cycle, it is not surprising that each of these tales exhibits some new and significant departures. The distinctions in narrative structure especially are interesting in themselves and illustrative of Babel's developing techniques. The second of the stories, "How It Was Done in Odessa," stands apart from the others in a number of ways. It is the only one of the four that has a special narrator and perhaps for that reason the only one that achieves the totally oral effect of immediate narration. Much of the story is given over to dialogue; when the narrator is not reporting the talk of others he himself is a master monologist. Factual description is kept to a bare minimum, and when it does appear it is dominated by the declamatory and mythic tones in which it is phrased. In spite of the fact that this is the longest of the four stories and that its ostensible subject is the character of the hero Benja Krik, there are no involved psychological analyses or complications of the underlying anecdotal base. Almost everything contributes to the effect of speech.

"How It Was Done in Odessa" tells of Benja's rise to fame, of his raid on the merchant Tartakovsky, and of the funeral he arranged for one of his victims. Reb Arye-Leib, the garrulous old man who narrates the tale, speaks with the same Jewish rhythms as the other Odessa characters; an interrogative intonation is common and major remarks are almost always prefaced with a question. When asked, for example, why only Benja Krik of all the gangsters rose to unprecedented heights of power and

8 The name Dvoira (or Deborah) means "bee" in ancient Hebrew. Benja's sister, with her bulging eyes and goitered neck, is thus not only a cat, but a queen bee, who in mating with the male drone will cause his death.

glory, Arye-Leib's answer begins with a question: "Why he? Why not they, you wish to know?" There is a hint of biblical magnificence in the rhythm of this response as there is in the parablelike quality of the eventual answer itself, for Arye-Leib never takes the simple or direct path in his explanations; he chooses the more circuitous method of illustration through comparison. He is a "reb," a teacher, and the biblical mode of narration comes to him naturally:

> And now I will speak as the Lord God spoke on Mount Sinai from the Burning Bush. Put my words in your ears. All I saw, I saw with my own eyes, sitting here on the wall of the Second Cemetery next to Little Lisping Mose and Samson from the undertaker's. I, Arye-Leib, saw this—I, a proud Jew dwelling by the dead (220).

The "biblical" tone alternates, however, with a comic vulgarity:

> ... [pretend that] your father is Mendel Krik the drayman. What does such a father think about? He thinks about drinking a good glass of vodka, of smashing somebody in the face, of his horses— and nothing more. You want to live, and he makes you die twenty times a day (212).

These examples from the narrative speech of Arye-Leib must be recognized as more than merely a means of characterizing the narrator linguistically. They indicate that oral devices permeate the entire compositional structure of the story and constitute its organizing principle. The sustained intonational rhythms, the digressions and bizarre detours, the pauses, the suggestions of gestures, the interpolated references to a listener, the bardic contrasting of a mundane present with an epic past, the repetition and word play—all point to the pronounced oral basis of the story, to its calculated effort to impose the illusion of improvised talk. So strong indeed are the effects of such oral devices that the story asks to be heard rather than read, or at least stimulates in the reader a desire to read it aloud.[9]

---

[9] Reminiscences of Babel by K. Paustovsky, I. Ehrenburg, and the Hungarian E. Sinkó contain numerous references to his abilities as a storyteller. Ehrenburg regrets the innumerable stories that Babel told but never found time to write; Paustovsky says that Babel's delivery made his stories when he told them even more

As is usually the case in Babel's work, it is not the outer subject of the tale that provokes the most interest, but the manner of its presentation. It is style that reveals the inner clash of opposing visions and gives a tale its peculiar radiance—and in "How It Was Done in Odessa" style is what the story is all about. Since the narrator and narrative devices occupy center stage and constitute the structural frame for this story, it is they that require the reader's first and closest attention.

No other story of the four has such a distinct and recognizable personality as Arye-Leib built as a focus into the story itself. Standing close to the center of events, he has none of that "outsider" quality to his voice and none of that neutrality of tone that occasionally appear in the other three tales. He is deeply immersed in the milieu he describes and he even speaks, as we have noted, with some of the same intonations as do his heroes— or, rather, the characters of his narrative speak within the broad range of Arye-Leib's voice. Ultimately, almost all of the talk is his: it is his voice, with its comically twisted, almost palpable words, that makes Babel's fantastic fictional Moldavanka come alive.

Another unique feature of "How It Was Done in Odessa" is the listener, the "I" who appears at the very beginning of the story and to whom Arye-Leib tells his tale. The invention of this new figure, separate and distinct from the narrator, greatly complicates and enriches the narrative structure by providing a kind of distorting echo chamber for transmitting events to the reader. Furthermore, the lyrical strain now emerges in its own right, and this new focal point within the story allows Babel to explore some additional ironic and dramatic conflicts. By introducing the listener-romantic, Babel provides a contrasting sounding

---

nearly flawless than when they were written; and Sinkó speaks of the writer's endless delight in anecdotes and gossip, which he related with all the gusto, gestures, and finesse of the born raconteur who savors each word and looks on his own happy formulations with the delight of a child. The talents of the actor, mimic, and caricaturist which made him such an excellent oral teller of tales are evident in Babel's written work as well, especially in his stories of Odessa. (See I. Ehrenburg, "Predislovie," *I. Babel': Izbrannoe*; E. Sinkó, *Roman eines Romans*; K. Paustovsky, *Vremja bol'šix ožidanij.*

EL CAMINO COLLEGE
LIBRARY

board for the narrator Arye-Leib, a foil against which the latter can exercise his wit and through which he can make his meanings sharper. Arye-Leib's language is by turns earthy and picturesque or solemn and biblical; it may even partake of the grand epic manner, but it is always consistent with the basic intonations of the Odessa jargon and Arye-Leib himself remains an integral part of the milieu he describes. The sympathetic listener, on the other hand, remains outside the tale's milieu: his language is literary and his discourse lyrical in intonation. It is the listening "I" who opens the story:

> It was I that began.
> "Reb Arye-Leib," I said to the old man, "let us talk of Benja Krik. Let us talk of his thunderclap beginning and his terrible end. Three black shadows block up the paths of my imagination. Here is the one-eyed Ephraim Rook. The russet steel of his actions, can it really not bear comparison with the strength of the King? Here is Nick Pakovsky. The simple-minded fury of that man held all that was necessary for him to wield power. And did not Haim Drong know how to distinguish the brilliance of the rising star? Why then did Benja Krik alone climb to the top of the rope ladder, while all the rest hung swaying on the lower rungs?" (212).

The speaker's style gives us a sense of his personality. The heightened language, despite its sophistication, reveals a poetic dreamer, a naïve and romantic youth. The opening of the story is furthermore broadly suggestive of the Seder, the Hebrew religious ceremony during which a youth asks his elders profound questions and receives by way of answer stories from the history of the Jews. The next words spoken by the "I," with their biblically phrased adages, reinforce these religious associations:

> Reb Arye-Leib was silent, sitting on the cemetery wall. Before us stretched the green stillness of the graves. A man who thirsts for an answer must stock himself with patience. A man possessing knowledge is suited by dignity. For this reason Reb Arye-Leib was silent, sitting on the cemetery wall (212).

The silence of Arye-Leib lasts but briefly. Having introduced the story and himself, the "I" assumes his role of listener and retreats to the periphery of the narrative. The rest of the words belong to Arye-Leib.

These opening lines set the stage for the recital of legendary events. We are shown Benja Krik in the early days of his career, during the period when he first revealed himself as an exceptional man and at the crucial moment of his emergence as a king. In keeping with this revelatory aspect of the narrative, a triumphant, even solemn, tone is sounded again and again. We have noted already the generally biblical quality of the opening; here and there one may detect more concrete hints of a biblical grandeur: in the solemn invocation of Benja's awesome beginning and his terrible end; in the reference to a new and shining star; and in the image of Benja ascending a ladder. Arye-Leib, whose narrative style is full of biblical intonation, is quick to reinforce our impression; he tells his young companion to imagine himself for a moment in Benja's place: "If rings were fastened to heaven and earth, you would grasp them and draw heaven and earth together" (212). Of course, given the specific context of the narrative, the effect of such a passage is mainly ironic and the tone one of mock rather than real solemnity. Benja's is an intentionally profane figure through which to suggest the uniting of the heavenly and the earthly, the spiritual and the physical.

Arye-Leib, in spite of the comic incongruity of epic treatment for a group of Odessa bandits, takes on the aspect of bardic singer. He treats events in a legendary manner, as if they had taken place long ago or far away. When he describes how Benja, early in his career, petitioned to join the illustrious band of Froim Grach, he speaks as of great and distant doings: "And the gangsters went into conference to consider the matter of Benja Krik. I wasn't at that conference, but they say that a conference was held" (213).

The band's decision is to try Benja by sending him on a raid against Ruvim Tartakovsky, and the reader will not be wrong in seeing in the assignment the outlines of a mythic encounter. At first glance one is tempted to see a kind of comic parallel to the initiation trial of a knight-errant, with Benja a kind of sullied Galahad being sent in quest of a more than spiritual treasure.[10] But there is another parallel, closer to home. The assignment given to Benja is a particularly difficult one: Tartakovsky has been afflicted by bandit raids nine times already; he has also had the distinction of a premature funeral service; and furthermore, though he is a rich man and has the soul of a murderer, he is one of them—an Odessa Jew. Indeed, Tartakovsky is a kind of legend himself, and although recognized as a merciless exploiter, he is given grudging respect by the community at large. Arye-Leib, with his comic rhetoric, makes it clear that he is a figure combining greed with power and that he is a worthy adversary for Benja:

> We used to call Tartakovsky "Jew-and-a-Half" . . . "Jew-and-a-Half" he was called because no single Jew could have had so much dash and so much cash as Tartakovsky. He was taller than the tallest cop in Odessa, and weighed more than the fattest of Jewesses (213).

Despite such constant intrusion of the comic into the conflict, Tartakovsky is a serious opponent. He is a rich and powerful oppressor of the poor and weak; half of Odessa, chained to his greed, labors endlessly in his shops. If Tartakovsky is really "Jew-and-a-Half," it is because he has sucked out the life of others, of slaves like his clerk Muginstein. In the story's symbolic and allegorical subtext, Tartakovsky even takes on a certain historical resonance, and through the tale's network of religious imagery, Babel makes of him a Pharaonic symbol. It is a circumstance with intentional ironic effect: "Tartakovsky has the soul of a murderer, but he is one of us. He originated with us. He is our blood. He is our flesh, as though one momma had born us" (214). It is his Jewishness that protects Tartakovsky from Jewish retribution. He is robbed, but his position is unassailed; he is buried, but only symbolically, so that he can rise from the grave to resume, like Pharaoh, his oppression of the people. In his

10 Like Galahad, too, Benja ends his adventure with investiture as a "king"; but unlike Galahad's, Benja's soul does not depart his body for the trip heavenward.

answer to Benja's extortion note, Tartakovsky assumes the role of fellow Jew and sufferer, of one condemned to a life of endless convict labor. A different conclusion, however, may be inferred from Tartakovsky's specific list of woes and tribulations. "Ulcers, sores, troubles and insomnia" afflict him in the same way that the plagues of the Lord afflicted Pharaoh—and, like Pharaoh, Tartakovsky remains unmoved.

It therefore falls upon Benja, who in this context becomes as much deliverer as bandit, to visit upon Tartakovsky an unprecedented tenth raid, something the other bandits, for all their boldness, have steadfastly refrained from undertaking. In his note Benja warns Tartakovsky that if he once more refuses to comply with the demands made upon him a great disappointment awaits him in his "family life." The tenth and final affliction visited upon Pharaoh was, of course, the slaying of the firstborn, and the implication is unavoidable that Benja in his wrath is capable of being no less terrible than the vengeful Yahweh. It is this finally that sets Benja apart from all of the other "aristocrats" of the Moldavanka: he does not waver before the ultimate grim necessity, even when the enemy is unhappily within instead of without the tribe. The result of the raid is indeed a slaying, though not precisely of Tartakovsky's firstborn. Tartakovsky, we are told, raises a hue and cry through all Odessa, while Benja, who is not to be cowed, argues with unwitting irony that even God makes mistakes.

The story progresses, under Arye-Leib's direction, by fits and starts. He steps in and out of his tale as it suits him, sometimes to slow down the pace, sometimes to mystify and heighten suspense, sometimes to make an appropriate observation. Occasionally he employs the device of the mock parable, which parodies the usual presentation of moral truths. True to his intonational style he often proceeds as if unraveling a riddle, he himself supplying both question and answer:

> When Ephraim informed him accordingly, he said "O.K." and went out, banging the door. Why did he bang the door? You will learn this if you come where I shall lead you (214).

All of Arye-Leib's narrative devices are justified by structure or effectiveness. His digressions, intrusions, pauses, and repetitions are the very stuff of which his tale is made. After giving a detailed report of Benja's bargaining with Tartakovsky over how much the murdered clerk's mother is to be paid (a bargain in which each side overstates its case before coming to businesslike agreement with the other), he produces the following typical comment: "Then they used bad language at one another hammer and tongs, Jew-and-a-Half and Benja. I wasn't present at this quarrel, but those who were remember it" (218). Those present, of course, were only the principals to the argument, but this does not prevent Arye-Leib from knowing exactly how Benja was dressed for the occasion or from knowing precisely where he paused in his argument for rhetorical effect. He has the right details, and if he has them secondhand this only emphasizes that he is telling the stuff of legends, of mythic battles—though the battle here, like almost everything else in Arye-Leib's tale, is a thing of words.

But Arye-Leib's most effective rhetorical device, one which serves as an ironic refrain throughout the entire narrative structure and which gives the story its tension and conflict, is the sarcastic assault that he periodically makes upon his young listener. The lyrical "I," whose voice opened the tale, is silent throughout the rest of its pages, but never out of sight; Arye-Leib is able to conjure up his person whenever he wishes to instruct through negative precept. The bookish romanticist and lyric poet, as seen through the eyes of Arye-Leib (and behind him, through the controlling vision of the author), emerges as the direct antithesis of the hero Benja Krik. Arye-Leib's very first words challenge his youthful listener to imagine Benja by turning himself inside out:

> Forget for a while that you have spectacles on your nose and autumn in your heart. Cease playing the rowdy at your desk and stammering while others are about. Imagine for a moment that you play the rowdy in public places and stammer on paper. You

are a tiger, you are a lion, you are a cat. You can spend the night with a Russian woman, and satisfy her (212).

He then asks the youth what he would have done if he had been cursed (or blessed) with a father like Benja's:

> What would you have done in Benja Krik's place? You would have done nothing. But *he* did something. That's why he's the King, while you thumb your nose in the privy (212).

Again, after telling how the guiltless Muginstein was murdered by a drunken member of Benja's gang, Arye-Leib asks the young listener:

> Now tell me, young master, you who snip coupons on other people's shares, how would you have acted in Benja Krik's place? You don't know how you would have acted. But he knew. That's why he's the King, while you and I are sitting on the wall of the Second Jewish Cemetery and keeping the sun off with our palms (217).

What Benja does, given the circumstances, is first to arrange for Muginstein's murderer to join him in the other world and then to organize for both the most sumptuous funeral Odessa had ever seen. Among the host of mourners are the employees of Ruvim Tartakovsky, dressed all in black and plodding along in shoes that "squeak like pigs in a poke." There are, says Arye-Leib, "a hundred of them, or two-hundred, or two thousand," but the actual figure is unimportant; they are a mass, not individuals, and the astonishing fertility imparted to them by Arye-Leib's rhetoric is a bitter and ironic comment on the promise that the Lord's people should increase and multiply.

Arye-Leib's tale rises to a fantastic climax as he describes how Benja, in the midst of the funeral ceremonies, dramatically arrives to deliver the oration. He appears amid a cloud of fumes in a sparkling red automobile; its wheels cast thunderbolts and its horn plays an aria from the opera *Pagliacci*. The ludicrous improbability of this visitation does not quite conceal the biblical parallel as Benja steps up on a mound of earth and with outstretched hands addresses the people.[11] The speech itself is a pure piece of verbal legerdemain, eloquently demonstrative of Benja's style, and on the surface utterly devoid of logic. But Benja's apparently incongruous eulogy—to the effect that Joseph Muginstein had died on behalf of the working-class—contains an underlying seriousness and truth. "There are people already condemned to death, and there are people who have not yet begun to live," declares Benja, and his words suggest the misery of all those lives doomed to pass within the shadow of ghetto walls.

Benja, on the other hand, is outrageously capable of living. He is a man, as Arye-Leib informs us with pride, who can "spend the night with a Russian woman and satisfy her"; he is one of those, in his own words, who "know how to drink vodka," who can take the experience of life straight. Benja refuses to endure oppression of any kind, and his emergence from behind the walls of spiritual as well as physical ghettos is his challenge to the past, to the monotony and passivity of Jewish suffering—and it is his call, as a contemporary king of kings, to a new exodus for his people.

Having delivered his oration Benja descends from the mound and disappears amid the smoke, the thunderbolts, and the music of his red chariot. It is then that little lisping Mose, the quiet figure who has always occupied the best seat on the cemetery wall, first utters the word "King" in reference to Benja Krik. When we recall that Arye-Leib has prefaced this final climax of his story with words that sound the laconic splendor of the Bible ("And now I will speak as the Lord God spoke on Mount Sinai from the Burning Bush"), we may well conclude that throughout his tale he has played an eloquent Aaron indeed to the less articulate, lisping Moses, and we may well remember that the voice from the burning bush spoke to the Jewish people of an end to their bondage and of a land of milk and honey that would one day be theirs.

11 From the Haggadah of the Passover again: "And the Lord took us out of Egypt with a strong hand, and with an out-stretched arm, and with great terror, and with signs, and with wonders."

The story's final paragraphs strike an ironic note and at the same time give the narrative Babel's favorite circular form. Arye-Leib descends from the elevated style of his most impassioned rhetorical moment to inform his listener that on the very day of the funeral, on the same day that Benja was first called king, Tartakovsky closed up shop. In Arye-Leib's very last words he expresses a lingering doubt that the young man who has heard his tale will have truly understood it:

> "Now you know all. You know who first uttered the word 'King.' It was Little Mose. You know why he didn't give that name to One-Eyed Rook, or to Crazy Nick. You know all. But what's the use, if you still have spectacles on your nose and autumn in your heart?" (222).

The ironic repercussions of this closing are rich and complex. The lyrical dreamer whose words opened the story had been asked by Arye-Leib to imagine that he was someone else, someone like Benja Krik, for only a concerted effort of the imagination could make this tale of adventure and passion real for such a timid, untried, bookish youth. And yet, paradoxically, the young man possesses qualities that are indispensable to the perception and appreciation of the multicolored, exotic world Arye-Leib describes. The autumn in his heart is the romantic pathos that allows such fantasies a measure of reality, and the spectacles on his nose, though they may be of colored glass and though they suggest the image of an academic and reserved intellectual, nevertheless represent the means to vision for the otherwise sightless.

On the other hand, says Arye-Leib, the imagination is insufficient: you may know everything, but unless the knowledge you have is a part of the reality of your being you know nothing; you remain an outsider, an on-looker. Imagination may lead you part of the way, but it can also take you into the comfortable rut of hollow pieties and deceptive traditions. To understand fully why Benja alone among many bold and violent men was the "King" requires more than a mere recognition of the Hebrew monotheistic tradition; it demands as well recognition of Benja's fundamental iconoclasm, of his pure and primeval contempt for degenerate tradition and dogma. Benja's wrath, like that of Yahweh, may be hurled against the people he loves as well as against their enemies; if he does battle with those enemies who attack the Jewish people from outside its communal structure, he rejects no less the complacent assumption of moral superiority so jealously guarded by hypocrites within the ghetto walls. Pharaoh is everywhere, within as well as without, and the road from slavery to freedom, from subjugation to redemption, demands that Pharaoh be resisted wherever he may be. The Jewish houses will not be passed over in the necessary slaying of the firstborn, not if it is to be the true passage "from sorrow to joy, and from mourning to festive day, and from darkness to a great light" (from the Haggadah of Passover). Of course if Arye-Leib's rhetoric has enticed the reader into accepting his fantastic fairy-tale for a kind of reality, it is ultimately due to the subtle craft of the author, who, hidden behind all of his characters, peers at us enigmatically through his own thick lenses. Arye-Leib's mocking criticism of the dreamy literary youth has partly blinded us to the fact that he, too, is an incorrigible romantic, a dreamer sitting on the sidelines atop the cemetery wall and singing the incomparable lay of Benja the King.

The two remaining Odessa stories share with "The King" and "How It Was Done in Odessa" many stylistic and thematic characteristics, but at the same time Babel is attempting, not without difficulty, to expand and deepen the possibilities of his material. Both "The Father" and "Ljubka the Cossack" also celebrate antitraditionalism and vigorous physicality, but this time the central characters are women. In "The Father," Benja Krik appears only toward the end; the dominant figure is Basja Grach, daughter of the one-eyed gangster Froim. Gigantic in her physique as well as her appetites, Basja, like Dvoira, is eager to find a mate. After casting about in the direction of an undersized grocery clerk (whose very name, Kaplun—Capon—is a mockery of her desires), she is matched with the King himself, the only character likely to survive the crush of her loving embrace. All of these women—Basja with her capon, Dvoira with her mouse-spouse, and the husbandless Ljubka—suffer from a lack of comparably vigorous male partners.

In the final story Benja does not appear at all, but the female protagonist, Ljubka, assumes a similar role. She is as rough and wild, as awesome in her way, as the King, and although the heroic, almost hagiographic, tone applied to Benja is absent here, the exaggerated, hyperbolic style is retained. Ljubka is presented as a figure larger than life and she partakes of a similar mythic-symbolic significance. The very nickname, "the Cossack," antithetical to "the Jew," suggests the same primitive attachment to physicality and force that characterized Benja and indicates that she has also rejected the cramped, segregated life of the ghetto. Ljubka's surname, in mocking contrast to her nickname, is Schneeweiss (Snow White). The two names, suggesting barbarous violence and gentle repose, reveal that typical fusion of incompatibilities that so often lies at the heart of Babel's vision. To be sure, there is an element of mockery; Snow White also evokes the image of Ljubka as a princess surrounded by dwarfs and freaks.[12] But there is still another, less obvious relevance to the allusion: Ljubka is identified with Snow White the eternally pure, with the sleeping beauty who required the touch of a Prince Charming to bring the blush of life to her cheeks. Although Ljubka apparently has no husband, she would seem, since she does have a son, to have been visited by some kind of Prince Charming. His identity is problematical, but to judge from Ljubka's formidable personality no mere mortal could have been her match. The religious travesty becomes obvious when the dominant image of the story is seen to be that of madonna and child, and Ljubka is finally associated with the virgin mother of Christian tradition and her son with the Messiah. The inn over which Ljubka reigns is a stopping place for wayfarers and pilgrims, and among those who arrive bringing tribute are three sailors from distant parts: the engineer Mr. Trottyburn and his

12 In a later story ("The Awakening"), where the indictment of Jewish culture seems more bitter, Babel actually uses the terms "dwarf" and "runt" to describe Odessa's brood of child violinists.

two companions, a Malayan and an English sailor. There are several indications that these travelers are to be identified with the biblical Magi, but the most compelling are the offerings they bring of tobacco, cocaine, and wine, and the orange star that gazes at them from the edge of the horizon.

Babel is once again in these allusions adjusting religious forms to modern secular usage, but what is strikingly new in this story is the admixture of specifically Christian motifs with the Hebraic elements used in the first two Odessa tales. If Benja had the aspect of an Old Testament Yahweh, Ljubka's son, who bears the royal name of David, suggests a sort of New Testament Messiah. He is admiringly described as "big as a Russian" and seems to be another of Babel's symbols for the emancipation from Jewish tradition. As in the biblical story, the young child and the hope he represents are threatened, but by the madonna-mother herself rather than by a Herod figure. Competing in the harsh world of smuggling, prostitution, and drink, Ljubka is more than a match for the roughest of her male customers, but she pays a price: she is unable, for all the amazon charms of her physique, to produce milk for her child. In performing an essentially male role she has lost a part of her femaleness, and it is a man, the wizened little Jew Tsudechkis (representing a transferred maternal figure much as Joseph in the Bible represents a transferred paternal figure), who weans the infant from breast to bottle. The weaning is typical of Babel, symbolic as well as actual, and suggests that the next generation will be the first to be truly emancipated, free not only of Egypt and the wilderness but of self-captivity as well. Little David remains, however, only a hope, tentative and unfulfilled, a promise rather than a revelation.[13]

This story, like "The Father," is interesting evidence of Babel's effort to go beyond the accomplishment of his first two Odessa tales. He did not completely succeed in his aim, and the problem

[13] The use of a child figure to symbolize hope occurs in almost all periods of Babel's creative life. He frequently represents the child as a possible future synthesis of conflicting values, especially in the later stories "Karl Yankel" and "Oil."

appears to lie in his attitude toward his material. In the first of *The Odessa Tales,* "The King," a controlling and sustaining feature is the author's sheer pleasure in the exuberance of his material; his captivating joy in the peculiarities of the Odessa speech contributes an essentially jocular spirit to the entire tale.[14] Much the same can be said of the second story, "How It Was Done in Odessa," in which Babel continues to exploit the natural potential of his material at the same time that he experiments with a deepening use of narrative and other stylistic devices. "How It Was Done in Odessa" is a sort of transitional story, more serious in its understructure than "The King," and offers greater possibilities for creative development. The last two stories, however, attempt to use the same kind of material in a different way. The jocularity remains, but it no longer seems congenial to other demands that Babel makes of his characters. He gives his essentially comic Odessa in these stories a greater weight than it can naturally bear. Part of the problem is that Babel's women protagonists are unsympathetic. They exist on a single plane and embody his themes in a somewhat schematic and unappealing manner.

Still, the themes suggested by Babel's women are important ones. His juxtaposition of the powerful, voracious female and the faint-hearted, puny male is especially revealing.[15] In such sexual encounters he sees a model for social reality, a way of portraying the conflict between aggressive and passive modes of behavior. In attempting to deny such basic, primitive facts, civilization itself in Babel's eyes becomes a source of turmoil and

14 In all editions the four stories appear in the same order: "The King," "How It Was Done in Odessa," "The Father," and "Ljubka the Cossack." This established sequence has no compelling function since each of the stories is complete in itself. Because this traditional sequence corresponds to the order in which the stories originally appeared when published separately, however, it seems quite likely that the established sequence represents the order of composition, which is corroborated by the author's own dating of the stories. The order of composition is important because it supports my speculation about the genesis of the stories and about the way in which Babel's artistic powers and methods were developing during a crucial time in his creative life.

15 For two other early and explicit treatments of this theme see "Tale of a Woman" and "The Sin of Jesus."

anguish. In the stories with women protagonists his inversion of the traditional male and female roles is thus an ironic statement that nature will somehow out, and the comedy of his mismatched couples contains more than a touch of bitterness and frustration. And yet, in their tragic contours, such portraits also reflect Babel's deep and ineradicable commitment to culture. Gentleness and aggression, the promptings of civilization and nature, are bound in unhappy union in the writer's heart.

With regard to solving this dilemma in his art Babel was one of those who, long before Andrej Sinjavsky,[16] recognized that the spirit of the age demanded a fantastic, phantasmagoric art, a vision of the grotesque. Profoundly cognizant of the discontents of civilization, he links the imagery of sexual rebellion with that of spiritual and political emancipation and creates a gallery of heroes who grope toward a new reality that is unclear even to themselves. *The Odessa Tales* is an optimistic work, one vesting the Revolution with hope. In his art Babel seeks in a sense to reconcile Freud and Marx, to redeem—not philosophically, but artistically—the harsh truths of the former with the noble hope of the latter. It is a sad commentary on the perspicacity of Soviet critics that they should find in Babel a writer whose talents were uncongenial to the epoch. The dilemma of Soviet life as well as Soviet art has always been that unfortunate contrast between the malingering present and the glowing future, and Babel, whose sin was an inability to nonchalantly confuse the two, doggedly insisted on locating his hopeful synthesis in the future.

[16] Cf. Abram Tertz, *On Socialist Realism* (New York, 1960).

# VI

# *Red Cavalry:* AN INTRODUCTION

*A simile must be as exact as a slide-rule and as natural as the smell of dill.*[1]

Babel's work on *Red Cavalry* overlapped and in part grew out of his work on *The Odessa Tales.* The two cycles have a number of common features, both thematically and stylistically. The stories in *Red Cavalry* no less than those in *The Odessa Tales* are for the most part episodic in structure, either plotless and impressionistic or built upon the merest anecdotal base. The narrative mixture of the solemn and the prosaic, the poetic and the vulgar, is even more in evidence, and the effectiveness of *skaz,* when used, is enhanced by a masterful use of still more varied linguistic material from dialect, jargon, and folksong. There is in both groups of stories the same penchant for the grotesque and for naturalistic or physiological detail, for the provocatively sensual. Once again the reader of *Red Cavalry* is assaulted by a barrage of sounds, smells, and sights, and by a particularly vivid and striking use of color.

Despite these similarities, however, there are significant differences between the two groups of stories. The *Red Cavalry* pieces exhibit a much greater structural variety than do the earlier tales, and Babel's exploitation of "poetic" principles of con-

[1] Babel's remark to K. Paustovsky, reported in *Vremja bol'šix ožidanij,* 137.

struction is carried to even further extremes. Several of the *Red Cavalry* stories, unlike anything in *The Odessa Tales*, are two- or three-page miniatures, but these compact, quickly read forms are saturated with emotional content. They utilize as framing devices anecdotes, letters, biographies, legends, and the reports of a war correspondent, as well as the eyewitness accounts and self-analyses of a diarist. A few pieces are mere sketches, some are prose poems, others are like fantastic Gothic dream scenes. In the miniatures especially, the lack of plot or action is obvious; the stories are built not upon traditional narrative conceptions, but upon the development of a peculiarly intense dramatic atmosphere.

Even the more epic, narrative tales, however, are extremely concentrated in effect. In them too the description of character and event and the sense of time are greatly foreshortened, and they often contain philosophical reflections or lyrical digressions. Some of the longer stories have a circular pattern in which a laconic narrative is framed by a solemn invocation and a poetically phrased conclusion, the latter usually giving a sudden lyrical or rhetorical emphasis to the story's basic theme. On the other hand, Babel will frequently allow the tensions of a story to remain unresolved, frustrating his reader's desire for a traditional climax or point. Almost always, however, the stylistic heterogeneity of Babel's tales requires both compactness of form and a powerful ending in order to keep the unstable mixture from exploding into incoherence.[2]

There is then no single structural pattern in the stories of *Red Cavalry*, and very few of them follow any sort of conventional narrative technique. A modernist, Babel adheres to the view that short prose fiction should strive for the steely surface of a consciously aestheticized style—should aspire, that is, to the condition of poetry. Since plot, characterization, and unity of theme play relatively unimportant roles in his compositional

---

2 For this summary description of Babel's forms I am much indebted to a number of illuminating studies by Soviet critics as well as to the previously mentioned essay by V. Terras.

technique, an extremely heavy burden falls in these stories, as it does in poetry, on the qualities of language itself. In the kind of tightly condensed fiction that Babel developed for *Red Cavalry*, particular attention is drawn to the smaller units of construction —to the paragraph and the sentence, and even to the individual word. Babel himself has described how carefully he worked over these small "building-blocks" of his prose:

> ...I check the freshness and accuracy of all my images, similes, and metaphors. If I cannot find the perfect simile, I don't use any at all. It's better to let a noun live by itself in its simplicity.
> ...I break my text into easy phrases. The more periods the better. I would make this rule a governing law for writers. Each phrase is one thought, one image, and no more. So don't be afraid of periods. ...
> ...All the paragraphs and punctuation must be done correctly, not out of some dead scholasticism, but so as to produce the maximum effect upon the reader. The paragraph is particularly magnificent. It lets you change rhythms easily, and often, like a flash of lightning, it reveals some well-known sight in a completely unexpected aspect.[3]

In *Red Cavalry*, the paragraph plays an extremely important role. Compositionally it is much like the stanza of a poem, serving as a rhythmic, syntactic, and thematic unit. Babel varies the intonational characteristics of successive paragraphs. He will follow an elaborate and self-contained rhetorical peroration or a lyrical evocation of the landscape, for example, with a short and stylistically neutral passage or with brief patches of dialogue. In constructing the larger unit of the story Babel often avoids composing transitional links between his paragraphs, preferring to intensify the effect by allowing any dissonance to remain. Even within the paragraph there may be intonational variety, a flat opening narrative phrase being followed by a striking image or by a philosophical epigram. In the stylized speech of Babel's Cossacks the poetic imagery and phrasing of folksongs and ballads alternate with the vulgar jargon of Revolutionary clichés, and both of these in turn contrast with the pathos of the author's

[3] K. Paustovsky, *Vremja bol'šix ožidanij*, 136, 137.

language. In general, phrasing is extremely condensed, often aphoristic, and considerable rhythmic force is developed by such devices as parallel construction, enumeration, and the refrain. As with the paragraphs, the sometimes abrupt transition between intonationally varied phrases contributes to the general effect of paradox and conflict.

With regard to the word as well Babel employs the techniques of poetic prose. Always cognizant of the sound and evocative power of individual words, he exploits to good effect the devices of alliteration, assonance, repetition, and inversion. His use of adjectives in particular is striking and unexpected, and his powerful imagery, rich in both metaphor and simile, imparts to the tales a heightened emotional coloring. Frequently images cluster together to form a network of subliminally suggestive leitmotifs; their effect is sometimes almost hallucinatory, conveying as in a nightmare an impression of terror, fantasy, and surrealistic intensity. Because of his method of agglomerating so many incongruous components into a single form, Babel's readers are often overwhelmed by a sense of shock and dislocation. Despite this reaction, however, the stories usually possess an underlying design, their variegated texture somewhat resembling that of a mosaic. The unifying center is, of course, the mind of the author, where all of the incongruities of styles, settings, motifs, and characters converge in a powerful vision. What Babel conveys through his pictorial style is an almost instantaneous visual perception. Like a sudden flash of light his miniatures briefly illuminate the several essentials of a scene in such a way as to leave the spectator stunned and grasping for a coherent explanation. Individual stories thereby attain a powerful immediacy of effect and thus largely defeat any attempt at an organized intellectual response.[4]

4 Babel's stories conform in a number of ways to prescriptions for the genre laid down by E. A. Poe: that a story's evocation of emotional response be accorded the same dignity as its development of intellectual and moral themes; an emphasis on the story's effect upon the reader and a belief that unity of *effect* rather than unity of *conception* plays the governing role in the construction of the

Not only stylistically and structurally, but in theme and tone as well, Babel's *Red Cavalry* stories combine a number of disparate elements. The starkly naturalistic vein in which he portrays the eroticism and brutality of his Cossacks contrasts with a pervasive symbolism, through which the figures acquire a mythic and heroic dimension. Similarly, he blends features from the epic, lyric, and dramatic modes. The lyric note is a dominant one in these stories and arises directly out of the heightened poetic pathos of the narration. Babel's use of the dramatic is seen not only in his portrayal of character through speech and action, but in the pronounced scenic quality of the tales. Furthermore, his stories' extreme stylistic and thematic tensions are themselves a source of great dramatic impact.

Babel's models for the epic vision are found not only in the ancient classics, but in the Russian tradition as well. From the time of *The Song of Igor's Campaign* (twelfth century) and through centuries in which the Russian folk epos thrived, a native epic tradition remained alive to nourish the literature of ensuing periods. Of Babel's nineteenth-century predecessors, two in particular found the past and its values of abiding interest, and these two, Gogol and Tolstoy, both exercised considerable influence on the young writer. We have seen already how, early in his career, Babel cited the "Southern" works of Gogol—his Ukrainian folktales and his semihistorical epic venture, *Taras Bulba*—as literary models, and in later years he often gave expression to what was obviously a deep and lasting admiration for Tolstoy. The latter fascinated Babel in part perhaps because of the size and scale of his work, so at odds with his own leanings toward the miniature; but despite the obvious differences in style and scope there is an essential kinship between the creator of *War and Peace* and the author of *Red Cavalry*.

In Tolstoy's epic naturalness Babel found the key to what made the great novelist, in his eyes, "the most marvelous writer

---

short story; and his strictures in the name of concentrated impression against length in either prose or poetry.

who ever lived."⁵ Upon rereading Tolstoy's novella *Hadji-Murat*, Babel spoke of being "shaken beyond description" by "the current that passed from the earth, through [Tolstoy's] hands, straight to the paper"; of how that power "stripped away mercilessly all outer layers with a sense of truth—a truth clothed in dress both transparent and beautiful."⁶ For Babel, Tolstoy was "pure literature," its "ideal conductor": "Reading Tolstoy, I always feel as if the world were writing through him. Do you understand what I mean? His books give the impression that the existence of a great multitude of the most varied people—and not only people, but animals, plants, clouds, mountains and constellations—has been poured onto paper through him."⁷

This sense of life, conveyed in all its immediacy and specificity, is a trait of the epic mode, and Babel, with his desire to apprehend life in a heroic mold, sought to impart this quality to his writing. His method of reestablishing such specificity is, of course, not identical with that of Tolstoy, but he shares with his predecessor a number of themes and devices.⁸ In his luminous treatment of physical passion, for example, and in his effort to attain calm in the face of terror, Babel comes close at times to that epic mood so marvelously conveyed in Tolstoy. The epic temper is more natural to Tolstoy, of course, who can sustain it for greater length, even outside the context of war; but in both men the tendency to analyze and moralize is at odds with the ancient Homeric naïveté. Furthermore, Babel, an urban being, is not born, like Tolstoy, with an intimate knowledge of nature and is less sure in his grasp of the calming effect of the pastoral scene. In his effort to reinvest abstractions and things with human functions and significance he at times merely decorates rather

⁵ From Babel's 1937 interview, published in *Naš sovremennik* No. 4 (1964), 97.
⁶ *Ibid.*
⁷ Quoted by G. Munblit in "Isaak Èmmanuilovič Babel' (Iz vospominanij)," *Znamja*, No. 8 (Aug. 1964), 120.
⁸ Babel's remarks about Tolstoy were made in the thirties, long after the completion of *Red Cavalry* and at a time when it was necessary to exercise considerable caution in expressing one's literary tastes. Although Tolstoy was one of the pre-Revolutionary writers whom it was "safe" to praise, Babel's admiration for Tolstoy's "epicality" is clearly both genuine and of early provenance.

than individualizes. Taken as a whole, however, Babel's feel for the epic is genuine, and its evocation in his work is extremely effective.

The epic features which contribute to that effectiveness include, along with a Homeric approach to character, certain thematic and stylistic traits as well. Babel's account of the taking and looting of towns is linked most obviously to the epic mode through the use of the martial theme—a tradition that embraces joyous ferocity quite as much as suffering and pathos. Furthermore, there are, in addition to the expected scenes of violence, heroism, and death, persistent if not unqualified signs of an antiurban, antimodern bias in Babel's tales. Not only his pastoral imagery and his landscape painting, but some of the more lusty and sensual passages as well help to create an impression of earthy simplicity which gives epic density and depth to his picture of life. The broad, panoramic canvas of splendidly posturing heroes and of cavalry squadrons wheeling into battle gives way at times, as is characteristic of the epic vision, to the microcosmic view of life's more eternal and everyday pursuits. Thus Babel is able to insert, in the middle of his description of a cavalry charge, the episode in which Sashka the nurse has her mare illicitly covered by the army commander's stallion. The sexual instincts and the violent passions evoked by war are thus seen to have a common source, and they are linked together to express the ambiguous relationship between the complementary impulses of both life and death. When the vantage point shifts again to the longer perspective at the story's end, the effect of the interlude is to give the closing lines an added poignancy and depth:

> The wind leaped between the boughs like a hare scared out of its senses. The Second Brigade flew between the Galician oaks, and the tranquil dust of the bombardment rose above the earth as though above a peaceful cottage. And at the Divisional Commander's signal we moved on to the attack—the unforgettable attack at Chesniki. ("Chesniki," 182.)

Throughout the book the vantage point is forever shifting in this way: the passing glances at pregnant Ukrainian peasant

women going about their chores; at Jews attending their synagogues and prayer meetings; at untutored soldiers with their
often surprisingly tender appreciation of nature; and the dazzling
vision of Budyonny ordering men to their deaths with his "flashing" smile, or of Kolesnikov, a young, recently promoted brigade
commander, "bathed in the flame of a crimson sunset," celebrating his new-won glory with "the masterful indifference of a
Tartar Khan." Such frequent shifts serve to etch the artist's canvas more deeply and help to tranquilize and subdue for a time
the raging violence that is always close to the surface.

A similar function is performed by Babel's striking epithets
and by his recurrent metaphors and similes. He uses a number
of descriptive but conventionally poetic adjectives which are
almost formulaic, rather like stock epithets. Words such as *unprecedented, indescribable, unparalleled, unforgettable, inestim-
able,* and *unfading* serve as a kind of recurring leitmotif,[9] and
along with other strikingly applied adjectives (e.g., "radiant riding breeches," "monstrous corpses," "the predatory pupils of
lighted candles") they contribute to the general hyperbolic and
dramatic stylization. So too with the names of illustrious heroes
given at the end of "The Brigade Commander"; the list is a
short but nonetheless Homeric catalog, in which the adjectives
become almost a part of the names: ". . . and I became conscious
of the training of the renowned Kniga, the headstrong Pavlichenko, and the captivating Savitsky."

Another device that Babel often employs, to either lyric or
epic effect, is poetic apostrophe, which he usually accompanies
with another short, poetic figure:

Hordes of paupers roll toward your ancient cities, O Poland . . . .
("The Church at Novograd," 45.)
. . . woe unto you, Prince Radziwill, and unto you, Prince

[9] Kenneth Burke, in his *Rhetoric of Religion* (Boston, 1961), has explored
the implications of the negative in theological conceptions: in the "shalt nots"
of the Mosaic code, and in the negative prefixes of traditional descriptions of God
(as *unbounded, incomprehensible, unknowable,* etc.). As elsewhere in his work,
Babel seems here to be secularizing a theological device.

Sapieha, risen for the space of an hour! ("The Church at Novograd," 45.)

O the rotted Talmuds of my childhood! O the dense melancholy of memories! ("Gedali," 69.)

O Brody! The mummies of your crushed passions breathed upon me their irremediable poison. ("The Road to Brody," 82.)

O regulations of the Russian Communist Party! You have laid down headlong rails through the sour pastry of our Russian tales. ("Evening," 127.)

Through the use of various types of parallel construction or the rhythmic repetition of key words and phrases (often with the addition or substitution of adjectives or other elements), Babel is able to impart a musical cadence to his prose:

"Away!" I said to myself. "Away from these ogling Madonnas deceived by common soldiers!" ("The Church at Novograd," 46.)

... and peace—Sabbath peace—rested upon the crazy roofs of the Zhitomir ghetto. ("The Rabbi," 78.)

Both of us looked upon the world as a meadow in May—a meadow traversed by women and horses. ("The Story of a Horse," 114.)

... and silence, almighty silence, had ascended its small-town throne. ("Berestechko," 119.)

The tireless wind—the clean wind of night—sings on, fraught with ringing, rocking souls. ("The Widow," 163.)

Do you remember Zhitomir, Vasily? Do you remember the River Teterev, Vasily, and that night when the Sabbath, the young Sabbath crept along the sunset, crushing the stars beneath her little red heel? ("The Rabbi's Son," 191.)

He died before we reached Rovno. He died—that last of the Princes—among his poetry, phylacteries, and coarse foot-wrappings. ("The Rabbi's Son," 193.)

Nature in the tales, again as in the epic, sometimes plays the role of chorus. The extended descriptions of landscape, however, are usually given in a lyrical key, and their general effect is to evoke a mood of nostalgia, a longing for that lost human involvement in the rhythmical patterns of nature. The stories project in this vein a constant refrain of dawns and sunsets:

Dawn drew a streak along the far end of the earth. ("Evening," 129.)

... the spiderweb stillness of a summer morning hung between the straight bright walls .... ("Pan Apolek," 55.)

Evening flew up to the sky like a flock of birds and darkness crowned me with its watery wreath. ("After the Battle," 187.)

The goblets of the sunset were tilted over the village. ("Zamoste," 168.)

The dying evening surrounded him with the rose-tinted haze of its sadness. ("The Rabbi," 77.)

Old Gedali ... meandered around his treasures in the roseate void of evening. ("Gedali," 70.)

And we were moving toward the sunset, whose foaming rivers flowed along the embroidered napkins of peasant fields. ("The Road to Brody," 82.)

Pierced by the flashes of the bombardment, night arched over the dying man. ("The Widow," 162.)

In the orange strife of the sunset a timid star lit up.... ("The Rabbi," 78.)

There are many references to the sun, moon, and stars. In the war-ravaged milieu of the stories they suggest a pre-Copernican, almost paganly animistic universe. Their cadenced reappearances serve both as emblems of eternity and as signals of the rhythmic passing of the days:

The slender horn of the moon bathed its darts in the dark waters of the river. ("The Rabbi's Son," 191.)

Humble little stars slid along the Milky Way.... ("Afonka Bida," 135.)

I roam through Zhitomir in search of a shy star. ("Gedali," 69.)

Over the town roamed the homeless moon. ("Pan Apolek," 64.)

The loitering moon crept out from behind the clouds and lingered on Sasha's knee. ("The Widow," 164.)

... the moon, clasping in her blue hands her round, bright, carefree face, wandered like a vagrant outside the window. ("Crossing Into Poland," 42.)

The heavenly bodies, intimately involved in the affairs of men, are not only personified, as in the examples above; they are frequently used in striking similes as well. Sometimes the imagery borders on the grotesque, but it is always appropriate to the particular tale in which it appears. Such imagery occurs, of course, only in the poetic language of the narrator; for him the stars (and especially the moon) have a spiritual significance:

> The orange sun rolled down the sky like a lopped-off head. . . . ("Crossing Into Poland," 41.)
> The dying sun, round and yellow as a pumpkin, was giving up its roseate ghost to the skies. ("My First Goose," 74.)
> Stars blaze like wedding rings in the darkness and, falling on Lyovka, are entangled in his hair and extinguished in his tousled head. ("The Widow," 163.)
> His rounded back was bathed in the light of the moon, stuck up on high like a pert shrew. . . . ("Evening," 128.)
> The misty moon loitered about the sky like a beggar-woman. ("The Widow," 164–65.)
> The moon, green as a lizard, rose over the pond. ("Berestechko," 121.)
> Already the moon hung above the yard like a cheap earring. ("My First Goose," 76.)
> The raw dawn floated over us like waves of chloroform. ("Zamoste," 169.)

The use of poetic devices such as these is far more prominent in the compact stories of *Red Cavalry* than in *The Odessa Tales*, and their effect is more potent. The earlier stories are perhaps best seen as a fruitful transitional phase that was necessary before Babel could attempt the larger task he set himself in *Red Cavalry. The Odessa Tales* had provided him with the first successful statement of his major themes, and they had demonstrated that he had found the ingredients of a style, if not the material, to embody them. Benja Krik and the other Odessa bandits had appealed to Babel largely because they represented his own desire to go beyond the confines of ghetto walls and because they signaled a new union between the Jew and the world at large. There was a kind of evasion, however, in picturing Benja as a sort of Robin Hood, and Babel's next stories show him moving away from material that was dangerously picturesque toward a more forthright statement. In turning away from his familiar Odessa setting he was seeking not so much new themes as a new

embodiment for old ones. Babel himself had earlier characterized the Odessans as men who dreamed of adventure only until
they married; for *Red Cavalry* he felt it necessary to shed still
more of the bourgeois residue, to seek as heroes either men who
had abandoned their families or men who didn't marry at all.
The very material of the cavalry stories—allowing for an honest
admission of horror as well as comedy—possesses a depth and
seriousness lacking in *The Odessa Tales*. The theme of war, with
its ambiguous mixture of the ugly and the beautiful, becomes
a stark metaphor for the struggle of life as well as the new setting
within which the author will confront at a deeper level the old
paradoxes and contradictions. *Red Cavalry* remains above all
the author's dialogue with himself, an inner debate or dialectic
concerning the nature and value both of life and of modes for
its perception.

We have seen that for Babel the key to both life and art is immersion in experience. Gorky had admonished him that in order
to write the artist had to acquire a knowledge of the world at
first hand, and in his new stories Babel was ready to record directly the sometimes painful consequences of the artist's search
for that knowledge. *Red Cavalry* reflects his continuing desire
to subject the individualism and self-absorption of the middle-
class intellectual to the test of living. Even the true nature of
the personal, he believed, could not emerge in isolation; in order
to be either affirmed or discredited, either transformed or transcended, it required the challenge of experience.

Almost all of Babel's work is consequently deeply rooted in
the autobiographical, not only in the narrow sense that it often
relies directly upon actual experience, but in the sense that it
proceeds from the writer's inmost needs and records his spiritual,
emotional, and physical odyssey.[10] Almost all of the remini-

10 The term "autobiographical" as applied to imaginative literature is hopelessly vague and ambiguous. Certainly all art is in some sense autobiographical,
but there is a problem as to its kind and degree. Despite the many pitfalls and
frustrations which lie in wait for an autobiographical approach to imaginative
fiction, it is too tempting, too interesting, and often too helpful to be finally and
fully ignored.

scences by Babel's friends and fellow writers emphasize his insatiable curiosity about life in the raw. For all his dedication to art he was always reluctant to be involved in the cliquish life of the professional literati. Jealously guarding his independence and his freedom of movement, Babel was something of a literary loner, a man who sought to avoid his associates not only in order to write, but also in order to preserve the anonymity he believed necessary to investigate life at the sources he found most interesting: in taverns and on waterfronts, in remote villages and byways, amid the unsophisticated and "unspoiled."

Konstantin Paustovsky has told us how Babel rented a room in the center of the Moldavanka thieves' district to study the life of its bandits and gather material for his Odessa stories; the model for Benja Krik, Paustovsky says, was an actual Odessa bandit, Mishka Yaponchik, the legendary leader of a Jewish self-defense league. Babel's cycle of childhood reminiscences ("Story of My Dovecote," "First Love," "In the Basement," and "The Awakening"), as well as numerous other works including *Red Cavalry*, bears the stamp of actual experience. This is not to imply that Babel's work is not fiction, that experience has not been subjected to the transforming analysis and crucial distortion of the artistic vision, but because Babel's art is so much of a piece and all of it so much the man it constitutes a kind of personal *Bildungsroman*. When art and life are held up to the light together each may help to reflect and illuminate the other.

Babel's search for knowledge often took him to the kind of places—the war-torn towns of southern Russia or, later, the headquarters of the Soviet secret police—that other intellectuals found abhorrent. Nadezhda Mandelstam, the widow of the famous poet, has recalled how in the thirties Babel liked to visit the officers of the Cheka, including their chief, the infamous Yezhov, and she offers a convincing explanation for this recurring pattern in Babel's behavior:

> [My husband] asked [Babel] why he was so drawn to "militiamen" [the word is a euphemism for Chekists]: was it a desire to see what it was like in the exclusive store where the merchandise was death?

ISAAC BABEL, RUSSIAN MASTER OF THE SHORT STORY

Did he just want to touch it with his fingers? "No," Babel replied, "I don't want to touch it with my fingers—I just like to have a sniff and see what it smells like." ... I am convinced that Babel went to see Yezhov ... out of sheer curiosity. ... Everything about Babel gave an impression of all-consuming curiosity—the way he held his head, his mouth and chin, and particularly his eyes. It is not often that one sees such undisguised curiosity in the eyes of a grownup. I had the feeling that Babel's main driving force was the unbridled curiosity with which he scrutinized life and people.[11]

All of this "curiosity" is ultimately devoted to art. Paustovsky has described how difficult Babel found it to come by his material, how he might spend a year or more on the composition of a single story, covering perhaps two hundred sheets in an effort to achieve but a few pages of distilled perfection. Babel himself has given eloquent testimony to the agony of creation, to the jealous care with which he treated the raw material of his art:

"I have no imagination," Babel once told me. "I'm very serious about this. I can't invent. I have to know everything, down to the last vein, otherwise I can't write a thing. My motto is authenticity. That's why I write so little and so slowly. Writing is very hard for me. After each short story, I feel several years older. Don't talk to me about creative work á la Mozart, about the blissful time spent over a manuscript, about the free flow of imagination! ... When I'm writing the shortest story, I still have to work at it as if I were required to dig up Mount Everest all by myself with a pick and shovel. When I start working I always feel that it's too much for me. Sometimes I get so tired I cry. All my blood vessels ache from the work. I have heart spasms when I can't manage a sentence. And how often they don't work, those wretched sentences!"[12]

Babel's creativity lies not in those areas productive of event or happening, not in the developing of story line or plot, but in the painstaking craftsmanship of actual compositional technique. His imagination is most potently at work in the stylistic elaboration of his themes; as a consequence he dazzles not so much with

11 Nadezhda Mandelstam, *Hope Against Hope: A Memoir*, trans. from the Russian by Max Hayward (New York, 1970), 321.
12 K. Paustovsky, *Vremja bol'šix ožidanij*, 133. Trans. by Andrew MacAndrew in *Dissonant Voices in Soviet Literature*, Patricia Blake and Max Hayward, eds., 46.

the variety of his invention as with the intensity and originality of its expression.

In *Red Cavalry* one of Babel's most important stylistic devices was the first-person narrative persona, a direction toward which he had been reaching for a long time. It will be recalled that his earliest surviving work, "Childhood at Grandmother's" (dated 1915), deals, not surprisingly, with the experiences of a first-person narrator, and "Inspiration," another early piece (published 1917), is a kind of artistic credo in the first person. In "Mama, Rimma and Alla" and "Ilja Isaakovich and Margarita Prokofievna," however, Babel had retreated from the use of the first person and sought a more neutral style within the "realistic" frame of third-person narration. In the four war stories published in the magazine *Lava* there is an identifiable narrative voice belonging to an "I," but the tone is detached and impersonal; we don't clearly perceive a persona behind the narrative mask. In "How It Was Done in Odessa" (published 1923), Babel had found a unifying device in the narrative *skaz* of Arye-Leib, while he allowed some of the tale's implicit conflicts to emerge through the other figure of his listening "I." The emergence of this new voice in the first person was a discovery of utmost importance to the subsequent development of Babel's art, and although the "I" of "How It Was Done in Odessa" is more evoked than evoking, Babel by this time undoubtedly had solved a major problem with regard to his use of the first-person narrative.[13]

By 1923, as a result of his own wartime experience and in connection with his work on *The Odessa Tales* and the first *Red Cavalry* stories, Babel had found a way to handle the personal in his writing, a solution that answered his stylistic and aesthetic demands at the same time that it satisfied his psychological need

[13] Only in 1923 did Babel begin to publish regularly, rather as if some dam had broken and the flow of his creativity finally been given outlet. Among the *Red Cavalry* stories first published in 1923 are several of the most important, including "The Church at Novograd," "The Dealth of Dolgushov," and "Pan Apolek," all of which exhibit his mastery of the "I." Several independent stories published in 1923 also display his burgeoning use of the first-person narrative: "Answer to an Inquiry," "Line and Color," and "Through the Fanlight."

for catharsis. The liberating devices which allowed the writer to embrace personal experience boldly in his art were irony and self-mockery; through the creation of a fictional persona who resembled but was not identical with himself, Babel was able to obtain a necessary degree of detachment.

The extent to which self-mockery is implicit in *The Odessa Tales* has been noted already. Indeed its presence seems essential to justify the rather cavalier morality those stories project on the surface. The irony is too diffuse, however, and its object has largely to be inferred from sources outside itself. Only in one story does the mocked "I" actually surface, and even then he is not the story's primary narrator but merely a foil for Arye-Leib. Babel needed in a sense to combine the two narrators of this story into a single persona who would express both the lyricism of the "listening I" and the epic grandeur of the bardic Ayre-Leib.[14] The listener alone, though the object of ironic mockery— and though the striking image of "spectacles on his nose and autumn in his heart" served to crystallize much that is central to the "I" of *Red Cavalry* as well—was not yet sufficiently close to the Babel who had already experienced war and revolution at first hand.

In *Red Cavalry*, then, the "I" is made a participant. The teller of other peoples' war stories is at last to tell his own; the curious and dreamy fellow in spectacles, the Jewish intellectual, is to leave the cemetery wall and submit himself to the test of living —not in the legendary land of a fairytale Odessa, not within a mock-heroic ghetto, but face to face with an actual, rather than metaphorical, war. The autobiographical is to become not a

14 "How It Was Done in Odessa" already represents a partial solution to these problems. It was a solution, however, that was incomplete and which was not repeated. Within the confines of the *skaz* which permeates this story, the voice of the bookish listener could hardly be identified with the peculiar syntax and jargon characterizing Arye-Leib, and indeed the latter's unique and vivid speech, with its colloquial syntax and diction, is a necessary contrast to the voice of the listener. Arye-Leib's contact with the living popular sources of language is itself a metaphor for his greater contact with life. Babel loved the peculiarities of popular language, but the persona he devised for *Red Cavalry*, though in part a combination of Arye-Leib and the listener, had necessarily to relinquish the popular *skaz* to the Cossack heroes themselves.

hindrance to larger meanings, but their agency; and experience is to be not merely art's prerequisite, but its substance. Babel's "I" in *Red Cavalry* remains an essentially passive figure. Like a dreamer, he has no personal control over experience and cannot himself initiate action. What happens always happens *to* or *around* him; all that he feels—excitement, terror, despair—is caused by forces outside him. Like many modern writers Babel avoids imposing a set of personal values upon events. Refusing to order a resolution for chaos, he uses the buffeted consciousness of the artist himself as antihero, and he hopes that out of his own torment will come a new revelation.

In his working plans and early drafts for *Red Cavalry* Babel constantly felt it necessary to remind himself to be as concise as possible. "Short chapters, saturated with content," is the way he described what he wanted to achieve, and in his pursuit of that aim he is ready to eliminate much that another writer would consider indispensable. He notes with reference to one tale that he must compose it "in separate fragments"; in the case of another that he must "pay attention to the story's discontinuity."[15] His finished work, with its deliberate avoidance of transitional links, contains so many apparently contradictory features and points of view that it resists an easy exposition. Babel was at pains to thwart his reader's expectations at many turns; often, in place of logical continuities, he gives what in one of his tales he calls "rational madness." As a result his stories require an almost motif-by-motif analysis.

[15] These remarks, indicative of many such comments in Babel's plans and drafts, are found in *Literaturnoe nasledstvo*, LXXIV, 492 and 495, respectively.

# VII

# Red Cavalry: COSSACK vs. JEW

*"A Jew who has mounted a horse has stopped being a Jew and has become a Russian."*[1]

*Red Cavalry* is built upon a number of thematic contrasts and paradoxes. The conflicts between culture and nature, between continuity and change, between a moral order and the chaos of experience, between the observer and the man of action, between the individual and the mass—all of these permeate the book. The stories depict two worlds, two different styles of life, locked in combat. In one there are towns, with churches, synagogues, houses, and markets. Life in this world is ordered and stable; civilization and culture have their roots in its traditional ways. But into these towns come men from another world—the Cossacks, self-assertive, proud horsemen, nomads who ride in search of nothing but the sense of their own natures. Babel's critique of civilization, his belief in the necessity of reasserting the claims of natural man, turns toward that broadest and deepest understratum of Russian life, the peasantry.[2]

---

[1] Remark made by Levka, brother to Benja Krik, in Babel's play *Sunset* (*I. Babel': Izbrannoe*, 290).

[2] An almost mystical belief in the peasantry, or at least a desire for the unification of the intelligentsia with the people, is a well-established tradition in Russian literature. Gogol's view of the religious spirit of the simple folk, Tolstoy's idealization of the peasant, and Dostoevsky's doctrine of a "return to the Russian soil" are variations on this theme. Although the hope of a unified culture failed

132

The Cossack soldiers of Babel's *Red Cavalry* are not a revolutionary corps of ideologically sophisticated, urban workers; they are the illiterate, heavy-fisted peasants of rural Russia, who, for all their ready violence, are endowed with vitality, passion, and a natural freedom and grace. The life of Babel's peasant soldiers is primitive and anarchic, a Darwinian jungle in which the strong prevail while the weak are condemned to suffering and destruction. The Cossacks accept this environment as natural; they claim only freedom of self-expression within it. As Babel sees it, their motive force in this demand for freedom is less a will to power than a will to joy, though he sees the two as perhaps inextricably mixed. Examining the range of figures who inhabit the stories—murderers, epileptics, rapists, parricides, and syphilitics—one is struck by how "Dostoevskian" their universe is, a universe of aggressive wills, of torturers on the one hand, and passive sufferers on the other—the latter most often being Jews.

Babel, however, rejects or seeks an alternative to the Dostoevskian religious "solution." Much of *Red Cavalry* is an anguished lament against just those self-denying, religious answers (passivity, acceptance, humility) that Dostoevsky proposes. Furthermore, the spare tone of Babel's stories is hardly Dostoevskian at all, and the poeticized surface of his miniatures seems almost the direct antithesis of a Dostoevskian narrative. But Babel is seeking to arrange much the same material, much the same analysis, in a different way so as to provide alternatives to Dostoevsky's answers.

Once again we are made aware that a new form announces a new content. One of the most immediately striking differences between Babel and Dostoevsky is in their treatment of character.

---

to survive the intelligentsia's estrangement from the institutions of national life, the idea of "the people" continued to exert a strong appeal. For many writers, Russia's semifeudal backwardness—the fact that capitalism and the state bureaucracy were superimposed upon an immense peasant society—gave hope that she might find an alternative to western European historical development in rural traditions. Babel could not accept the vestiges of the 19th-century pastoral ideal (which was hardly viable in its own day), but in his rejection of middle-class urban life he does turn once again to the peasant.

In Babel there is little or none of that psychologizing which helps to establish a set of psychic mechanisms for the operation of the Dostoevskian universe. Babel prefers to leave the question of motivation unprobed, to allow the act itself both a kind of integrity and a degree of spontaneity. Furthermore, psychological analysis would tend to diminish or expose his heroes, and Babel is more intent on conveying a sense of awe toward them. In Dostoevsky the willful heroes themselves are tortured by inner doubts, by moral and metaphysical dilemmas, whereas in Babel the heroes are unaware that doubt, remorse, or conscience exists. Despite their brutality his Cossacks remain, if not innocent, at least childlike in their ferocity. They are not moved, as many of Dostoevsky's heroes are, by a conscious choice of evil as a self-defining act, but by a spontaneous, unknowing self-indulgence. Even in their ferocity a desire for joy is manifest. In answer to the narrator's anguished question as to why the Cossacks whip their own infantry, Afonka Bida, in the story that bears his name, answers grandly, "for laughs." Similarly, the Cossack Konkin toys with a prisoner before killing him, much as a child might play with a wounded insect, or a cat with a mouse. In "Two Ivans" the warlike Akinfiev promises to have a good time in torturing the cowardly, yet stoical malingerer Ageev. In none of the Cossacks is there any recognition that such acts are evil or immoral.

There is one figure in *Red Cavalry*—and only one—who does engage in introspective analysis, one character who agonizes, doubts, and torments himself with moral questionings: the author. It is in the intellectual-narrator that the reader finds a Dostoevskian character to match a Dostoevskian world, and it is in him too that the book contains its dialectical pattern. The narrator is a man burdened with consciousness, with an inhibiting moral awareness, and in his readiness to condemn or suffer the "sins" of others he finds reason for insistent self-mockery. Refusing to grant himself a moral superiority, he ridicules the "Christ-like" aura in his makeup and suspects that not a higher standard of conduct, but weakness may be the cause of his special sensitivity. Still, despite the acuity of his self-criticism, the accursed questions remain, and the narrator is unable to shake his need to find a justification for the suffering and cruelty he sees. Given the nature of life, two responses are available to him: either he can remake himself so as to be able to accept more equably the terror he encounters in reality, or he can transform his perception of that reality. *Red Cavalry* tests both these possibilities within a continuing moral dialectic.

The question of modes of perception is a crucial one in *Red Cavalry*, but here too the pattern is paradoxical and dialectically complex. The narrator fears the functions of imagination and mind; he wishes to be an active participant in life, not a mere observer, to discover a connection with the world, not suffer alienation from it.[3] There are, on the other hand, certain things a civilized man can never do; he can only know *of* them. And Babel's narrator seeks this kind of knowledge too: he responds to that strange precept which Babel's grandmother had instilled in his mind in childhood: "You must know everything. . . . Trust no one and have no friends." The grim, inhuman coldness of this knowing is perhaps best expressed in *Red Cavalry* by Matthew Pavlichenko, the Cossack general who speaks of trampling his former master to death "for an hour or more" so that he might "learn what life is really like." Although he does not, of course, perform such acts himself, the desire for this same awful, gruesome, unintellectual "knowledge," for knowing real life beyond all possibility of illusion, seems at times to motivate Babel also. In his need to apprehend reality he grows impatient with

---

[3] The attack upon imagination as inferior to experience is one of Babel's pervasive themes. His constant attention to the carnal is itself a reflection of his fear of the spiritual imagination. In his stories he is always immersed in the physical details of his heroes, in their very flesh and clothing. But the estranged-observer motif always remains. Arye-Leib, like his listener, is only a witness of Benja Krik's glory. In another early story ("Through the Fanlight") the narrator spies on the room of a prostitute while she entertains clients. The narrator of *Red Cavalry* too is mainly a spectator amid the Cossack troop; he collects their stories, writes their letters, and in one case even reads their mail (Babel himself once confessed that he knew no greater joy than to read the letters of other people). Visual imagery is one of *Red Cavalry*'s major leitmotifs, and its language is permeated with verbs of seeing and perception.

mere "mental" knowledge and is prepared to abandon the traditional proprieties of bourgeois culture.

But in opposition to this "realist" who wishes to know life at its horrible center, Babel gives us the romantic who, with his "confused poetic brains," seeks to perceive reality in the light of some sustaining ideal. When the suggested ideal tends toward the overtly humanistic—or, even more, when it tends toward the moral—it is rejected as a grossly romantic illusion. But the poetic impulse itself, whether lyric or epic, is never crushed, and the aesthetic dimension remains essential to Babel's hope for a new revelation.

"Crossing the Zbruch," the book's opening tale, is an excellent example of the richly suggestive short story that Babel developed in *Red Cavalry*. In its two pages it introduces an atmosphere, a series of motifs, and an array of structural qualities that are characteristic of the book as a whole. The impression of sketchiness is more apparent than real, for like many of Babel's stories this one opens up into widening circles of meaning; it expands under the retroactive influence of subsequent stories or through the added insight of successive readings into much richer and deeper significances than at first appear. Many of the connective links in the story's chain of logic have been foreshortened or omitted altogether, and the reader is rushed along a path of wildly fluctuating sensations without guidance from the author.[4]

In the story's title large events are hidden behind the seemingly trivial. The phrase "crossing the Zbruch" does not reveal that the movement described is actually the beginning of the great Soviet counteroffensive of the 1920 war. The invasion of Poland, which throughout the book is to be implied as a moment

---

[4] Talking to D. Furmanov in Dec. 1924 when he was working to complete *Red Cavalry* and when most of the stories had already appeared in journals, Babel asserted that the difference between his *Red Cavalry* and Furmanov's *Chapayev* was that Furmanov's book was a first draft, whereas his own was a second or third rewriting. He then cautioned Furmanov to work more slowly and above all to avoid "explanations": "Please, don't give any explanations—just show things, and let the reader figure it all out for himself!" (D. M. Furmanov, *Sobranie Sočinenij v četyrex tomax*, IV, 343.)

of great historical import, is thus introduced only by suggestion.[5] Furthermore, the title contains a symbolic significance as well. The book's very first word, "crossing," suggests one of the major themes of the work: it implies not only transition, but transformation. For the narrator of the story the experience of the crossing has the quality of a symbolic act, is both an initiation and an adventure, a departure from one world and a tentative entry into another, a farewell to the past and a headlong rush into the future. This future, which the narrator has committed himself to enter and which he hopes to accept, is a world filled with darkness, horror, and death. His acceptance involves both a stepping-over of normal moral boundaries and a possible transference of allegiance.[6]

The opening paragraphs invoke the expectation of a ride toward destiny, of a fateful encounter to be experienced at an unknown destination. The first two sentences move from the brusque beginning of a military dispatch to the suggestion of a historically relevant tradition of violence and oppression:

> The Commander of the VI Division reported: Novograd-Volynsk was taken at dawn today. The staff had left Krapivno, and our baggage train was spread out in a noisy rearguard along the highroad, along the unfading highroad from Brest to Warsaw built by Nicholas I upon the bones of peasants (41).

This highroad built upon bones leads through a lavish landscape, the description of which abounds in fantastic, dreamlike imagery. The almost baroque coloring marks the spatial movement of the crossing with a corresponding temporal transition from dawn to dusk, from light to darkness:

> Fields flowered around us, crimson with poppies; a noontide breeze played in the yellowing rye; on the horizon virginal buckwheat

---

[5] One of the English translations of *Red Cavalry* (*Isaac Babel: The Collected Stories*, ed. and trans. Walter Morison) renders the story's title as "Crossing into Poland," which, though it gains in specificity and helps the foreign reader, loses some of the power of Babel's indirection.

[6] It is possible too to hear in the Russian word for "crossing"—*perexod*—a semantic echo of Dostoevsky's *prestuplenie*: the stepping over which is a transgression or crime. (The word appears in the title of Dostoevsky's novel, *Crime and Punishment.*)

137

rose like the wall of a distant monastery. The Volyn's peaceful stream moved away from us in sinuous curves and was lost in the pearly haze of the birch groves; crawling between flowery slopes, it wound weary arms through a wilderness of hops. The orange sun rolled down the sky like a lopped-off head, and mild light glowed from the cloud gorges. The standards of the sunset flew above our heads. Into the cool of evening dripped the smell of yesterday's blood and of slaughtered horses. The blackened Zbruch roared, twisting itself into foamy knots at the falls. The bridges were down, and we waded across the river. On the waves rested a majestic moon. The horses were in to the cruppers, and the noisy torrent gurgled among hundreds of horses' legs. Somebody sank, loudly defaming the Mother of God. The river was dotted with the square black patches of the wagons, and was full of confused sounds, of whistling and singing, that rose above the gleaming hollows, the serpentine trails of the moon (41).

That the movement described is a kind of descent into darkness and terror as well as a rite would seem clear from the progression of images: the flowering fields with their ripening grains give way to the smell of blood 'and of yesterday's slaughtered horses; the myriad colors of a resplendent summer give way to ultimate blackness; the peaceful Volyn recedes into the background as the turbulent Zbruch heaves itself into the fore; the monastery wall imaged in the virginal buckwheat succumbs to the voice of someone sinking and loudly defaming the Mother of God; and the beheaded sun rolls down the horizon to be replaced by the serpentine moon and its gleaming pits. The crossing of the river Zbruch, then, like the crossing of the Styx, will mark the passage into a place of terror and death.

The narrator reaches his destination and has his encounter with destiny and a vision of hell:

> Far on in the night we reached Novograd. In the house where I was billeted I found a pregnant woman and two red-haired, scraggy-necked Jews. A third, huddled to the wall with his head covered up, was already asleep. In the room I was given I discovered turned-out wardrobes, scraps of women's fur coats on the floor, human filth, fragments of the occult crockery the Jews use only once a year, at Passover.

"Clear this up," I said to the woman. "What a filthy way to live!" The two Jews rose from their places and, hopping on their felt soles, cleared the mess from the floor. They skipped about noiselessly, monkey-fashion, like Japs in a circus act, their necks swelling and twisting. They put down for me a feather bed that had been disemboweled, and I lay down by the wall next to the third Jew, the one who was asleep. Faint-hearted poverty closed in over my couch (42).

The encounter is a significant one. The narrator of "Crossing the Zbruch," a figure as yet unnamed and still unknown to the reader, ultimately will be revealed as the Jewish comrade-in-arms of Cossack cavalrymen, and the vision of horror that he here encounters is the world of Jewish poverty and deprivation which he knows from his own experience. What he sees is not unlike what Virgil's Aeneas saw on his trip to the underworld:

... in the entry of the jaws of hell, Grief and avenging Cares have made their bed; there dwell wan Sickness and gloomy Eld, and Fear, and ill-counselling Hunger, and loathly Penury, shapes terrible to see; and Death and Travail, and thereby Sleep, Death's kinsman. . . .[7]

The narrator fears that in the wretched, suffering Jews whose room he shares, in these grotesque shapes mutilated by poverty, sickness, and fear, he sees the terrible fate of Jewish life. It is this world that he has elected to forsake in pursuit of the newer, brighter one that the Revolution gives promise of bringing. Again like Virgil's Aeneas he enters hell as a part of his journey into the light of the future.[8] To embrace the vision of the new world, however, means to abandon all deceptive visions of the millennium, and in a harsh and bitter image Babel appears to reject the Hebrew belief in a final justification of history. Among the scraps of clothing and bits of human excrement lie fragments of the "occult crockery" which the Jews use in celebration of

7 J. W. Mackail, trans., *Virgil's Works* (New York, 1950), 111. The heroes of myth and epic who visit the dead (e.g., Ulysses, Aeneas, Dante), like the narrator here, all encounter tormented relatives or friends.

8 Aeneas in Book Six of Virgil's epic is granted in the Sybil's words a prophecy of the travails that yet await him: "Wars, grim wars I discern, and Tiber afoam with streams of blood" (Mackail, 106).

Passover, broken remnants of a dream of escape into a promised land.

Lying down on the gutted mattress beside the sleeping Jew, the narrator falls into a fitful, nightmare-ridden sleep. In a dream he sees Savitsky, the commander of the Sixth Division, fire twice at the head of the brigade commander, both of whose eyes fall to the ground.[9] "Why did you turn back the brigade?" shouts Savitsky to the wounded man, and with this the narrator awakens to find the pregnant woman groping over his face with her fingers.

Upon the interruption of his dream the narrator awakens from his nightmare into a terrible reality. With the woman's hands groping over his face, he is somehow related to the figure whose eyes were destroyed in the dream, and yet now he is to have a kind of revelation. The woman takes the blanket from the old Jew at whose side he has been sleeping, and he sees a dead man:

> Lying on his back was an old man, a dead old man. His throat had been torn out and his face cleft in two; in his beard blue blood was clotted like a lump of lead (43).

The narrator's laconic, almost clinical description is expressive of an almost wordless terror; but with all of the story's earlier turbulent energy we have been prepared for some such catastrophe and we receive it almost with relief. As the story draws quickly to its close still another revelation is made: the pregnant Jewess explains that the dead man was her father and that at the moment of his death he had begged the Poles in vain to kill him in the yard so that his daughter would not see him die. The old man's death is thus imbued with a somber beauty, with the sacredness of a martyr's self-sacrifice, and the narrator's awareness of death is accompanied by a vision of that which transfigures death. Amid the degrading filth of wretched surroundings an epiphanic revelation has emerged. Violence too exhibits the mark of paradox, a mixture of something holy with something

---

9 The same image of the falling eyes appears in Book Sixteen of the *Iliad*, in the passage where Patroclus, with the throw of a rock, crushes the head of Cebriones, Hector's charioteer.

terrible. The story ends, however, as it must, with the unresolved question of the orphaned Jewess:

> "... And now I should wish to know," cried the woman with sudden and terrible violence, "I should wish to know where in the whole world you could find another father like my father?" (43).

The woman's cry is not only a statement of loss, but a statement of pride as well. It also remains an unanswerable question, one to which Babel returns again and again in this book: Where is the justification for cruelty and suffering? Or, in a variant form: How is the brutality of violent death to be made bearable? That the old man knew how to die nobly suggests the possibility of a terrible, awesome beauty in human suffering, but it does not remove death's sting, nor does it answer the daughter's persistent, forthright question. Perhaps the answer the story obliquely offers is found in the pregnant woman's womb, in the vague promise of the future, in the hope that is one of the story's themes, the theme of rebirth.

It is in connection with the narrator himself that the story suggests the pattern of a ritual rebirth.[10] His passage through the river at the story's opening is like the symbolic immersion that traditionally precedes a spiritual transformation.[11] Later, in his requisitioned quarters, he beds down beside death and falls into a troubled sleep. Awakened from his nightmare by the pregnant Jewess, like a delirious child roused by its mother, he is transferred from his ripped-open mattress (a uterine image and, with the dead old father beside him, an image of the tomb as well) to a safer place. These figures of a father and an expectant mother

[10] Stylistically and structurally the story seeks to deliver a meaning out of chaos, tension, and upheaval. The verbs which describe the rivers, for example, with their gurgling, bending, crawling, roaring, and twisting into knots, seem an analogue of the pains of maternal labor.

[11] Even the landscape description that precedes the river crossing may be seen as an augury of rebirth. At the very entrance to hell, the ripening grains are a symbol of life. The crimson poppies and yellowing rye that figure so prominently in Babel's landscape are often associated with Demeter, the Greek deity of vegetation and fertility, who with her daughter Persephone suggests the myth of rebirth. The underworld journey itself may be interpreted as a descent that presages an ascent, a journey into the self and the past which the hero must undertake before launching upon a new life.

give the story an overtly familial cast; the narrator thus implies
the person of the absent son, the figure who is waiting to be born.
The house where he has spent the night is a rude, filthy hovel,
but such too is the birthplace of gods. This very setting, in which
holy crockery lies amid scraps of excrement, supplies the means
through which reality is transcended, through which, by the
story's end, the death of a pathetic old man has become ennobled
in the narrator's transformed consciousness.

As befits the opening story of an interconnected cycle, "Crossing the Zbruch" defines a number of major themes and presents
a frame for their interpretation. The narrator of the tale has
crossed into another world and has seen a vision of wondrous
terrors, but he has been merely a passive witness so far. He has
embarked upon his novitiate, but the period of his personal test-
ing remains to be faced. The theme of initiation rites and trials
thus becomes a refrain repeated throughout *Red Cavalry*, and
the motif of rebirth, of a need for remaking, is enacted in a number of important stories: "My First Goose," "The Death of
Dolgushov," "Evening," and "After the Battle."[12] The first of
these offers the clearest example of the initiatory ordeal.

In "My First Goose" the narrator is appointed to the staff of
one of the combat divisions. He arrives to present his papers as
the divisional commander is dictating an order instructing one
of his subordinates to attack and destroy an enemy unit, threatening him with death should he return unsuccessful. The narrator

[12] The narrating "I" of the stories remains nameless through more than half
of the book. When a name does appear it is the same one (Ljutov) which Babel
himself used, both as a military correspondent in the 1920 war and later as a
reporter in Tiflis. For Babel, as for his fictional "I," the pseudonym served to
conceal his Jewishness from anti-Semitic companions. Because of its association
with Babel's own pseudonym and because of its belated appearance in the book
(after trials have been passed), the narrator's name in *Red Cavalry* suggests the
ritual name of an initiate. The adoption of a new name is a common feature in
rites of initiation, symbolizing the transformed nature of the initiated man. (Note
too how Benja Krik as a mark of his maturity and stature had conferred upon
him the title of "King.")
A further mark of the initiate is his knowledge of the mysteries of the elect.
The "mystery" in the world of the cavalry, manifest throughout the cycle and
made a final test of personal achievement at its end, is the ability to ride a horse
well.

envies "the iron and flower" of the commander's youth and stands before him in an open admiration bordering on worship:

> ...I wondered at the beauty of his giant's body. He rose, the purple of his riding breeches and the crimson of his tilted cap and the decorations stuck on his chest cleaving the hut as a standard cleaves the sky. A smell of scent and the sickly sweet freshness of soap emanated from him. His long legs were like girls sheathed to the neck in shining riding boots (73).

The narrator himself, a bespectacled graduate of the St. Petersburg University Law School, is a striking contrast to the athletic figure of the commander, who treats him with an easy condescension:

> "Oh, are you one of those grinds?" he laughed. "Specs on your nose, too! What a nasty little object! They've sent you along without making any enquiries; and this is a hot place for specs. Think you'll get on with us?" (73).

The narrator accepts the commander's challenge and goes off with the quartermaster to find a billet for the night among the Cossack troop. The quartermaster echoes the commander's thoughts and gives the newcomer a piece of advice:

> "Nuisance with specs. Can't do anything to stop it either. Not a life for the brainy type here. But you go and mess up a lady, and a good lady too, and you'll have the boys patting you on the back" (74).

As soon as the quartermaster has left, the narrator is subjected to a barrage of taunts and insults. One of the Cossacks tosses his trunk over the gate, and in humiliating self-abasement he crawls along the ground gathering his scattered clothing and manuscripts. When he tries to settle down to read a speech by Lenin printed in *Pravda*, the Cossacks step on his feet and make fun of him. Unable to concentrate on his reading, the narrator sees Lenin's words, in an image expressive of self-pity, as trying to reach him "along a thorny path." Resolving upon a face-saving action he puts aside his paper and accosts the landlady with a demand for food. When she responds with a mildly muttered complaint he seizes a nearby sword and appropriates an unfortunate goose roaming about the yard:

A severe-looking goose was waddling about the yard, inoffensively preening its feathers. I overtook it and pressed it to the ground. Its head cracked beneath my boot, cracked and emptied itself. The white neck lay stretched out in the dung, the wings twitched. "Christ!" I said, digging into the goose with my sword. "Go and cook it for me, landlady" (75).

The sacrifice produces the desired effect. The Cossacks, "immobile and stiff as heathen priests," invite him at last to join them, to share their food, and to read aloud to them from the text of Lenin's speech. But his action sits heavy on the narrator's conscience. As night approaches, the moon hangs "over the yard like a cheap earring."

As an initiatory ritual of blood sacrifice, the narrator's action has been facile, cheap, and even perverse. The young hero has faced no monstrous dragon, only a goose, and the killing is linked to a grim, repressed sexuality. The narrator has responded to the quartermaster's suggestion that he despoil a lady by killing a bird instead, but the result suggests a kind of self-mutilation more than it does the attainment of manhood.[13] Nor is the narrator's success in joining the Cossack brotherhood very deep or lasting. A desire for the recovery of childlike innocence quickens with the coming of night ("Evening laid a mother's hand upon my burning forehead"), and the narrator retreats to the intellectual's subtle and solitary pleasures when, reading aloud from Lenin's speech, he exultantly catches "the secret curve of Lenin's straight line." The Cossacks, however, admire Lenin's directness, the way he "strikes at truth straight off, like a hen at grain."

[13] The very title of the story is a mocking suggestion of a tale of sexual initiation. One of Babel's later, autobiographical tales, "The Story of My Dovecote," recalls this one. There too the killing of a bird is linked to the discovery of harsh truths and to sexuality. In the later story it is the narrator, a young boy, who has his bird killed; Makarenko, the killer of the bird, is significantly a legless cripple. In "My First Goose" the theme of sexual assault upon a woman ("the purest" he can find, he is advised by the Cossack quartermaster) further suggests a matricidal motif: the destruction of the maternal sway in order to gain the affection of the Cossack brotherhood.

The narrator thus has not become one with the Cossacks after all; their "straight" way is not his, neither in harsh action nor in its justification. His imitation of their behavior was only a mockery, and he remains cursed with his consciousness. When he lies down with the others to sleep, for all their physical closeness, he is still alone, troubled by harsh and discordant dreams:

> We slept, all six of us, beneath a wooden roof that let in the stars, warming one another, our legs intermingled. I dreamed; and in my dreams saw women. But my heart, stained with bloodshed, grated and brimmed over (77).

The estrangement of the sensitive, intellectual narrator from his unsophisticated, semiliterate companions is a frequently repeated theme. In the exposition of this theme the narrator himself is often revealed in a less than favorable light. At times the apparently irresolvable conflict threatens his very life. In "The Death of Dolgushov" the narrator is asked by a mortally wounded comrade to end his suffering with a well-placed shot:

> "You'll have to waste a cartridge on me," said Dolgushov.
> He was leaning up against a tree, his boots thrust out apart. Without lowering his eyes from mine he warily rolled back his shirt. His belly had been torn out. The entrails hung over his knees, and the heartbeats were visible.
> "The Poles'll turn up and play their dirty tricks. Here are my papers. You'll write and tell my mother how things were" (89).

The narrator, however, cannot bring himself to kill, even in mercy, and as he rides off from the wounded man he hears the latter's hiss of contempt: "Sneaking off, eh?...Well, sneak off then, you swine" (89). The narrator then watches as his friend Afonka Bida shoots Dolgushov through the mouth. The narrator's failure, his inability to adhere to a code of comradeship, turns his friend Afonka into a mortal enemy:

> "Afonka," I said with a wry smile, and rode over to the Cossack. "I couldn't, you see."
> "Get out of my sight," he said, growing pale, "or I'll kill you. You guys in specs have about as much pity for chaps like us as a cat has for a mouse."

And he cocked his rifle.
I rode away slowly, not turning around, feeling the chill of death in my back (90).

Once again the image of the spectacles serves to set off the "civilized" man from his less sophisticated companions; the gulf between them implies not only separation, but open hostility. Afonka is restrained by the driver Grishchuk, who, left alone with the narrator as the story closes, offers him a shriveled apple —a touching gesture, but also perhaps a biblical allusion and a suggestion that to sin is human:

"Eat it," he said to me. "Do please eat it."
And I accepted Grishchuk's offering and ate his apple in sadness and reverence (90).

In war the tests that a civilized man faces, his confrontations with others and with himself, grow ever more severe. He may sink finally into an unresponding torpor or fall into a mindless despair, but the trials themselves are unrelenting. In "After the Battle" the narrator is once again confronted with the necessity of killing, this time in battle with the enemy, and once again his decision to remain personally undefiled is the cause of estrangement from a comrade-in-arms. The story opens with a magnificent, spasmodic, almost dreamlike description of the rout suffered by the Soviet troops at the hands of a Cossack brigade which had earlier deserted to the Poles. The narrator, shown now as actually experiencing a battle, has at last been baptized with a name and is seen attempting with others to rally the fleeing troops.[14]

At the battle's end, however, Ljutov's solidarity with his fellow warriors is challenged by the soldier Akinfiev, who accuses him of riding into battle with an unloaded revolver. In refusing to accept his comrades' enemies as his own he has once again been a traitor to their code. Even Sashka, the regimental nurse and camp follower who had hitherto seemed selfish and uninvolved, wishes she had had a gun to help turn the tide of battle

[14] The narrator's name (Ljutov), applied as it is to a man who refuses to kill, is distinctly ironic (cf. the adjective "ljutyj"—fierce, ferocious, or cruel).

and proves herself capable of a noble passion that is beyond
Ljutov. The story comes to a close inside the narrator's mind,
where self-pity and a sense of moral rectitude struggle against
the recognition of a real deficiency:

> Evening flew up to the sky like a flock of birds, and darkness
> crowned me with its watery wreath. I felt my strength all ebbing
> away. Bent beneath the funereal garland, I continued on my way,
> imploring fate to grant me the simplest of proficiencies—the ability
> to kill my fellow-men (187).

The narrator's lament over his inability to kill even an enemy
is more than merely an easy, self-serving irony. It expresses a
genuine sense of deficiency, a sort of moral handicap, and it
brings to mind the tortured self-questioning of Dostoevsky's
Raskolnikov, who similarly sought a heightened sense of identity
in an act of violence. Raskolnikov attempted to establish his
*right* to disregard a moral code, whereas Babel's hero questions
his *ability* to do so. But both characters seek a sense of superior
manhood, an act to take them beyond the limits of civilized con-
ventionality. For Babel's narrator the question posed by the
war is not so much his capacity to bear pain (as a Jew he knows
that he can do this) as it is his ability to inflict it, and it is this
threatening sense of inferiority which in large measure deter-
mines the strange admiration he feels for his more violent comrades.[15] One of the narrator's desires is to undo his excessive
moral sensibilities so that he can find a place among his Cossack
friends; he seeks to fit into the world he inhabits as into a picture
—to blend properly, aesthetically.

For many Soviet critics the private dilemmas of Babel's narrator in *Red Cavalry* are simply a reflection of the character's

---

15 The narrator's open admiration for the Cossacks is usually expressed (as in
"My First Goose") in terms of an envy of their manly grace and beauty, but it
also includes an awed respect for their cruelty (e.g., the figure Dyakov in "The
Remount Officer"). Babel's narrator in *Red Cavalry* is still very much like the
youthful listener of "How It Was Done in Odessa," who marveled at the glorious
deeds of Froim Grach, Kolka Pakovsky, and Benja Krik; in "The Brigade Commander" even the form recalls the earlier tale, for once again a legendary trio
haunts the narrator's imagination ("the famous Kniga, the headstrong Pavlichenko and the captivating Savitsky").

(and by extension the author's) lack of Revolutionary zeal. Reduced to its crudest form the argument states that, as a petty bourgeois, Babel (or his surrogate Ljutov) is a decadent individualist who is psychologically incapable of appreciating either the Revolutionary mass or the guiding force of communism that directs it. But this simplistic view is grossly inadequate. By totally identifying the author with his narrator it fails to acknowledge the irony and criticism that Babel directs toward his own fictional persona, and by adopting a narrow, vulgar concept of Revolutionary orthodoxy it severely diminishes the genuine Revolutionary commitment that Babel does have. It is true, of course, that he refuses to mindlessly follow the dictates of Party slogans and that he allows unpredictability, confusion, and irrationality to play a major role in events; but his denial of the Party's all-knowing and all-powerful hand at the helm is far from being a lack of commitment. Babel is a revolutionary; he is desperately committed to the destruction of the old world and to rapid change; but he is also an artist, and he refuses to will his desires into being or to preach what he does not know to be true. Destruction is not yet creation, the present is not yet the future, and Babel remains true to these distinctions.[16]

The narrator of *Red Cavalry*, in part resembling Babel and in part diverging from him, does seek to understand not only the unlettered peasants and workers whom he perceives as the potential but unknowing bearers of a new order, but also those single-minded, convinced Communists who may be its more conscious agents. In "Evening" the narrator introduces several of his co-workers on the army newspaper: "wall-eyed Galin, consumptive Slinkin and Suchov with the gnawed-away intestines" are passionate propagandists, bringers of political wisdom to the masses. The story focuses on Galin, who rants tirelessly about

[16] What particularly irks some Soviet critics of *Red Cavalry* is the lyrical aspect of its first-person narrative. They complain that Babel himself, rather than the Revolutionary Army, is the central figure of the book, and they label this decadent individualism. Under the rigidly ideological Soviet regime, where the cultural front is fiercely policed and the state's literary image jealously guarded, such a charge is tantamount to complete rejection.

the fate of Russia's emperors and with whom, as with the Cossacks
in other stories, the narrator comes into conflict:

> With my confused poetic brains I was digesting the class struggle
> when Galin approached with his gleaming wall-eyes.
>    "Galin," I said, overwhelmed by loneliness and self-pity, "I'm
> ill. It seems the end has come, and I'm so sick of being in our
> Cavalry Army. . . ."
>    "You're a driveler," replied Galin, the watch on his thin wrist
> showing 1:00 A.M., "you're a driveler, and we're fated to have to
> put up with you drivelers. We're busy shelling and getting at
> the kernel for you. Not long will pass and then you'll see those
> cleaned kernels and take your fingers out of your nose and sing
> of the new life in no ordinary prose. In the meantime sit still, you
> driveler, and stop whimpering around us" (129).

Galin's wall-eye may be said to represent the single–minded-
ness of his vision, his rejection of that confused periphery which
so bedevils the narrator's "poetic brains." But at the same time
Galin suffers in a personal sense for his wall-eyed view of life:
the washerwoman Irina, whom he loves, prefers to bed down
with the cook, Vasily, and Galin is left to warm himself with his
prophetic vision of the future, when today's undisciplined allies
will have to become Galins or be thrust aside:

> "The Cavalry Army," then said Galin to me, "the Cavalry Army
> is the social focus effected by the Central Committee of our Party.
> The revolutionary curve has thrown into the first rank the free
> Cossacks still soaked in many prejudices, but the Central Com-
> mittee's maneuvering will rub them down with a brush of iron"
> (130).

As is clear from the stories examined thus far, one of the major
battlefields of *Red Cavalry* is in the narrator's mind. His search
amid death for a way to live is what motivates a number of the
tales. He is the spectator who wishes to become involved, the
outsider who wishes to join, and he is also the disillusioned modern youth searching for men uncorrupted by civilization. At the
same time the narrator himself remains a man of the city, a Jew
and an intellectual; he is caught between two worlds, each of
which fills him at times with horror or disgust. If he seeks among

his army comrades to escape the suffering and deprivation of the closed old Jewish world, he collides with the harshness and cruelty of the Cossack way of life. The book is propelled forward through a recurring pattern of advance and retreat, of expansion and contraction, of hope alternating with despair.

It is no surprise that a number of the stories in *Red Cavalry* deal not with the fortunes of warring soldiers, but with the fate of those ghetto-sealed Jewish communities in the Polish towns through which the Revolutionary army passes. Whenever the narrator's sense of humanity is violated beyond endurance, he retreats to the Jewish ghetto, where he seeks a kind of companionship that the Cossacks cannot provide. He reemerges each time, it is true, but the pattern of withdrawal is recurrent. A knowledge of Babel's personal reaction to the Polish campaign of 1920 will help put this pattern into perspective and clarify the creative distortion that his art imposed upon experience.

In addition to *Red Cavalry* there exist fragments of a diary that Babel kept during the campaign, as well as some early plans and drafts for the stories. Not all of this material has been published, but enough is available to give at least an idea of how Babel's views developed and took on literary form. The diary excerpts, especially, give a record, however cryptic, of immediate impressions. Although the Babel who later reworked this material into his stories was a different man from the Babel of 1920 who hurriedly jotted down his impressions while on the move, the diary nevertheless illuminates the shape of *Red Cavalry*. For all his evident sympathy with his narrator, Babel the author is not to be totally identified with that character. But the Babel of the 1920 diary is very close indeed to the Ljutov of *Red Cavalry*, and many of the latter's attitudes and dilemmas have their source in the mind of the former.

Besides constant indication of his intention to write about what he has seen (reminders to "write this," "describe that," "capture that"), the diary contains the recognizable kernels of several of the stories of *Red Cavalry*; a host of names, figures, events, and details were jotted down for later use, and often they appear in the final book in a way that is both strikingly similar and, because of the addition of authorial irony, significantly different. Many of the diary notations have to do with Babel's reactions to the Polish Jews, whose life seemed to him so deprived and joyless. Under the heading "July 30, Brody," for instance, he notes:

> ... The city has been destroyed and plundered. It is an immensely interesting place. Polish culture. An ancient, wealthy, and distinctive Jewish settlement. Those horrible bazaars; dwarfs in house-coats, house-coats and earlocks; ancient old men; the street on which the school is situated; 96 [?] synagogues. Everything is half demolished.[17]

Again in a note dated "June 27" we read:

> These people lead a preposterous life—like animals. Filthy rooms, thousands of flies, disgusting food—and they want nothing better. Just greed and that repulsive, unvarying arrangement of living quarters.[18]

And in one of his jottings for the story "Brody," he observes:

> I have never seen a more melancholy town. The sources of Jewry— I will not forget this for the rest of my life.[19]

Babel especially abhors the stagnancy and lethargy which often accompany misery, the unwillingness or inability of people who are mired in poverty and wretchedness even to desire change. At times in the diary he despairs completely and doubts the possibility of happiness for the suffering people he sees. For the Jewish inhabitants of ghettos and small villages it is the dead weight of an unchanging history that Babel finds so oppressive. In some of his notes for a story never written ("Demidovka") he draws a biblical and historical parallel. On the eve of the holy day set aside for fasting and mourning in memory of the fall of Jerusalem, a religious family reads from the Book of Lamentations. While looting, killing, and rapine envelop the town, the

---

[17] Quoted by I. Smirin, in "I. Babel' Novye materialy," *Literaturnoe nasledstvo,* LXXIV, 498.
[18] Quoted by L. Livšic, in "Materialy k tvorčeskoj biografii," 114–15.
[19] *Literaturnoe nasledstvo,* LXXIV, 492.

mournful dirge evokes the destruction of the Temple and the ruin of Israel. Babel's attitude to the destruction is ambivalent; he cannot help but abhor the violence and cruelty, and yet he is equally repelled by the ancient squalor and changelessness of Jewish fate and welcomes their doom. He is both repelled and fascinated by what he sees, and as a Jew himself he finds his own fate (as his diary entries of June 4 and July 26 record) closely involved with the world-shaking war and revolution that he has experienced:

> Life flows on before me, but what does it mean?
> I have to sort it all out: the Polish compaign, the World War, and my personal fate.[20]

The effect of war upon ancient traditions is endlessly fascinating for Babel, and he has an especially keen eye for observing the weird tangle of historical threads entwined in contemporary events. In the war-torn towns of Poland he catches the sights, sounds, and smells of an ancient decay, of a world in its death throes: the Jewish quarters, with their shops and their synagogues; the last lingering traces of an aristocratic, feudal Polish culture; and the free, wild life of the fighting Cossacks—all are enmeshed in the convulsions of change. The diary provides a striking instance of how certain of Babel's impressions passed with amazing ease into one of the finished stories of *Red Cavalry*. Under the diary heading "7 August, Berestechko" we read:

> A memorable day. In the morning we transferred from Khotin to Berestechko [. . .] The body of a slain Pole, a terrible body, monstrously swollen and naked [. . .] the historical plains of Berestechko, Cossack graves. And in essentials, nothing has changed— it's still the Cossacks against the Poles, even more the serf against the master. I shall never forget this town; its covered courtyards— long, narrow, and stinking. All this is one or two hundred years old. The population is sturdier here than other places. The main thing is the architecture—white, watery-blue houses, tiny streets, synagogues. Peasant girls.
> [. . .] Everything exudes antiquity, tradition; the town is satu-

20 *Ibid.*, 476.

rated with the bloody history of a Jewish-Polish ghetto [. . .]
The ancient church, the fenced-off graves of Polish officers—the
mounds are still fresh, only about ten days old; crosses of white
birch. How terrible it all is. The house of the priest is destroyed.
I find old books, priceless Latin manuscripts.
. . . Night in the town. The church is closed. Before evening I
go to the castle of the Counts Raciborski. A seventy-year-old bachelor and his ninety-year-old mother. Only two of them left; the
people say they are mad. Describe this pair. The ancient Polish
house of the Counts—probably more than a hundred years old.
Antlers, old paintings—still bright—on the ceiling, bits of antlers.
Tiny rooms upstairs for the servants, slabs of stone, passageways,
excrement on the floor, Jewish kids, a Steinway piano, sofas ripped
open to the springs. Remember the light oaken doors, all white;
the French letters from the year 1820. [. . .] My God, who wrote
them, when were they written? Wrinkled letters, I took some
relics, a century old. The Mother—the Countess.
The Steinway piano. The park. The pond.
I can't tear myself away—I recall Hauptmann, Helga.
A political meeting in the castle park. The Jews of Berestechko.
The witless Vinokurov. Kids running all around. They're electing
the Revolutionary Committee. The Jewish men wind their beards
on their fingers; the Jewish women listen to a speech about the
Russian paradise, about the international situation, and about
the uprising in India.[21]

This passage from the diary has been quoted at length because
almost all of it finds its way into one or another of the stories,
most noticeably "Berestechko," where the same multinational
and incongruous mixture of "ancient" cultures acquires a heightened poetic expression: the yellowed leaves of a lady's French
letters; Cossack warriors and Hasidic Jews; a wretched town
whose inhabitants reek of rotten herring; and towering above it
the castle of the Counts Raciborski, lit by a lizard-green moon
and presided over by the aged and maddened last of the line.
The story even adds to the aura of historical analysis and acquires
a heightened tension through the suppression of the narrator's
passionate personal reactions. In an added episode the Cossack
Kudrya murders an old Jewish man, slitting his throat with care

21 *Ibid.*

so as to avoid soiling his trousers, and the narrator's description of the scene has a similar precision and lack of expressed emotion. The Babel of the diaries, however, found such sights unbearable. Again and again the notebooks record his despair at the depths of human cruelty, and for all his celebration of the Cossack army and its martial beauty he frequently gives expression in the diary to hatred for what war brings. An unfinished and unmailed letter found among his diary papers, dated August 13, 1920, gives a clear indication of how profoundly alienated Babel felt at times from the war, the Revolution, and his comrades:

> . . . Above us are captivating skies, and a mild sun. Pine trees rustle around us and we can hear the snorting of hundreds of steppe horses. One could really live here, but all our thoughts are directed to murder. My words may sound foolish, but war is sometimes truly beautiful. It is always, however, harmful.
>
> I have just lived through two weeks of utter despair—because of the fierce cruelty which never lets up here for even a minute. It has made me realize how unsuited I am for this business of destruction, and how hard it is for me to tear myself from old ways. . . . These ways may have been evil, but for me they breathed poetry, just as the beehive does honey. I'm pulling back now, but what does it matter—others will make the Revolution, and I will sing about what is off to the side. This is what I can do and there will be time and a place to do it. . . . I have come to myself; in my heart I feel a hundred-horsepower strong, and once again I am thinking my own thoughts. The two devils, or rather bombs, which exploded a half hour ago just a hundred paces away, cannot impede me.[22]

This desire to abandon the Revolution to others and turn instead to poetry and the past is also found in *Red Cavalry*, in that pattern of advance and retreat which defines the movement of the book. When the weight of the war's cruelties becomes too heavy to bear, Ljutov flees to those very Polish Jews whom he otherwise sees as warped and deprived; something of his own past responds to their calm and dignified suffering:

> The Jews of Volhynia and Galicia moved jerkily, in a way that offended taste; but their capacity for suffering was full of a sombre

22 Excerpted from the text of the letter as quoted in Livšic, "Materialy," 123.

greatness, and their unvoiced contempt for the Polish gentry unbounded. Watching them, I understood the poignant history of
this region... ("Discourse on the *Tachanka*," 86).

In "Gedali," Ljutov roams on a Sabbath eve through the
streets of Zhitomir in search of the past, "in search of a shy star"
or "a bit of that pensioned-off God in a glass of tea":

> On Sabbath eves I am oppressed by the dense melancholy of
> memories. In bygone days on these occasions my grandfather would
> stroke the volumes of Ibn Ezra with his yellow beard. His old
> woman in her lace cap would trace fortunes with her knotty fin-
> gers over the Sabbath candles, and sob softly to herself. On those
> evenings my child's heart was rocked like a little ship upon en-
> chanted waves. O the rotted Talmuds of my childhood! O the
> dense melancholy of memories! (69).

He makes his way to the market place, its booths emptied by the
war of both people and goods. There, in a small Dickensian
curiosity shop, he finds one lone hold-out, the old Jewish proprietor Gedali, who has remained, the last guard of the dying
bazaar, to keep the faith with his relics from the past and his
dreams.[23] As always in Babel, culture is here writ small—in the
microcosm of a wretched little junk shop. Its proprietor Gedali
believes in the impossible, in the joy-giving Revolution, in an
International of good people. As he explains to Ljutov:

> "The Revolution—we will say 'yes' to it, but are we to say 'no'
> to the Sabbath?" began Gedali, winding about me the silken straps
> of his smoke-hidden eyes. "Yes, I cry to the Revolution. Yes, I cry
> to it, but it hides its face from Gedali and sends out on front
> nought but shooting..." (70).

The narrator's reply, that the Revolution cannot do without
shooting, fails to reconcile gunpowder with the Sabbath. Like
Dostoevsky's Christ in "The Grand Inquisitor," Gedali, though
blinded by the Poles, has an ennobling vision of human possi-

---

[23] Here too the kernel of the story is found in an actual encounter recorded
by Babel in his diary. Under the entry for July 20 is the following note: "A little
old Jewish philosopher. An inconceivable shop—Dickens, brooms, and golden slip-
pers. His philosophy: Everyone says he is fighting for truth, and everyone
plunders." (Quoted by Ehrenburg in his Introduction to *I. Babel': Izbrannoe*, 6.)

bilities. Ljutov, who has hitched his star to the Revolution, returns to his war while Gedali departs on a different path:

> ... a tiny, lonely visionary in a black top hat, carrying a big prayer-book under his arm.
> The Sabbath is coming. Gedali, the founder of an impossible International, has gone to the synagogue to pray (72).

Babel's Ljutov has chosen another road, but Gedali remains a sadly beautiful figure out of the author's own past, for we have seen how Babel himself in an earlier day had expressed a view of the Revolution not unlike Gedali's:

> ... It may not be a bad idea sometimes to grab a rifle and start shooting at each other. But that's not all there is to revolution. Who knows, perhaps that's not revolution at all.[24]

If Babel now turns his back on his youthful dreams, in Gedali he allows the past all its elegiac beauty, and the ethos of that past, so antithetical to that of Babel's beautiful but cruel Cossacks, will continue to make its appeal to the narrator of *Red Cavalry* more than once before he bids it a final farewell. In "The Rabbi" he has his narrator Ljutov again venture into the ancient world of the Hasidic synagogue. As the "Sabbath peace settles upon the crooked roofs of the Zhitomir ghetto," Ljutov, in the company of Gedali, visits the home of Rabbi Motale Bratslavsky, who presides at a meeting of "the liars and the possessed." All is not peaceful, however, in the rabbi's house, for his own son, "the cursed and disobedient last son," is in attendance only under protest. He is likened to a "recaptured prisoner brought back to his cell," and his face, "emaciated as a nun's," suggests an image of emasculation. Ljutov's estrangement from the world of Jewish tradition is thus echoed by that of the rabbi's own son. When the rabbi solemnly asks him, "What is the Jew seeking?" the narrator answers, "Merriment." And in reply to the further question, "What is the Jew's occupation?" he claims to be "putting into verse the adventures of Hersch of Ostropol." In reality, of course, Ljutov's work at the time was

---

[24] "Dvorec materinstva," *Novaja žizn'*, March 31, 1918.

writing political articles for the army paper. The obvious intent of the irony is to undermine those values which the rabbi holds dear, but the effect cuts both ways, for the values of the narrator's war propaganda are equally called into question.

Ljutov escapes, but the "vague odor of corruption" that he had noticed in Gedali's shop will trouble him again. In the very next story, "The Road to Brody," the supposedly dead past will be evoked once more in the closing lyrical digression:

> O Brody! The mummies of your crushed passions breathed upon me their irremediable poison. I could already sense the deathly chill of orbits suffused with tears grown cold. And here am I being borne away at a jolting gallop, far from the dented stones of your synagogues (82).

We can see in Babel's diary again how the "realist" in him rejected and ridiculed those religious values associated with the past:

> An argument between a Jewish youth and the Cossack Prishchepa. The boy wears glasses, his eyelids are red and inflamed. He is black-haired, nervous; his Russian is incorrect. He believes in God: God is an ideal which we carry in our hearts, and each man in his heart has his own idea of God; if you behave badly, God is offended. These stupidities are expressed by the boy in pain and exultation.[25]

The Babel who "knows" life recognizes only too well that his Cossack friends carry no such Jewish god in their souls. When thus limited to the Jews such a belief becomes only a guarantee of suffering, and he rejects it as absurd. One can hardly fail to note once again how self-directed the ridicule is, how close the picture of the Jewish youth is to the portrait Babel gives of himself in *Red Cavalry*.

For all his desire to exorcize his inherited traits, Babel remains their prisoner. In the struggle between his mind and his heart the Jews are seen both as contemptible self-victimizers and as sympathetic. He makes a certain distinction between the institutional faith as represented by the rabbi and its human visage as

25 *Literaturnoe nasledstvo,* LXXIV, 499.

exemplified in Gedali. The simple Jewish shopkeeper, whose dreams are eloquently humane, draws Ljutov to him; the rabbi, who speaks in formulas, drives his own son away. Gedali in his black hat and green frock coat at least still has some life left in him. The rabbi, dressed in shroudlike white and wearing a sable cap, is the "last of the Chernobyl dynasty"; his house has a broken portal and the room where he presides over a court of fools is likened to a morgue. It is Gedali who, in affirming his faith, nevertheless describes the end of the rabbi's reign:

> The passionate edifice of Hasidism has had its doors and windows burst open, but it is as immortal as the soul of the mother. With oozing orbits Hasidism still stands at the crossroads of the turbulent winds of history ("The Rabbi," 77).

In the book's penultimate story, "The Rabbi's Son," this demon of the past will return to haunt Ljutov.[26] Amid the tattered humanity of a bedraggled peasant army he encounters once more the unruly son of Rabbi Motale, now mortally wounded. Among the scattered belongings of the dying man the old paradoxes and contrasts find their consummate expression:

> His things were strewn about pell-mell—mandates of the propagandist and notebooks of the Jewish poet, the portraits of Lenin and Maimonides lay side by side, the knotted iron of Lenin's skull beside the dull silk of the portraits of Maimonides. A lock of woman's hair lay in a book, the Resolutions of the Party's Sixth Congress, and the margins of Communist leaflets were crowded with crooked lines of ancient Hebrew verse. They fell upon me in a mean and depressing rain—pages of the Song of Songs and revolver cartridges (192–93).

Ilya Bratslavsky has made his escape, the last of the rabbinical princes has become a Red soldier, and in his dying words he attempts to refute Gedali's view that "only the mother is eternal." "In a revolution," he tells Ljutov, "a mother is only an episode." And Ilya's struggle to renounce the world of his childhood is Ljutov's as well:

26 In the first several editions of Red Cavalry, "The Rabbi's Son" was the final story of the book; but in the fifth edition (1931) Babel added a new story, "Argamak," which in subsequent editions has ended the cycle.

He died before we reached Rovno. He—that last of the Princes —died among his poetry, phylacteries, and coarse foot-wrappings. We buried him at some forgotten station. And I, who can scarce contain the tempests of my imagination within this age-old body of mine, I was there beside my brother when he breathed his last (193).

Even in this story the resolution remains uncertain and the final effect ambiguous. If Ilya Bratslavsky has indeed escaped, it is only through the agency of death; his search for a new identity has returned him to the bosom of the eternal mother—earth. With his dying breath Bratslavsky exclaims in despair that his command of a regiment had come too late, too late to turn the tide of battle and too late for his own salvation. Nothing has really changed and he carries with him to the grave the scattered belongings of a Jewish poet and "the stunted virility of a wasted Semite."

# VIII

# Red Cavalry: CHRISTIANITY, CULTURE, AND HISTORY

*"O death, O covetous one, O greedy thief, why couldst thou not have spared us, just for once?"*[1]

Babel viewed the past with an ambivalent mixture of hostility and respect. Deeply committed to the humanistic concerns which distinguished the Russian intelligentsia at its best, he nevertheless shared in the prevailing mood of cultural disillusionment. Like other artists and intellectuals of the twenties, he had come to believe that the renewal and furtherance of humane values required abandoning the very institutions that were the traditional guardians of those values. Repelled by the asceticism and decay of established religious tradition and by the hypocrisy, deceit, and injustice of Russia's aging feudal and emergent middle-class society, Babel vested great hope in the Revolution's promise of a social renewal. In his profound desire for a cultural transformation he also sought support beyond the boundaries of Marxist ideology, and behind the disquieting ambiguities and the iconoclastic idealism of his art may be sensed the commanding presence and seductive thought of Friedrich Nietzsche.

Since shortly after his death in 1900, and increasingly with the passage of time, Nietzsche's impact upon literature has been ex-

---

[1] Closing paragraph of "The Cemetery at Kozin," from Morison, ed. and trans., *Collected Stories*, 107.

tremely powerful. Reaching an early peak in the 1920s, it has left
its mark upon most of the major modern figures. Perhaps Nietzsche was the first to express in an electrifying and persuasive way
the feeling that had been growing among intellectuals that Western culture had reached a state of crisis. His insights into the
spiritual and psychological condition of contemporary Western
man and his call for a "transvaluation of all values" struck a
chord to which twentieth-century artists profoundly responded.
His dictum, in *The Birth of Tragedy*, that life was justifiable
only as an aesthetic phenomenon, might serve as an epigraph to
an entire range of the avant-garde art of the twenties.

Isaac Babel, who was deeply immersed in the currents of mod-
ernism, shares many of the Nietzschean attitudes. His search for
a heroic possibility in life and for heroic figures to embody that
possibility in art bears comparison with a major tenet of Nietzsche's thought; both *The Odessa Tales* and *Red Cavalry*, with
their monumental heroes, seem to owe something to the Nietzschean concept of the *Übermensch*. Furthermore, the effort to
transcend traditional moral categories or, in the terms of the
Revolution, the need to overcome prejudicial middle-class no-
tions of right and wrong, follows in Babel the Nietzschean pattern of seeking alternatives in the deeper recesses of human nature. The German philosopher's "Dionysian" affirmation of the
joy "beyond all terror and pity—that joy which includes even joy
in destroying,"[2] finds a startling echo in the pages of Babel's *Red
Cavalry*. In a memorable phrase of the narrator's ("oxvačennyj
gibel'nym vostorgom"—seized by a destructive joy), it even acquires an actual expression that strikingly recalls Nietzsche. Although he never abandoned a belief in humanism, Babel did
move beyond it in order to embrace as well the kind of radical
aestheticism which Nietzsche proposed. The parallels between
the two men are indeed so compelling that some of their ramifi-
cations need to be examined more closely.

In his very first book Nietzsche sought to uncover, through an

[2] *The Basic Writings of Nietzsche*, trans. Walter Kaufmann (New York, 1968),
729.

exploration of the culture of ancient Greece, a vision of life which would fundamentally challenge the spirit of his own time. His famous formulation, in *The Birth of Tragedy*, of the Dionysian and Apollonian antithesis, of that fruitful tension between the thrust of demonic passion and the calm of ordered harmony, was an original and successful attempt to alter the prevailing views on Greek civilization and on the nature and origin of its art. In the god Dionysus, Nietzsche found a symbol for those darker urges upon which he conceived the refined and classic beauty of the Apollonian ideal to rest. The worship of Dionysus, having its source in the demonic promptings of a primitive savagery and expressed through the pulse and rhythm of music and dance, gave birth in time to the Greek art of tragedy while the worship of the god Apollo, symbol of harmony and repose, gave rise to sculpture and other plastic arts.

Babel too was keenly responsive to the subterranean workings of primitive nature on the behavior of men, and he had a fine sense as well of that opposition Nietzsche described between the dynamic and the static states of existence, of that tension between the chaotic flux of becoming and the ethereal beauty of being. Although many of his stories portray the clash of these rival perceptions, he attempted, like Nietzsche, to discover them in union.[3] Some of the Cossack figures of *Red Cavalry*, combining a readiness for the spontaneous release of elemental, often violent emotion with the grace and charm of great physical beauty, seem to represent for Babel something of the same bipolarity that Nietzsche sees as the Greek ideal.

Nietzsche's comparison of the Greek and contemporary worlds involved, in its further elaboration, still another dualism, one which is also reflected in Babel in an intensely personal way. In the second edition of *Birth of Tragedy*, Nietzsche added a new subtitle along with a belated foreword entitled "Attempt at a

---

[3] "Line and Color," written at the same time as *Red Cavalry* but not a part of that cycle, displays a facet of this conflict in arguing the need of line to supplement the perception of color, of a purpose perhaps to supplement art. But Babel himself, though he struggled against it, was deeply committed to the claims of color, and here as elsewhere reveals a major feature of his Nietzschean temper.

Self-Criticism." Both the new subtitle, "Hellenism and Pessimism," and the new foreword reflected the change that had taken place in Nietzsche's thinking during the fourteen years since the book's first publication. The major antithesis, as Nietzsche now expressed it, was no longer between Dionysus and Apollo, but between both of these, as the twin poles of Hellenism, and the Hebraic-Christian moral tradition that in Western history came to supplant them.[4] Speaking in his preface of Christianity in particular, but elsewhere including Hebraism in his denunciation, Nietzsche proclaims that:

> Behind this mode of thought and valuation, . . . I never fail to sense a *hostility to life*—a furious, vengeful antipathy to life itself. . . . Christianity was from the beginning, essentially and fundamentally, life's nausea and disgust with life, merely concealed behind, masked by, dressed up as, faith in "another" or "better" life. Hatred of "the world," condemnations of the passions, fear of beauty and sensuality, a beyond invented the better to slander this life, at bottom a craving for the nothing, for the end, for respite, for "the sabbath of sabbaths"—all this always struck me, no less than the unconditional will of Christianity to recognize *only* moral values, as the most dangerous and uncanny form of all possible forms of a "will to decline" —at the very least a sign of abysmal sickness, weariness, discouragement, exhaustion, and the impoverishment of life. For confronted with morality (especially Christian, or unconditional, morality), life *must* continually and inevitably be in the wrong, because life *is* something essentially amoral—and eventually, crushed by the weight of contempt and the eternal No, life *must* then be felt to be unworthy of desire and altogether worthless.[5]

This is an indictment with which Babel largely agrees. And he is attracted as well by the Nietzschean counterargument: that the deities of the pagan Greeks offer an alternative value system in the aesthetic apprehension of reality, and that in so doing they

---

4 Noteworthy discussions of this same dichotomy, one pre- and one post-Nietzschean, are: Matthew Arnold, "Hebraism and Hellenism" (*Culture and Anarchy*, 1869), and Lev Shestov, *Athens and Jerusalem* (1937). Although on opposite sides of the issue, both writers pose the conflict as one between morality and some alternative force: in Shestov's terms, between religion and rational philosophy; in Arnold's between "strictness of conscience" and "spontaneity of consciousness."

5 *The Basic Writings of Nietzsche*, 23.

symbolize the affirmation rather than the rejection of life. The opposition between the two modes of thinking is for Nietzsche total. Morality, he declares, "is neither Apollonian nor Dionysian; it negates all aesthetic values—the only values recognized in *The Birth of Tragedy*: it is nihilistic in the most profound sense, while in the Dionysian symbol the ultimate limit of affirmation is attained."[6]

Babel's assault upon religious institutions, like Nietzsche's, involves not only a repudiation of Jewish tradition, but a confrontation with Christian culture as well. Several of the stories in *Red Cavalry* actually take place in and around Catholic churches, and their prevailing attitude is one of rejection. The tone is sometimes even more mocking than with the Jewish tales, and the reason for this is not hard to find. In the stories reflecting on Jewish life Babel was dealing with material that was full of the most intense personal concern and involvement. In the Catholic tales he was able to view his material from a certain distance and to give his anticlericalism a freer rein.

In "The Church at Novograd," Babel has his narrator enter, with a mixture of repulsion and fascination, the forbidden *sanctum sanctorum* of Catholic mysteries. A dominant image of the story is that of the crucifixion and resurrection, seen in a threatening light. The opening sentence announces the appropriation of the priest's house by a Red Army commissar; the priest himself has escaped. Pani Eliza, the Jesuit's former housekeeper, greets the narrator, who has come to report to the commissar, with an offering of tea and biscuits: "Those sponges of hers had an odor of crucifixes. A subtle juice was in them, together with the aromatic fierceness of the Vatican" (43). The suggestion of a Eucharistic communion is increased with the arrival of the absent priest's assistant, Pan Romuald, who, tracing upon a map the circles of the Polish debacle, proudly "enumerates his country's wounds." This "eunuch with a giant's body," symbol of an ascetic, fleshless, emasculated institution, is identified in another

[6] *Ibid.*, 727.

164

story with the figure of John the Baptist. Here, as the narrator drinks rum with him:

> The breath of an invisible order of things glimmered beneath the crumbling ruin of the priest's house, and its soothing seduction unmanned me. O crucifixes, tiny as the talismans of light ladies; parchment of Papal Bulls; satin of feminine letters rotting in the blue silk of waistcoats! (44).[7]

The narrator continues:

> I can see you now, faithless monk, in your mauve cassock, with your plump hands and your soul as gentle and pitiless as the soul of a cat; I can see the wounds of your god oozing seed, a fragrant poison to intoxicate virgins (44).

This unsettling conglomeration of virgins, whores, and eunuchs about a crucified god is a fearful yet fascinating nightmare for the narrator. In the garden outside the house "thirsty roses" stir beneath "the black passion of the sky," "green lightning flashes upon the cupolas," and "at the foot of a slope huddles a disrobed corpse"—all of which suggest another image of the crucifixion. This then is the narrator's vision of Catholic Poland as he spreads his mattress in a church abandoned by its priest and seeks comfort in the thought that "hordes of paupers roll toward the ancient cities" to threaten the princes Radziwill and Sapieha, who have "risen for an hour." Frightened by the thought that the old order may yet return to prove the new era stillborn, the narrator flees to the church, where more terrors await him: two silver skulls gleam upon the lid of a broken coffin, another suggestion of crucifixion and resurrection, and high above the altar, in the very dome itself, shines a multitude of lights.

But the nightmare is finally dispelled. Ljutov, locating the commissar, discovers that the lights are not angels on high, but a detachment of Red Cossacks searching the church with candles in their hands. Having uncovered piles of army uniforms in the

[7] Some of the details in this passage recall the diary entry which played so large a part in the development of the story "Berestechko."

priest's apartment, they have decided to look into the church itself, and Ljutov now joins them as they explore its "subterranean passages and mildewed caverns." Inside the echoing building they find jewel-encrusted images of the Virgin and icons which split down the middle to reveal hidden niches. Flashing the horsehead insignia on their cuffs—pagan talismans against Christian magic—they continue their penetration of the innards of the temple—a rape, perhaps, of Mother Church. In the Holy of Holies they find gold, gems, and banknotes, a desecration of the altar by its own votaries, and with the mystery thus unveiled the narrator is enabled, at least for the moment, to overcome its seductive power:

> O foolish priest, to hang the bodices of your parishioners upon the nails in the Savior's cross! . . .
> "Away!" I said to myself. "Away from these ogling Madonnas deceived by common soldiers!" (46).

This tale, with its subterranean passages, its missing priest, and its generally supernatural atmosphere, has many of the trappings of a Gothic satire. Through the story's somewhat sinister symbolism, the Christian temple becomes its obverse, a demonic, dungeonlike cellar. The search through the temple's crypts suggests the winding quest through a monster's lair—or through the labyrinthine entrails of the monster itself. The latter surmise is buttressed by the story's network of odor motifs: "the aromatic fierceness of the Vatican," "the odor of crucifixes," "the breath of an invisible odor," the rotting letters, the "fragrant poison" of oozing seed, the decaying edifice of the church itself. The *essence* of Christianity is thus revealed in the story by its scent, and the search for that essence entails a *descent* into the bowels of Mother Church.[8] Thus an imagery of debasement presents

---

[8] The feminine imagery with which Babel describes the Church is manifest throughout the story. Churches, castles, and palaces, psychologists tell us, are often symbols of the female sexual organs. The motif of wandering down into a maze or labyrinth may symbolize the return to the mother's womb, and the ascent out of it the effort to be born, to emerge into light. Babel's narrator, spreading his mattress in a church abandoned by its priest (the father) describes himself, significantly in this connection, as "a violent intruder."

the spiritual institution of the church in crudely physiological terms, and the gold and gems which the Cossacks uncover in the Holy of Holies may be seen as a corollary, but reverse motif—that is, as a displaced image of excrement.

In another Catholic story, "St. Valentine's Church," the narrator is outwardly more sympathetic to the religious feelings of an invaded population. But his sympathy is a rather cold one, prompted by the consideration that it is good policy to refrain from insulting a conquered people's deeply held convictions. The narrator's tone seems more dispassionate here; he is less personally involved. But his attitude is actually no less sacrilegious than the behavior of the Cossacks, whose despoiling of the church he deplores. "Saints in this temple," he tells us, "went to their deaths with all the picturesqueness of Italian singers." The hallowed bones of the church's patron remind him of "the bones of a hen." The actual desecration of the church by the Cossacks is merely an outward manifestation of the narrator's inner thoughts. Only once is he moved by genuine emotion—when he encounters, in a painted statue, "the most extraordinary image of God I have ever seen in my life." The Christ of this statue is a curly-headed Jew, a bearded figure in an orange greatcoat; pursued and overtaken by hatred, he has raised a bloodied hand to ward off another impending blow.

Babel's response to the spiritual power of this last image is extremely significant. It reveals the common ground upon which both the Hebrew and Christian traditions rest; it also reveals the continuing power of both traditions to affect Babel deeply. The ambivalence of his writing, as we have seen repeatedly, is based upon the extraordinary attraction exerted upon him simultaneously by conflicting traditions and values. Even with regard to Christianity, Babel's attitudes remain essentially ambiguous. He sees the living force of the church exhausted in institutionalism, its community-forming mission of providing an ordered sense of human destiny abandoned. But if the church clings to a decaying past, to the yellowing parchment of Latinate papal bulls, Babel finds it impossible to reject its former splendor. He still responds to the spiritual magnificence of church art and architecture and to the glimmerings of vitality in its ancient traditions. His atheism and his Revolutionary commitment notwithstanding, Babel remains devoted to what might ultimately be called a "religious" search for life's meaning. That so much of *Red Cavalry* takes place in or around synagogues and churches is itself a mark of the appeal that a religious view of the cosmos exercises upon Babel's imagination. If it is true that he often mocks, it is equally true that he can never quite slay his monster, and he returns obsessively in his stories to the religious figures and holy temples that symbolize the serious and sacred view of human fate.

Even the Revolution must have for Babel a quasi-religious, a messianic or eschatological, dimension if it is to become a truly significant human event.[9] The destruction and strife that abound in war, the pain and suffering that the Revolution imposes: these gain meaning only as a battle, a struggle to create a just world. One of the great symbolic images woven through Babel's *oeuvre* is the heroic figure of the pregnant woman, and just as she is destined to give birth in pain and blood so too man, to create, must suffer and sacrifice. The creativity of woman as childbearer is emblematic in another sense as well, for it exemplifies the mundane circumstance in which the sublime fact is often located and from which it emerges. Babel, as noted in "Crossing the Zbruch," is one of those artists for whom the epiphany plays a major role both spiritually and technically. That the heroic can be found within a sordid setting and that a potentially godlike creativity can reside even in destruction almost become for Babel articles of religious hope, and it is this hope that constitutes the major part of that awe with which Babel's attitude toward his Cossack warriors is imbued. These primitive men, who may be

9 There is a possibly religious image of the Revolution in "Gedali." The old Jewish shopkeeper, affirming his desire to embrace the Revolution, complains to Ljutov that it conceals itself from him and sends out in front nothing but shooting. The image is reminiscent of the Lord's words to Moses (Exodus 33:22): "And I will take away mine hand, and thou shalt see my back parts: but my face shall not be seen."

the creators of a new era, have something of that terror-inspiring quality shared by demons and gods, and if Babel flees the demands of an institutional faith he nevertheless continues to evince a need for gods—but for living gods who will minister to his nostalgia for pure and vital beginnings.

Babel thus views his Cossack comrades as primitive in a positive as well as a negative sense. He sees their brutality as a concomitant of their potential for creativity. Despite the historic conquest of Western civilization by Christianity, the Cossacks, as Babel perceives them, retain at least some of the elements of pre-Christian pagan belief, notably a closeness to nature and an almost animistic view of the universe.[10] This accords well with Babel's own attempt to seek meaning in experience, to seek God, as it were, not in the abstractions of philosophers or in textual religions, but in life. He can even, as we have seen, share in the mocking contempt which the Cossacks express for people like himself, for writers and intellectuals, for those baleful, bookish "guys in specs."

Babel's critique of the self-absorbed intellectual and his artistic "deification" of more primitive men have a precedent in the conception of "God-building" *(bogostroitel'stvo)* proposed by Maxim Gorky. He too had sought an alternative to the Dostoevskian doctrine of religious resignation and attempted to find it in a kind of mystical humanism in which man and his works would assume the place of the traditional deity. Seeking to preserve the ethical and cultural values he saw endangered by Revolutionary extremism, Gorky had tried to graft on to the Revolution, already replete with messianic fervor, a renewed, albeit human, godhead. Even before the Soviet seizure of power this attempt at a synthesis of Marxism and Christianity had provoked a sharply hostile reaction from Lenin, at whose insistence Gorky eventually abandoned the project. Such thinking, however, because it provided grounds for a spiritual affirmation of the politi-

---

[10] Note the special relationship between Afonka Bida and his horse, or the simple reverence with which he tells his legend of the bees in "The Road to Brody."

cal and social cataclysm, continued to appeal to Russian intellectuals well into the first post-Revolutionary decade, and there
are clear echoes of it in Babel's *Red Cavalry*.[11]

We have already observed that Babel's work suggests another,
more iconoclastic, inspiration, that his celebration of warlike
Cossack manhood recalls Nietzsche's morally ambiguous glorifi-
cation of the *Übermensch*.[12] Preeminently a man of the troubled
twenties, Babel was compelled to consider a challenge to traditional moral categories far more extreme than Gorky's. Confronted in his youth with the actual horror of revolutionary reality, Babel found the kind of mystical humanism espoused by
Gorky an insufficient response, and he turned, however tentatively, toward the radical individualism and stark aestheticism
advanced by Nietzsche. Throughout *Red Cavalry*, Babel is torn
by conflicting impulses, by the necessity to choose between spiri-
tualizing the Revolution or apprehending an otherwise unbearable reality in aesthetic terms. Finally, Babel cannot abandon
either course and the tensions between them remain. Against the
anarchic Nietzschean flight "beyond good and evil" sounds the
ancient Hebraic call to the Law, and against the aesthetic preoc-
cupations of a Francophile artist who celebrates life's splendid

11 Gorky's dispute with Lenin on this question of "god-building" was to be
symptomatic of the dilemmas and contradictions residing in the spiritual heart
of the Revolution. In retrospect Gorky's capitulation seems an ominous portent
of the fate that awaited Revolutionary humanism in the years ahead. Gorky's
ideas and the conflict with Lenin are summarized by Dan Levin, in *Stormy Petrel:
The Life and Work of Maxim Gorky* (London, 1967), 143–63.

12 There is an intriguing passage in the Moscow diary of Ervin Sinkó (*Roman
eines Romans*, 336) that touches upon the question of Babel's attitude toward
Nietzsche. In a 1936 meeting between Gorky and André Malraux, for which Babel
served as interpreter, the German philosopher became the object of a heated exchange. They were discussing the problem of the individual under socialism, and
Gorky, in the name of socialist humanism, expressed vehement opposition to
Nietzsche's thought. Malraux argued that Nietzsche's was a powerful voice in
the struggle for man's spiritual emancipation, and Babel, in his capacity as interpreter, had to exert a good deal of tact in order to avert a break between the
two men. In his later account of the meeting Babel, says Sinkó, identified fully
with Gorky's position, but Sinkó is persuaded that Babel's respect for the Russian
made him less than candid. Whatever Babel's views were at the time of this
meeting—and it is true that by 1936 they had changed considerably—his writing
of the twenties is something else again.

chaos sounds the added moral imperative of a Russian literary tradition deeply hostile to the tenets of art for art's sake.[13]

For all his cover of aesthetic detachment Babel never succeeds in stifling his awareness of actual experience. He could never fully assent to Nietzsche's "You say it is the good cause that hallows any war? I say unto you: it is the good war that hallows any cause."[14] Neither, of course, could he agree with the anti-Socialist animus of Nietzsche's thought. The appeal of Marxism and the final justification of the war being fought in its name are, in Babel's view, necessarily linked to the promise they hold for the future. In his art, since Babel is neither crude propagandist nor falsifying apologist, this connection is made only implicitly; but a hope in the future is as vibrant beneath his book's laconic surface as in the more explicit diary that he kept during the months of campaigning.

This justification of a harsh present in the name of a happier future raises questions of belief that are once again akin to the religious. The Marxist vision of a finally just and felicitous human order is in fact, as has been observed, not unlike the Hebraic-Christian promise of paradise.[15] Furthermore, both philosophies accept the notion of an irreversible flow of history, yet both posit a mystical ending to its progression and in so

[13] It is no surprise that the French should have been the first to respond to Nietzsche's profound aestheticism. It may be that Babel absorbed his own "Nietzscheanism" partly through French intermediaries, his love of that country and its culture allowing perhaps for an easier adoption than would a directly German source. Nietzsche himself preferred French over German culture, sharing with Babel even a particular fondness for Maupassant. The eventual appropriation of Nietzsche by the Nazis, as well as the ominous political developments in Russia, may, by the mid-thirties, have produced changes in Babel which contributed both to his increasingly negative assessment of his earlier work and to his private artistic crisis.

[14] Walter Kaufmann, ed. and trans., *The Portable Nietzsche* (New York, 1954), 159.

[15] "The Rabbi's Son" demonstrates, despite the antithetical worlds implied by the catalogue of the dying man's effects, that rival versions of a similar vision are at stake. Ilya Bratslavsky has deserted his faith but continues to wear on his brow a likeness to Spinoza—and to carry in his pocket the portrait of Maimonides. Perhaps the two great Jewish philosophers, both supreme rationalists, are not after all so unlike the Russian Marxist whose image takes pride of place along with theirs.

doing provide men with a sense of relief from the nightmare of a relentless history in whose wake all is at last consumed. But for contemporary, nonreligious man such an eschatological conception of time seems ever less efficacious in mitigating the terrors of history, and alternative theories of time, older than the linear historical conception, have in the modern period attracted a considerable revival of interest.[16] The cyclical theory of time, in contrast to historistic views, postulates a cosmic time of everlasting repetitions, allowing for the conception of both an eternal present and a re-creatable past, and thus escapes history by denying it altogether. Such a conception of time lay at the base of ancient religious views of the world and, experienced in this way, allowed primitive, religious man "periodically to experience the cosmos as it was *in principio*—that is, at the mythical moment of Creation."[17] Whether by ritual reenactment of the past or through interpretation of concrete, historical personages and events in terms of mythical categories, the pressures of the actual present were given a metaphysical meaning.

Such a cyclical theory of time, offering release from the pressure of intolerable contemporary conditions, has exerted a powerful attraction upon many modern artists. Once again, it is Nietzsche, with his theory of the eternal recurrence, who has done most to revive the concept and to lend it particular relevance to the twentieth century. For the artist it has the special attraction of appealing strongly to the poetic need for pattern and rhythm; and for an artist such as Babel it answers both the nostalgia for a purer, "precivilized" age and, because it is eternal as well as present, allows a faithful and truthful concern for the given moment.

Attempting to fix and preserve the moment against history, to allow it its particular truth, and yet simultaneously aware of and even desiring the increasingly rapid and powerful pressures

16 For this discussion of time and history I am much indebted to two stimulating books by Mircea Eliade: *Cosmos and History* (New York, 1959) and *The Sacred and The Profane* (New York, 1961).
17 Eliade, *The Sacred and The Profane*, 65.

toward change, Babel found a cyclical view of time especially adaptable to the needs of his art and used it in a manner reminiscent of its original religious functions. Cyclical theories of time need not be religious in application, but it is significant that they may be and that their origin is invested with religious purpose. If shorn of its mythoreligious qualities—and this is what Nietzsche sought with his "eternal recurrence"—a cyclical theory no longer offers escape from an endless chain of meaningless suffering, and one is forced back to a linear, historical view which requires a religious belief in immortality and paradise if one is to avoid the specter of irredeemable injustice. The cyclical view in any case denies the possibility of a belief in historical progress, and Babel, who profoundly yearns for change, is once again caught in a series of paradoxes with no consistent solution available.

We have already noted, in "Berestechko," for example, how Babel achieves a special intensity through his use of historical analogies; indeed, in his diary entry for 7 August, quoted earlier, he even remarks that events are forever repeating themselves. Repeatedly he draws parallels between the present and the past: a religious dispute that is to figure in a projected story brings forth a comparison with the eighteenth century;[18] another planned story ("Demidovka"), dealing with the effects of the war on a small Jewish town, elicits the remark that "all is the same as it was at the destruction of the Temple at Jerusalem."[19] So strong is Babel's tendency to view events through the prism of historical parallels that he even cautions himself against it, remarking in one of his plans for "Brody" that the story must be done "without comparisons or historical parallels—just a story."[20] But for Babel the appeal to historical analogies remains irresistible, and the tales of *Red Cavalry*, for all their immediacy, are resonant with echoes of the past. War is perhaps the most terrible of those recurring phenomena with which the pages of history

---

[18] From Babel's plans and drafts as printed in *Literaturnoe nasledstvo*, LXXIV, 493.
[19] *Ibid.*, 499.  [20] *Ibid.*, 492.

abound, and in seeking a meaning for the destruction and suffering that it brings Babel turns to the past, partly to deny, as it were, history itself.

The most useful commentaries on Babel's art have tended to concentrate on his forceful imagery and on the specifics of his unusual and highly effective style. But such analyses have been only partially successful, either limiting themselves to a mere catalogue of devices or succumbing in despair before the proliferating ironies, ambiguities, and contrasts of his style. The brilliance of Babel's style dazzles indeed, but it also blinds the reader to other dimensions of his work, to levels which, operating below the surface sparkle of the tales, help to unify and define them within a larger context. Much has been made of Babel's use of metaphor, of his saying two things or linking two worlds in a single terse phrase. The symbolic level of his work extends this double voice, or dual vision, to the framework of an entire story, and in so doing it adds a degree of objectivity to the subjective tone of the narrative frame.

The Odessa cycle, as we saw earlier, was probably composed in the two or three years prior to Babel's major work on *Red Cavalry*, and would seem to represent his experiment with a new method. The earliest Odessa piece ("The King," 1921), though it does have a symbolic subtext, is written in a more jocular vein than the other tales and compositionally stands somewhat apart from them. Although it does possess a biblical or religious strain, the essential motivation is almost exclusively one of mockery; furthermore, it seems to have only a Hebraic base. By 1923–24, however, when the later Odessa tales and the first *Red Cavalry* stories began to appear, a growing complication in the symbolic subtexts is noticeable. Christian and Hebrew themes begin to intertwine, echoes of both the Old and the New Testaments begin to be heard, and the stories seem less mocking in intent. "How It Was Done in Odessa" is a key transitional story. Still predominantly Old Testament and Hebraic in its allusions, it nevertheless strikes a new note both in the introduction of the lyrical "I," who prefigures the *Red Cavalry* narrator, and in its more extensively developed network of symbolical parallels. Arye-Leib is a loquacious Aaron set beside a lisping Moses, and Tartakovsky and Benja may be seen, respectively, as Pharaoh and Yahweh. In "Ljubka the Cossack" (1924) a specifically Christian motif is introduced through the use of a Madonna-and-child image (one which even includes, in Mr. Trottyburn and his sailor companions, the three attendant Magi).[21]

*Red Cavalry* and later stories add an overt political dimension that is only implied in *The Odessa Tales,* but once again religious figures play a major role. It would not be wise to suggest that *Red Cavalry* is a sustained allegory, but, as with *The Odessa Tales,* the cavalry cycle has a network of allusions and parallels which constantly asks for symbolic readings.[22] Part of the problem in discussing Babel's symbolism is due to the peculiar genre he employs—neither novel nor fully independent short stories. Taken individually the stories do not seem able to bear the weight of their symbolic undertones, and only as a whole, in a larger philosophic context, does the symbolic level gain the density necessary for its support. The connected cycle of stories is thus uniquely appropriate to the essentially dual focus of Babel's vision: it gives that immediate short view—confused, inchoate, in flux—which is true to experience, and it simultaneously provides a more coherent, longer perspective. One is tempted to see an analogy with film techniques, where the rush of rapid sequences and minutely detailed close-ups can alternate with sweeping panoramas; or with the epic tradition in general, where specific, physical, often violent reality is set against the rhythms of nature and the eternal, recurrent tides of time.

Babel's attitude toward history, as it permeates the structure of *Red Cavalry,* is one of the ways his work acquires a symbolic import and through which his dual vision is achieved. By sug-

21 In a later addition to the Odessa group ("Froim Grach," ca. 1933), Christian symbolism still has a part to play: the passing of the bandit chieftain is linked, through its setting, to the crucifixion of Christ.
22 In the light of Babel's immersion in Hebrew tradition and his addiction to biblical allusion, the example of parable is suggestive, pointing as it does to the kind of moral questions with which Babel is ultimately concerned.

gesting a pattern of analogies and recurrences and by interweaving his own life, time, and place with other historical moments, Babel seeks both to dedicate his art to actual experience and to gain access to an antihistorical perception of reality. His stories almost always contain a level of personal experience, a happening or event in which he himself is either a participant or to which he is a witness. This finite, single, specific event is usually expanded to embrace the experience of a larger community (e.g., the Jews, Russia, or even the world in the first critical stages of the Revolution), and this second level is anchored in a mythic or symbolic substructure, sometimes with elements of travesty, but seldom with real parody.[23] As a part of this process in his work events and personages are interpreted in terms of symbolic analogies. Babel identifies his characters with other figures—real and fictional, historical and mythical, literary and religious. He will often mix several of these mythosymbolic features into a single ambiguous, but highly expressive, composite figure.[24]

The symbolic referents are often of a religious type and, interestingly enough, they frequently involve an interweaving of images derived from Judaism, Christianity, and communism. In "The Rabbi," for example, some of the Jews are described as resembling "fishermen and apostles"; the rabbi has "monkish fingers" and his son "the wan face of a nun"; in "Evening" the Communist propagandists of the army newspaper are introduced as "three bachelor hearts with the passions of Ryazan Jesuses"; and in "Sashka the Christ" an extensive array of details, going well beyond the casual and ironic use of the nickname, links the tale's hero with the figure of Jesus. A more detailed examination of "Sashka the Christ" will illustrate how Babel extends a symbolic motif throughout the structure of an extremely short story.

Called the Christ because of his mildness, Sashka is the step-

23 A major motif running through the work is the desire to extend the witness element into a personal participation at all levels—hence the constant emergence of his narrator's private moral dilemmas.
24 The method used by Babel is strikingly similar to that antihistorical, cyclical view of history that Eliade describes as typical of earlier religious man.

son of a village carpenter (his true father remains unidentified), and he himself becomes the communal shepherd in a Cossack settlement. Having always wished to become a shepherd ("all of the Saints used to be," he pleads), Sashka finally succeeds at about the age of fourteen in persuading his stepfather to let him go. But this occurs only after both of them have contracted a venereal disease from a wandering beggarwoman. By threatening to report the facts to his mother Sashka secures the right to leave from his stepfather, Tarakanych. Many more of the story's details contribute to the symbolic parallels. Tarakanych, for example, jokingly refers to his wife as "Your Highness" (vaše vysokoblagorodie), and Sashka, more seriously, makes a point of his mother's purity as against his own and his stepfather's taintedness:

> ... but did you see the body mother has. Her feet are clean, and her breast is clean. Don't wrong her, Tarakanych. We're tainted (98). [The Russian word for "clean" is also used in the sense of "pure."]

The effect of these passages suggests the Marian tradition, and the familial identification is further confirmed by Sashka's night-time vision, during which he sees in a dreamlike tableau the horse collars beneath his mother's rude bed, the star that appears in the window of their hut, and himself lying in a cradle suspended from the sky. The star, the cradle, and the cross are dominant images in the story's framework, and when Sashka leaves on the morning following his vision it is to become the village herdsman, in which capacity he will minister comfort to the peasants and gain for himself renown for his simplicity, his love, and his illness.

Even Sashka's betrayal of his mother links him with Christ, recalling as it does Jesus' refusal to recognize his own mother (Matthew 12:47–48) and his admonition that those who would follow him must forsake their families (Matthew 19:29).[25] Sashka's venereal disease, with its implication of insanity, suggests

25 I am indebted to Mr. Donald Fiene of Indiana University, a fellow Babel student, for drawing my attention to the biblical references given here.

the tradition of the holy fool and functions in part somewhat like the epilepsy of Dostoevsky's fools in Christ. At the same time, however, the particular nature of the disease lends a certain ambiguity to the image. Babel frequently juxtaposes religious and sexual themes, and in so doing seems to insist on a specific involvement of the Christian deities in sexual adventure—an immersion in the reality of flesh—to cleanse them, as it were, of the abstraction of spirit. The tradition of asceticism is central to almost all conceptions of the religious experience, and Babel views it, especially in its Christian version, with a kind of horrified fascination. Christ is the human incarnation of God; he is made to suffer the sins and agonies of man; and yet he is singularly free of that one experience which is the most human of all. Christian symbolism, as Nietzsche so forcefully insisted, is tightly fenced in by a peculiarly sexless atmosphere; not only is the Christ himself exempted from fleshly involvement, but he is born of a virgin mother, who is herself accorded an especial purity by the doctrine of her own Immaculate Conception. Toward these strange and protective purities Babel's attitude is frequently one of mockery: there are his leering Madonnas; Christ's wounds, in a line from "The Church at Novograd," ooze seed to captivate virgins; and the Jesus of Pan Apolek's apocryphal tale (in "Pan Apolek") lies with the maid Deborah and fathers her child.[26]

Despite his distaste for much in Christian ideology and for the church as an institution, Babel's attitude toward Christianity is not exclusively one of mockery.[27] Like many members of the

[26] Another believer in the life of the body, D. H. Lawrence, tells in a similar tale—"The Man Who Died"—of how Jesus becomes the lover of a priestess of Isis, to whom he gives a child, and of how he then learns to live in acceptance of the phenomenal world. Apolek's Jesus, in contrast, retires in sadness after his experience of the flesh to join John in the desert east of Judea. Babel's ironic use of Christian motifs does not, it might be added, come to an end with *Red Cavalry*; they are to be found as well in the plays *Sunset* and *Maria*. In two other stories of the *Red Cavalry* period ("The Tale of a Woman" and "The Sin of Jesus") there are still further variations, rather crudely done, on the theme of Christian celibacy.

[27] As noted earlier, the narrator Ljutov is also sometimes ironically identified

Russian intelligentsia in the Revolutionary era, he gives evidence of an almost obsessive interest in the figure of the Christ or Messiah. With Alexander Blok, who also confessed his dislike of the meek and pitying effeminate Christ and who yet placed his image at the climax of his poem "The Twelve," Babel finds the great religious champion of the oppressed an irresistible symbol and returns to his figure again and again in *Red Cavalry* and elsewhere. In addition to its use in "Sashka the Christ" and some of the Ljutov stories, Christ imagery appears as well in "The Letter," "Squadron Commander Trunov," "Pan Apolek," and in other stories. Often, as with "Sashka the Christ," the religious symbolism is essentially sympathetic.

Sometimes Babel will show a religious image travestied and defiled, but the image itself remains a powerful symbol. In "Salt," for example, a woman gains entry to a crowded transport train when the Cossacks take pity on her for the newborn infant she carries in her arms. When it is finally discovered that she has deceived them and that the swaddling clothes contain not a child but a bag of salt, the soldier who had first admitted her pushes her from the train and in a fit of rage kills her with a shot from his rifle. In the woman we find still another of Babel's many Madonna figures, but a false one. Yet the role of motherhood itself, which elsewhere in Babel is given special status through the use of just such Madonna-related imagery, remains a sacred function.

The separate stories, fragmentary and episodic though they appear to be, hover constantly around the same image patterns. No single large, heroic figure dominates the fictional landscape; now one, now another of the characters performs a part in the symbolic ritual. Often it is in their interrelatedness that they gain the fullness necessary to their symbolic import. Khlebnikov and Savitsky, for example, who figure prominently in "The Story of a Horse" and its sequel, depend upon each other for their symbolic function, and they depend in turn upon Sashka,

with a suffering, Christlike figure, and in such instances the mockery, as is often the case with Babel, is mostly self-directed.

Pan Apolek, and others. Babel's major symbolic referents are actually few in number, but their specific habitations keep changing and many characters partake of the same symbolic role. The proliferation of Christ figures may thus be seen, at least in part, as an examination of the Revolution's messianic principle, and an attempt to penetrate beyond irony and perversity to what is truly significant.

By representing incongruous characters as figures of religious import, Babel is attempting both to humanize the conception of divinity and at the same time to associate the hopes of the Revolution with religious promises.[28] The mild Sashka, throwing in his lot with the Reds and enlisting in the Cossack cavalry to become a minister to the militant, remains a gentle man, and in so doing he relates the Marxist vision of justice to that of Christ. In a similar way old Gedali's longing for the International of good people relates it to the Hebrew vision of the Promised Land. If the Revolution cannot do without killing, Babel is alert to the historical parallels with the bloody battles of the Old Testament and with the Christian holy wars, but he insists on retaining as well the messianic dream, a belief that the repetitious suffering is an apocalyptic prelude to still another recurrence, to a kind of secular second coming.

One of the most remarkable stories in *Red Cavalry*—and one of the most perplexing—is "Pan Apolek." Richly allusive and suggestive, it asks, more than any of the other tales, for an allegorical reading. The Pan Apolek of the title, one of those wandering beggars who speaks of God, is an itinerant painter whose genial mockery of the institutional church captures the narrator's fancy:

> Apolek worked zealously, and at the end of a month the new church was filled with the bleating of flocks, the hazy gold of sunsets, and the straw-colored udders of cows. Buffaloes with threadbare hides plodded beneath the yoke, dogs with pink noses ran before the flock, and plump babes swung in cradles suspended

---

[28] One recalls Arye-Leib's description of Benja Krik as a man who would grasp the rings of heaven and earth and draw the two together.

from the upright trunks of palm trees. The brown rags of Franciscan monks surrounded a cradle. The crowd of Wise Men was gashed
with bald heads, with wrinkles blood-red like wounds. Among this
crowd glimmered the foxily smiling, little old face of Leo XIII;
and the Novograd priest himself, fingering in one hand a Chinese-
carved rosary, was blessing with his other hand the newborn Jesus
(58–59).

The flocks, cows, and the threadbare buffaloes who plod beneath the yoke are Apolek's rueful comment on the communal
herd laboring under the weight of the cross, while the pink-nosed
dogs who run before them are a mocking apotheosis of the
Church's princes, its popes and bishops. In the Franciscan monks
(as with John the Baptist in another of his paintings) the artist
gives form to the Church's ascetic renunciation of the phenomenal world, and the inclusion in the crowd of wise men of a foxy
Leo XIII, the reforming pope who in the late nineteenth century sought to stem the growing tide of secularization with a
series of liberal social and political policies, suggests that Apolek
has little faith in the Church's intention really to change.

In his paintings for the Novograd priest, Apolek draws inspiration for his religious figures from living people. Although the
Church benignly accepts the inclusion of Pope Leo in a crowd
of worshipers or the Novograd priest himself as one of the Magi
or his assistant Pan Romuald as the decapitated head of John
the Baptist, it anathematizes the idiosyncratic painter when he
also depicts the town prostitute, a Jewish girl named Elka, as
Mary Magdalene and the lame convert Yanek as St. Paul. Apolek
refuses to remove his frescoes, however, and for three decades
carries on a running battle with the Church, peopling the huts
of the town with icons in which the village peasants, for a modest
fee, see themselves enshrined as Josephs and Marys or their enemies depicted as Judas Iscariots. The struggle against the priest
(the multitude not unexpectedly sides with Apolek) is finally
brought to an end when the "Cossack flood drives the old monk
from his aromatic nest of stone," whereupon Apolek trium-
phantly takes up his abode in the priest's home.

In the dispute between Apolek and the priest there is clearly a seriocomic allusion to the famous conflict between Michelangelo and Pope Julius II. Confined to his wooden scaffolding beneath the dome of the Novograd church, Apolek, like Michelangelo in the Sistine Chapel, pursues his own vision of the holy. The priest, pleased at first to see himself immortalized in one of the frescoes, sends a goblet of cognac to the painter at work beneath the dome; but in the end his personal vanity and his pompous sense of respectability cannot abide the artist's humanizing spirit, and he dismisses Apolek from his commission. The painter whom the priest appoints in Apolek's stead—like Michelangelo's great contemporary, Raphael—cannot repress his admiration for his rival's achievement, and he allows the paintings of Elka and Yanek to stand.

The story clearly advances the same humanizing doctrine that appears in some of Babel's other tales. As with "Sashka the Christ," or earlier in *The Odessa Tales*, the human and the divine are brought into close proximity so that each, however bizarrely, might enrich the other. In Apolek's art the humblest of sinners is enveloped in holy robes, and through the painter's sly mockery of religious hypocrisy the divine is reimbued with human features. It is certainly not difficult to see here something of Gorky's humanistic "god-building," but the story is more wildly textured than has thus far been suggested, and Apolek himself is a more complicated figure than at first appears. He captivates the imagination of the narrator not only with the negative critique of his anticlericalism, but with a rival "gospel" that has long lain "hidden from the world."

The painter is accompanied in his wanderings by old Gottfried, a blind, silent accordion player, and not only his companion's name but several other allusions suggest Germany as their place of origin: the two friends, for instance, wear hobnailed German boots; Apolek has a diploma from a Munich academy; on the blind man's bald head flutters a feathered Tyrolean hat; and when the companions carouse in a Jewish alehouse they give thundering voice to "the songs of Heidelberg." Behind this strange duo is a playful adumbration of a Nietzschean paganism; in the complementary but bipolar union that Apolek and Gottfried represent, Babel has given an extended expression of Nietzsche's Apollo-Dionysus synthesis which he uses as a mocking contrast to the Christian deity.[29]

Apolek, whose very name suggests Apollo, is an itinerant painter, a master of light and color. Wandering the globe or traversing the dome of the Novograd church in his wooden seat, with an "endless" canary-colored scarf about his neck, he is like a dazzling human incarnation of the solar deity. At the same time Gottfried, the blind musician and "eternal friend" whom Apolek leads with his left hand and whose accordion expands and contracts like the moon in its phases, is clearly identified as a representative of the lesser, lunar deity.[30] Vision and blindness, day and night, painting and music, sun and moon—all of these, as well as the several references to wine in association with Apolek, suggest aspects of the two Greek deities, and when the friends sing their German songs in the Jewish pothouse, one hears a further suggestion of that conflict between Hebraic and Hellenic cultures which Nietzsche had described.[31]

When they first arrived in the town, some thirty years earlier, the two friends had made their way to the Jewish tavern, where Apolek, undressing from head to foot, had poured water over

[29] Nietzsche, incidentally, considered his family to be of Polish origin, a fact in which he took some pride. A "Nietzschean" tale with a Pan artist as its hero may thus possess a curious fitness.

[30] The phases of the moon have traditionally been associated with both the form of musical instruments and the shape of the Hebrew letters—a linking of music and literature that further corroborates Nietzsche's thesis on "the birth of tragedy out of the spirit of Music."

[31] Although one may force some of these parallelisms into too rigid a mold, it is nonetheless tempting to see still another Dionysus-Apollo contrast in the Michelangelo-Raphael theme: the former's turbulent passion and the latter's serenely placid harmonies illustrate the Nietzschean dichotomy in a singularly appropriate way. Furthermore, Apolek's stories—"about the romantic age of the Polish nobility, about the fierceness of female fanaticism, about the painter Luca della Robbia, and about the family of the Bethlehem carpenter"—supply still more antitheses. The wildly independent and brutal Polish nobles might easily bring to mind the petty kings of Homer's Greece, and the fanatical women might suggest those devotees of Dionysus, the Bacchantes. Oscillating wildly to the opposite extreme, Apolek's other subjects suggest serene and devout religiosity.

his "rosy, slight, and puny body." Now this parody of a baptism is not exclusively Christian in its implications, for Dionysus too was the "twice born," "water-given" god. Although Dionysus, like Jesus, is a god of the simple people and a symbol of resurrection, he has none of the ascetic features common to the post-Hellenic religions. He is a fertility god who symbolizes rebirth through the processes of nature, through the rhythmic return of the seasons and the cycles of vegetation. Apolek, when he pays for his dinner at the inn with a pencil portrait of the innkeeper's wife, promises to return to redo his work in color and to add, like fruit to the tree, pearls to the lady's hair and an emerald necklace on her breast. The innkeeper, upset at losing his money, chases after his guests with a stick. But then, his mind troubled by the recollection of Apolek's "rosy body streaming with water, the sunshine in his little yard, and the low hum of the accordion," he drops his stick and, as if sensing the visitation of a god, returns to his home. Apolek and Gottfried, like the sun and moon, continue their eternal wandering and like Apollo-Dionysus, they become a symbol of the pagan eternal return which defies both history and the Hebraic-Christian end of the world.

For all the story's aura of Nietzschean paganism, in the end Babel has to view his artist, the "bearer of a new gospel," with ironic detachment. Usurping at last the priest's place in the house of Pani Eliza (the Mary of his paintings), Apolek comes perilously close to being himself an image of Christ. No longer a wanderer, he now spends his time in the housekeeper's kitchen and of an evening regales the narrator with his stories, including the tale of Jesus' marriage to Deborah. Ljutov remains enchanted with Apolek's blasphemies and awaits his initiation into the mystery of Jesus' marriage with an air of solemn, almost ritualistic anticipation:

> My interest whetted by the opening of Apolek's story, I stride up and down the kitchen awaiting the appointed hour. Beyond the window, night stands like a black column; beyond the window, the live dark garden has grown still. Beneath the moon the road to the church flows in a milky, luminous stream. A shadowy radi-

ance lies on the earth, and hanging from the bushes are necklaces
of gleaming fruit (62).

Ljutov's tone and imagery continue to suggest a pagan religious
cosmography. The black column of the night recalls the pillar
of the world, the *axis mundi* which connects and supports the
cosmic regions of heaven, earth, and the underworld; the milky,
moonlit road to the church resembles the Milky Way, the path
of ascension to the heavenly moon. The moon itself, in pagan
theology, is regarded as the receptacle for the dead, as both casket
and regenerating matrix for the spirits that traverse the circle
of heaven and earth, of death and life. The necklaces of gleaming fruit recall the promise of fecundity which Apolek-Dionysus
gave the innkeeper's wife when he proposed pearls for her hair
and a necklace for her breast.

But as Ljutov waits for Apolek in Pani Eliza's kitchen the
scent of Christian lilies, "pure" but "poisonous," overpowers the
resinous pagan aroma of fir logs. Purity triumphs in Apolek's
tales as well, for after lying with Deborah from a sense of pity,
Jesus, "the bee of sorrow" having stung his heart, departs to
join John in the wilderness.[32] The child born of his union with
Deborah is hidden away by the priests, for the Church has no
need of renewing its myths. Having adopted Jesus as the eternal
Son of God, the Church must deny his fatherhood, for this
would imply an unacceptable recurrence, a chain of replacements
and transferences. What the Church seeks, Apolek's tale implies,
is to establish its myth in perpetuity; through renunciation of
the flesh it hopes to fix it forever as an eschatological denial of
time. Thus in the Christian era the worship of the ascetic Jesus

32 The reader will recall that Babel had once before used the name Deborah
(which in Hebrew means "bee") to refer to a vigorous female who is paired with
a timid male ("The King"). The bee, furthermore, was one of the forms in which
Aphrodite, the death-in-life goddess, was worshiped. Like the queen bee, Aphrodite
was said to have destroyed the sacred king who mated with her by tearing out
his genitals. She also mated with the god Dionysus and gave birth to his son
Priapus, whose symbol was the phallus. The asceticism of Christianity is linked
to the motif of the bee in still another *Red Cavalry* story. In "The Road to
Brody," Afonka Bida tells Ljutov that according to a legend of the Cossack
womenfolk, the bee refused to sting Christ upon his cross.

has supplanted that of Dionysus, and Babel, clearly preferring the latter as a symbol of life and resurrection, regards the change as an impoverishment. Still, in Apolek's apocryphal tale, he suggests that they both have a common origin, and he does bring the image of Christ closer to that of the pagan god. In taking pity upon the forsaken Deborah and becoming her lover, Jesus resembles the Dionysus who similarly consoled Ariadne after Theseus had abandoned her. In Jesus' siring of a son (even if the priests do spirit him away) there is the promise of a natural alternative to the Christian concept of immortality—the regenerative powers of nature.

Babel, however, remains in doubt as to whether Apolek's challenge can be taken seriously. "Fate *nearly*," his narrator tells us, "made the humble vagabond Apolek the founder of a new heresy," and "he then *would have been*," he adds, "the most devious and the wittiest combatant of all those with whom the Roman Church in her evasive and seditious history has had to deal." (Italics added.) But Apolek is a vagabond no more; complacently ensconced in the absent priest's house, he seems a tamed, enfeebled rebel. The painter, we have been told, along with his brushes and paints carries a pair of white mice. Reminding us that the divine Apollo was Smintheus the Mouse God, they also foretell that the Church—in the person of its beadle Pan Robacki, who can yawn like a cat as he threatens Apolek—will have little difficulty in swallowing him up.[33]

What Apolek has proposed as a replacement for religious belief is a doctrine of nature, but as an artist he also proposes as a means of apprehending this doctrine, a gospel of art. And this is his limitation. Despite the appeal that the aesthetic makes to his modern sensibility, Babel, with his unquenchable hope for pro-

[33] Another of Babel's manifold ironies, this one self-directed: toward the story's close, the author has Apolek offer to paint the narrator as St. Francis of Assisi, with a bird on his sleeve. The saint with the failing eyes, who exhibited the stigmata of Christ and who loved with a surpassing tenderness all living things—especially birds, which he sought to protect against wanton killing—is a most engaging image for the creator of "My First Goose" and of "The Story of My Dovecote" to bestow upon his surrogate.

gress, finds in the end that aestheticism alone does not suffice. Neither Apolek, nor Luca della Robbia, nor even Michelangelo, can completely contain the "tempests of imagination" within his "age-old body." As the story draws to its close, Babel's narrator is once more cast adrift from all vows. Abandoning the crafty painter, the beadle Pan Robacki, and all the others, he leaves to spend the night with his "plundered Jews," accompanied on his way by a now "vagrant and homeless" moon, warming up in his heart as always "impracticable dreams and discordant songs."

The lyrical note with which this story ends reminds us once again of the central role played by the narrator's consciousness in developing the book's tensions. In stories such as "Pan Apolek" the actual war and the Cossacks fighting it recede, and the narrator's mind becomes the major battlefield, his thoughts and reveries the main combatants. But Babel also criticizes his narrator. Throughout *Red Cavalry* he struggles against allowing the lyrical impulse complete sway, and to interpret Ljutov as the single hero (or antihero) of the work would greatly diminish that suprapersonal, epic quality that Babel is obviously at pains to create. Ljutov is after all only one of many figures caught up in the chaos of events, in the whirlwind of the cavalry's devastating advance and retreat. In several of the stories he appears only fleetingly or not at all, and in these the Cossacks themselves return to the fore. These are the author's hard-won visions of another reality, his witnessings of that world outside of himself which, in spite of his private reactions to either its horror or grandeur, simply exists.

In a distinct group of stories, perhaps the most popular among orthodox Soviet critics, the Cossack soldiers themselves step forward as narrators. Frequently the frame that Babel employs for these Cossack *skaz* stories is epistolary. His soldiers become letter writers, and through their manner of expression, as well as through what they say, both their personalities and their wartime circumstances are revealed. Even in writing the Cossacks retain an oral style, but the forms of peasant speech, the colloquial distortions of syntax and morphology, become mixed in their letters with "literary" affectations, with the borrowed phrases of newspaper clichés or with the ill-digested rhetoric of Revolutionary sloganeering.

In one of the best *skaz* stories, "Salt," the Cossack Balmashev sends a letter to the editor of a party newspaper in which he justifies his killing of a peasant woman. Deceived into thinking her bag of salt was an infant child, he had allowed her to board an overcrowded troop train and through the night had protected her from the threat of rape. Undeceived by morning, he had rectified his mistake with a shot from his rifle. The self-righteous phrasemongering of Balmashev's letter produces an impression of both comic and appalling irony. Yet the effect is not limited to this; beneath the murderer's crude, bombastic self-justification lies a genuine indignation at the costs inflicted by war, a deeply felt sympathy for the suffering and injustice that war, especially revolution, brings to soldier and civilian alike. Because the brutality of his crime emerges as the corollary of his earlier tenderness, Balmashev's awful fulmination contains a poetic power, and the sweeping crescendo of his absurd, ungrammatical rhetoric achieves a touch of genuine pathos:

> And seeing that scatheless woman going along like that and Russia around her like I don't know what, and the peasant fields without an ear of corn and the outraged girls and the comrades lots of which go to the front but few return, I had a mind to jump out of the truck and put an end to my life or else put an end to hers. But the Cossacks took pity on me and said:
> "Give it her with your rifle."
> So I took my faithful rifle off the wall and washed away that stain from the face of the workers' land and the republic (126).

In "The Letter," another of the epistolary *skaz* pieces, an almost mindlessly brutish peasant lad, Vasily Kurdyukov, dictates to Ljutov a letter home. Reporting to his mother on life at the front, the boy grotesquely mixes the serious and the comic, the relevant and the irrelevant. Bits of chitchat and gossipy news and an elaborate inquiry after the health of a favorite horse (which appears at first to be a person) give way belatedly to the calm recital of family horrors: Vasily's brother Fyodor has been murdered by their father, and he in turn has been killed by another of his sons, Simon. In the peasant youth's uncomprehending account the family tragedies attending the civil war find a vivid, if emotionless, expression.

Despite the brutish dullness of the entire Kurdyukov clan, their passion has the somberness of a Dostoevskian drama, of an eternal, even religious conflict between father and sons. Timothy Kurdyukov (the given name in Greek means "honoring God") was a policeman under the old regime and remained a fierce opponent of the Revolution to which his three sons had given their allegiance. Sacrificing his first-born Fyodor (in Greek, "the gift of God") upon the altar of his fanaticism, he threatens the destruction of all his offspring. The Revolutionary advance, however, forces him to flee. Disguised and in hiding, he is cornered at last when a friend of the family reveals his whereabouts to his son. Simon and his men, preferring, like the ancient Jews, tribal justice to the laws of the state, demand that the Party tribunal turn the old man over to them for execution. In this tale of family hatred and betrayal, only Simon, the Revolutionary scourge and parricide, shows a trace of feeling: at the last moment, he makes his younger brother Vasily leave the troop so that he will not see the slaying of their father. The theme of the brothers who band together to slay their father suggests the atmosphere of ancient myth, and such "Greek" themes are latent throughout *Red Cavalry*.[34]

Besides those stories framed as letters, others are cast in the form of an oral *skaz*. In "Konkin," for example, and in "Matthew Pavlichenko's Autobiography," the language is heavily salted with colloquial speech. In the latter the Cossack narrator

---

[34] It is significant that Babel chooses to depict the familial strife occasioned by the civil war not in the usual terms of fratricide, but through the motifs of filicide and parricide. In his later work Babel was to continue to exploit such "mythic" material, and in his play *Sunset* he was to return, though without the Revolutionary context, to the subject of family conflict and generational rivalry.

even speaks in the rhythms and images of the Russian *byliny* or folk epic:

> And what d'you think, you Stavropol boys, comrades, fellow-countrymen, my own dear brethren? The master kept me hanging on like that with my debts for five years. Five lost years I was like a lost soul, till at last the year Eighteen came along to visit me, lost soul that I was. It came along on lively stallions, on its Kabardin horses, bringing along a big train of wagons and all sorts of songs. Eh you, little year Eighteen, my sweetheart! Can it be that we shan't be walking out with you any more, my own little drop of blood, my year Eighteen? We've been free with your songs and drunk up your wine and made out your laws, and only your chroniclers are left. Eh, my sweetheart! (103).

Poetic devices such as inversion or the rhythmic use of refrain and repetition often appear in dialogue as well, and the normally rude speech of unlettered soldiers and peasants may give way, especially in moments of deep emotion, to a language that borders on verse. The effect of such poeticized speech, as of Ljutov's ornamental narration, is two-fold: it introduces into the rampant brutality a genuine note of gentleness, thereby helping to humanize the barbaric, and at the same time it ennobles and glorifies both the events and the men of war. The poetic style, whether in narrative or in dialogue, is thus a major part of that broad epic frame with which *Red Cavalry* is constructed. Our exploration of that frame would remain incomplete, however, without some further discussion of the book's thematic and structural characteristics.

We have noted how Babel frequently develops a powerfully symbolic subtext which gives to his stories a broader historical resonance and a deeper internal tension. Several of his characters are drawn with a Hebraic or Christian configuration, and this religious "mythicizing," though often tinged with mockery, helps to invest the Revolution with a kind of sacred meaning. Not all of Babel's heroes lend themselves to depiction in terms such as these, however, and many of the tales exhibit another dimension, a counterweight, as it were, to the religious aspect, in their use of a Homeric frame. In the stories with Cossack protagonists not only the imitation of an epic style, but the very dramas they relate, both of men and happenings, often become a symbolic reenactment of the Homeric poem. Interpreting contemporary events in terms of models from the past, Babel describes the Revolution as a "timeless" war, as a part of the unchanging fate of mankind, and its Cossack horsemen—their human traits enlarged to mythic proportions—become Homeric heroes.

Throughout *Red Cavalry* there are numerous instances in which Babel shows his Cossacks bathed in a lustrous light. Some have been indicated already: Savitsky, his giant body commanding the gaping admiration of mild, bespectacled Ljutov; Kolesnikov, who wears the martial glory won by his valor with careless arrogance; the former athlete Dyakov (in "The Remount Officer"), a dashing figure in silver-striped scarlet trousers, leaping from his fiery Arabian stallion and whirling his black opera cloak as he disappears from view. And there are countless others, from the dazzling commanders Voroshilov and Budyonny to the common soldier Levka who, "surrounding himself with night as with a nimbus," is almost godlike.

But there are larger epic parallels as well: tales of family strife ("The Letter"), of bloody retribution ("Matthew Pavlichenko's Autobiography" and "Prishchepa"), and of the slaughter of prisoners ("Squadron Commander Trunov" and "Konkin"). In "Konkin" the hero and his comrade, like Ulysses and Diomides in the *Iliad*, play a game of suspense with an enemy captive, and like them they kill him in the end. In "Squadron Commander Trunov" the slayer of prisoners himself seeks a violent death, perishing in unequal, heroic combat with a supernatural monster (an American warplane). Still another Homeric parallel occurs in "The Widow," where the sordid squabble over the belongings of a dying regimental commander recalls the rivalry for the armor of the slain Achilles.

Behind "The Story of a Horse" lies an extended Homeric parallel. The dispute between Savitsky and Khlebnikov over possession of a white stallion, one of the spoils of war, calls to

mind that fateful feud over a captured woman that made enemies of Agamemnon and Achilles. Khlebnikov is too proud to
accept a black mare as a substitute for his trophy and retires
bitterly from the Party and the war. The higher military authorities, like the Homeric gods, refuse to adjudicate the opponents' dispute, and misfortune falls upon both of them. After
leading an unsuccessful campaign Savitsky too is dismissed from
his command and withdraws into the splendid isolation of a dis-
graced warrior king. Surrounding himself with his private herd
of thoroughbred stallions and nursing his grievance in the love
of a Cossack woman whom he has taken from another man, he
resembles Achilles awaiting the call to return to battle and glory.
In a delayed sequel to the story the two men finally become reconciled, which is to imply perhaps that the gods will now smile upon
the Revolution's cause as they did upon that of the Greeks.[35]
Despite elements of travesty, which sometimes hide the epic
contours of the stories, Babel has a genuine commitment to the
heroic vision, and the mundane setting to which his Homeric
Cossacks are bound is only a partial, ironic concession to the antiheroic modern age.[36]

By interpreting the modern Russian experience in terms of
the heroic age of Greece, Babel succeeded in mitigating the
horror and brutality of Revolutionary events. By viewing contemporary reality from an epic perspective he helped also to
blunt that insistent moralism which was always a part of his own
lyric temperament. Babel was not blind to the harsh realities of

---

[35] The black and white horses which figure in the quarrel may also suggest
the horses of the Apocalypse. He who sits upon the white horse, says the Book
of Revelation, shall wear a crown and be a conquerer, while the rider of the
black horse holds in his hand a pair of balances, symbolizing right and justice.
Khlebnikov, the reasonable man who seeks a just and rational solution, "a regular
Karl Marx," as he is called, in time becomes reconciled to his loss (he leaves the
army to become chairman of a local Revolutionary Committee); while Savitsky,
no longer astride the white stallion, rides toward chaos and death, toward an
apocalypse which he himself can mock.

[36] Many of these Homeric parallels have been pointed out by Victor Terras in
"Line and Color: The Structure of I. Babel's Short Stories in *Red Cavalry,*" *Studies in Short Fiction,* III, No. 1 (Fall 1965), 141–56. He has also done much to
elucidate Babel's use of epic "travesty."

the war, but he chose to see them ennobled and invested with in-corruptible meaning, to see them distanced and secured from the vicissitudes of history. We know from his diary how difficult it was for Babel to accept what he encountered at the front, and it is all the more remarkable, in view of his personal revulsion at violence, that he should have been able to impart to his tales as much of an epic cast as he did. An examination of the writer's diary and other source material sheds a good deal of light on how *Red Cavalry* came into being.

The diaries show that many of Babel's characters and situa-tions were drawn from life. Budyonny and Voroshilov, who ap-pear in *Red Cavalry* under their own names, are the most ob-vious examples, but many of the thematically more important figures, as well as their stories, were also suggested by actual persons—Savitsky by Division Commander Timoshenko, for ex-ample, and Khlebnikov by a Commander Melnikov. Behind the good fortune in war of the young Kolesnikov lie the actual ad-ventures of a soldier by that name, while some of the details in Pavlichenko's autobiography come from the life of Commander Apanasenko as told in the propaganda paper for which Babel worked.[37] More interesting than such factual similarities, how-ever, are similarities in attitude. Often the very atmosphere as well as the events of a tale are present in the diary in embryonic form. One finds in a brief notation dated July 16, 1920, the kernel for the story "The Remount Officer," and in the entry of a few days before this description of its hero:

> Remount officer Dyakov—a bewitching picture, red riding breeches with silver stripes, a notched belt. Comes from Stavropol, is 45 years old, wears short gray mustaches, and has the figure of Apollo. Has a son and a nephew, swears like a madman.[38]

Prishchepa and Konkin are characterized in the diary with an equal precision and clarity, and they too closely resemble their

---

[37] In developing his fictional version of Apanasenko's life, however, Babel pointedly ignored the newspaper's simplistic account of the commander's awakened class consciousness.

[38] *Literaturnoe nasledstvo,* LXXIV, 474.

fictional counterparts. The former's contempt for a fellow soldier who "neither loves nor understands horses" and the latter's clownish manner of speaking in proverbs are noted briefly and preserved for future use. It was not easy, of course, for Babel to assimilate all of his observations into his art; the terrible suffering that he witnessed and the endless cruelty inflicted upon the inhabitants of captured towns are recorded in his diary with obvious anguish. On July 21 he writes: "What is our Cossack? Layers of trashiness, daring, professionalism, revolutionary spirit, bestial cruelty."[39] He is forever asking, in either hope or fear, what events mean, whether the motley crew of cruel, peasant warriors around him can actually be the bearers of a new and humane era. And then he notes that his Cossack friends are not only bestial, but that they possess "an awesome force," "an unutterable beauty," and are capable of "magnificent comradeship."[40] In despair one day, he will observe on the next that "the filth, apathy, and hopelessness of Russian life are unbearable" and that surely "the Revolution will do something" to end them (entry of July 28).[41] And so it goes, back and forth, disgust and despair alternating with admiration and hope.

At the time of the actual campaigning Babel was not yet in a position to transmute his raw experience into art. He required some distance from the cruelty and killing before he could undertake an assessment of what he had seen. In the diary, where his immediate impressions are recorded, life is viewed as an almost continuous funeral; in the finished book, where he has attained the needed perspective, the horror and destruction are subordinated to an affirmation of life. The transformation, insofar as it does take place, is the result of Babel's insistence that human endeavor is potentially heroic. His alterations of fact and his changes of emphasis through various drafts almost always reveal this pattern of searching for an immanent heroism. A story about the slaughter of military prisoners, for example, underwent sev-

[39] Quoted by Smirin, in *ibid.*, 477.     [40] *Ibid.*
[41] Quoted by Livšic, in "Materialy k tvorčeskoj biografii I. Babelja," *Voprosy literatury*, VIII, No. 4 (1964), 115.

eral modifications and eventually produced two finished versions. In the earlier, called "There Were Nine," the narrator Ljutov stands in the foreground; his outraged reaction to the murder dominates the story's close:

> The nine prisoners are dead. I know it in my heart. This morning I decided to conduct a requiem in their memory. In our cavalry army there is no one but me to do this. Our troop has made camp in a demolished country estate. I took my diary and went into the garden, which had survived. Hyacinths and blue roses grew there.
>
> I began to make notes about the platoon commander and the nine dead men, but right away a familiar noise interrupted me. Cherkashin, the staff today, was attacking the bee hives. Mitya, a ruddy-faced peasant from Orel, was following him with a smoking torch in his hands. Their heads were wrapped in their greatcoats. The slits of their eyes blazed. Thousands of bees were trying to beat off their conquerors and were dying by their hives. I put aside my pen. I was stricken with horror at the multitude of requiems stretching before me.[42]

In the version finally used in *Red Cavalry* the murder of the prisoners is made part of an entirely different story. In "Squadron Commander Trunov" the main figure is the murderer himself, shown as a man whose cruelty results from a passion for justice. The slaying of the prisoners in a moment of rage is not condoned, but it is redeemed in a sense when the hero, sacrificing his own life on behalf of his comrades and their cause, fulfills himself in a heroic death. All of the dead, including the slayer now as well as his victims, are linked in a somber tribute to creative sacrifice, and the image of Trunov, with all its contradictions, acquires a tragic dignity. The narrator Ljutov, confronted with a more complex reality than he might wish, is no longer as quick to judge as in the earlier version.

More than once in the diary there are moving lamentations like that quoted above on the destruction of the bees. But again

42 Although excerpts of this story have been quoted by Soviet critics, it has never been published in full in the Soviet Union. The passage quoted above is taken from the Russian text as published in the New York émigré magazine, *Novyj Žurnal*, No. 95 (June 1969), 19–20.

the diary impressions undergo subtle modification when incorporated into *Red Cavalry*. Compare the following two passages, the first an entry from the diary and the second the opening section of "The Road to Brody":

> An orchard and an apiary, the destruction of the bee gardens. It's terrible, the bees buzzing in despair as they are blown up with gunpowder. . . . A bacchanal, they're battering hives about with their swords, the honey pouring into the ground, the bees stinging. They smoke them out with tarred and burning rags.
>
> $\cdot\quad\cdot\quad\cdot\quad\cdot\quad\cdot\quad\cdot$
>
> I felt sorry about the bees. The fighting armies treated them most brutally. There are no bees left in Volhynia.
>
> We defiled the indescribable hives. We destroyed them with sulphur and blew them up with gunpowder. The smell of singed rags reeked in the sacred republic of the bees. Dying, they flew around slowly, humming so that you could hardly hear. And we who had no bread extracted the honey with our swords. . . . There are no bees left in Volhynia (80–81).[43]

In the latter passage, by including the hungry human marauders in his expression of sorrow and by involving himself in the destruction, Babel has significantly changed the effect. Furthermore, the story has a pervasive lyric tone and, closing with Afonka Bida's legend of the bee that refused to sting Christ, it rises to a compassion that embraces once again defiler and defiled alike:

> "Got to understand the bee," concluded Afonka, my platoon commander.
>
> "Well, and the bee's got to stick it now; it's for them too that we're messing about here" (81).[44]

Throughout *Red Cavalry*, the narrator Ljutov, like his creator, is constantly confronted with the problem of how to perceive

---

[43] For the comparison of these two passages, and for much else pertaining to the diary, I am indebted to the article by L. Livšic, "Materialy k tvorčeskoj biografii I. Babelja," VIII, No. 4 (1964), 128.

[44] The beehive is a traditional symbol of the ideal republic of order and justice and is seen as confirmation of the myth of the golden age when honey fell from the trees. The particularly sad irony in the Cossacks' destruction of the "sacred republic of the bee" is that for all his attempted avowal of the new cause, Babel cannot refrain from lamenting the death throes of ancient cultures—not only that of the bees, but also of Hasidism and even of feudal, Catholic Poland.

reality. Uprooted by the war from his familiar life in the traditional culture of the city, he is besieged by doubt and confusion, by an overwhelming sense of dislocation. A student of the law, of that labyrinthine network of rules and traditions which is supposed to make urban civilization work, Ljutov is forever seeking order and a pattern in events, but what he mostly finds is chaos and anarchy. His civilized system of values is primarily a negative one, made up of legal and moral injunctions, of "shalt nots," and it constantly brings him into conflict with a system which he cannot comprehend. He fights with the Cossacks on their execution of prioners, refusing thereby to acknowledge a concept of justice which differs from his own;[45] riding into battle with an unloaded weapon he transgresses against that inviolable code whereby men at war share each other's enemies; leaving the mortally wounded Dolgushov to the merciful shot of a fellow Cossack he shows himself a stranger to the deepest loyalty of a comrade-in-arms. With his violation of their ways Ljutov is fatally estranged from a life he would share, earning the undying hostility of his Cossack companions.

The Cossack code of values is not the same as that of the civilized, of course, but Babel grants it a nobility of its own. In his lyric depiction of the epic lives and deaths of legendary saints, sinners, and heroes, he sought to acknowledge the value of a forgotten ideal, of a way of life in which men—violent yet brave, brutal yet gay, primitive yet poetic—were a splendid breed. His imagination takes him back to the grandeur of an earlier day, to a time when men were virile and free, when the hero could ride a horse faultlessly and face or inflict death with the assur-

[45] Instances of battlefield justice in *Red Cavalry* and of disagreement with "civilized authority" are numerous: the dispute in "The Letter"—for example, over custody of the elder Kurdyukov—is not so much a disagreement on the sentence to be pronounced (death) as on the means of carrying it out. But in expressing their contempt for the bureaucratic regulations of a distant authority, the Cossacks still adhere to their own private code of justice. Pavlichenko, Prischepa, and Balmashev, having no use for legal niceties, all serve as both judge and executioner. Akinfiev (in "After the Battle") has his own law against malingerers, and Levka (in "The Widow") will himself be the executor of his dead commander's last will. For the Cossacks such action is not the dethronement of justice, but its swift and unrelenting execution.

rance of an ultimate grace. In his vision of war Babel allows the possibility of a stark beauty. The life of his cavalry army has a bold and awesome simplicity. It is enacted against the backdrop of broad expanses of land, and its rhythms are the ancient, nomadic rhythms of the march—open, sweeping, and free. As Babel well knew, the Revolution was to be the last great battle in which the cavalry would play an important role, and his nostalgic evocation of its ancient ethos imparts a lyrical tone to his book. The Cossack and his mount, forming a union that is at once both practical and mystic, create an image in which prosaic necessity and poetic form ride together in harmony.

Still, the last great ride is an anachronism, for even at the time of the Russian Revolution the cavalry was already a small, atypical element of warfare. Vast regiments of infantry, similar to those which had made their appearance in the trenches of World War I, well-defined fronts, and extended lines of battle—these were the true face and form of modern warfare. These contradictions are reflected in Babel's book by the conflicts that erupt between the cavalrymen and the footsoldiers of their own army. The Cossacks, those élite, self-possessed masters of the terrain, free to roam wherever their mounts will take them, cannot conceal their contempt for the regimented, earth-bound infantrymen. In "Afonka Bida" they make sport with the footsoldiers by whipping them about like cattle, asserting thereby their anarchic selfhood and their rejection of the colorless mass.[46] The Cossacks themselves, however, are also victimized, the prey of history. In "Squadron Commander Trunov" they are forced to give battle to the airplane, and this quixotic struggle of man against machine becomes a metaphor for a gallant but futile combat with time. In a paradoxical way, of course, these are not unrelated opponents, for the plane is the truly mobile, modern horse, and its flier the cavalryman of an age just begun.

---

[46] Babel also finds room in this story to express a familiar irony. In the role of "hetman of the mouzhiks," commander of a wretched and ill-equipped infantry, he casts "a weak-eyed Jewish youth with the wan and rapt face of a Talmudist."

Babel, however, remains entranced with his vision of Cossack manhood and seeks to impart to his captivating heroes a timeless beauty. Their capacity for life is a welcome antithesis to the stunted, joyless existence which he otherwise fears is his fated lot. Horror remains, brutality is unavoidable, but unlike the horror and brutality of religious resignation that of the Cossacks contains a present and living beauty which is much to be preferred to the promised beauty of a future paradise. Such at least is Babel's hope, for despite its harshness *Red Cavalry* is his most optimistic construction of life's possibilities, his youthful cry of affirmation. In "Argamak," with which the book closes, the journey of Babel's narrator comes at last to a hopeful end.[47] All those tales of trial and initiation find their ultimate symbolic fulfillment: he has learned to ride. A recurrent dream, the narrator tells us, has sustained him through all the ineptitudes of his waking hours; in it the Cossacks pay him no mind as he passes by them on his horse, and gradually it dawns upon him that he rides like everyone else. By the end of the book dream and reality have merged, and when it finally comes the longed-for achievement is the result not of a willed success, but of the attainment of grace. The very horse he has maimed has taught him to ride; redeeming his sin against beauty the bespectacled narrator becomes fit at last to enter a sacred world. Ljutov—and perhaps Babel too, at least for the moment—has triumphed in his quest. He himself belongs to the vision.

47 The earliest editions of *Red Cavalry*, it should be noted, ended with "The Rabbi's Son"; only in 1931, with the fifth edition, did Babel add the more rounded conclusion provided by "Argamak." The story's long delay in appearing in print (it was dated by the author "1924–1930") would seem to indicate a continuing doubt in Babel's mind as to its fitness, but its final inclusion would seem equally to indicate a dissatisfaction with having the more somber "Rabbi's Son" as the concluding tale. In its over-all effects *Red Cavalry* remains a deeply perplexed and self-contradictory work, and it is likely that Babel's insertion of the new ending was designed to tilt the scale ever so slightly toward the affirmative resolution that was his deepest and yet most precariously balanced hope.

# IX

# AFTER *Red Cavalry*

*I started writing as a youth, then stopped for a number of years, then wrote in a torrent for several years, then stopped again. Now I'm beginning the second act of the comedy or tragedy— I don't know which it will be.*[1]

*If you talk about silence, you cannot avoid speaking of me—the great master of that genre.*[2]

"Babel is the rage of Moscow. Everyone is mad about him," wrote Konstantin Fedin to Gorky in July 1924,[3] and indeed, with the rapid succession of tales from *Red Cavalry* then appearing in print, Babel had become something of a literary celebrity. When a few years later his stories appeared in book form they were almost universally received by the critics as masterpieces of the new literature, and Babel himself received numerous invitations to discuss his work at literary symposia and to speak before groups of aspiring writers. With his burgeoning reputation, Babel now found his stories in great demand among the editors of leading literary journals, and on the promise of his future successes he was assured of a fairly steady income from the state publishing houses and writers' organizations. Like other prominent authors in the Soviet Union, Babel was granted a sort of retainer, in return for which he was expected in due course to perform properly.

[1] From a transcript of Babel's 1937 interview with a group of young writers, printed in *Naš sovremennik*, No. 4 (1964), 97.
[2] From Babel's speech to the 1934 Congress of Soviet Writers, held in Moscow. The speech has been reprinted in the most recent Soviet edition of Babel's works: *I. Babel': Izbrannoe* (Moscow, 1966), 410.
[3] *Literaturnoe nasledstvo*, LXX, 475.

In 1924 Babel had settled in Moscow, and although he was to complain often about life in the capital and to make frequent and sometimes prolonged trips away from it, this was to be the nearest thing to a permanent home that he would have for the remainder of his life. The first years in Moscow, the period between 1924 and 1926, were particularly crucial ones for Babel, professionally and personally. No longer living in the relative obscurity of provincial towns but in the seat of Soviet authority, and with his new-won fame, he could hardly fail to be drawn into the literary-political debates which were becoming increasingly menacing. Writers were being asked to join the vanguard of social and political activism, and in the highly polemical atmosphere of the time they found themselves assailed on all sides by demands that their art reflect the goals and ideals of the state. Early in 1924, Babel himself was the target of a vicious attack by none other than General Budyonny, who accused him of a lack of Revolutionary zeal and of lampooning in his stories the Soviet cavalry.[4] Such attacks upon writers were becoming widespread, and they affected the atmosphere even within the literary community itself. Thus in May 1924, along with a number of other, similarly disturbed literary people, Babel felt compelled to sign a statement of protest against one of the groups then attacking nonconformist writers.[5] This brush with the self-appointed guardians of Soviet culture could hardly have seemed as important to Babel then as it strikes us now. For the most part he was busily engaged with personal affairs: preparing for the first book publication of *Red Cavalry*, planning new work, and arranging a host of troubling private matters.

4 The charge appeared in an article entitled "Babizm Babelja" (Babel's Womanism), *Oktjabr'* (No. 3, 1924), 196–97. Budyonny was to return to the attack with an open letter to the newspaper *Krasnaja Gazeta* in October 1928, at which time Babel was eloquently defended by Gorky in an answer which he sent to *Pravda* in November of that year.

5 The statement singled out the "On-Guardists," a leading group of proletarian writers of the twenties who sought to suppress all but their own brand of highly class-conscious writing. While they were for a time held at bay, the "Onguardist" espousal of a state-controlled literature was to become eventually the official party position. The 1924 letter of protest, which Babel and 35 other writers signed, is in L. Timofeev's *Sovetskaja literatura* (Moscow, 1964), 163–64.

In the brief span of a year and a half, almost coinciding with the first moments of his literary success, Babel was to lose the companionship of the closest members of his family. Beginning in February 1925 and following in quick succession, Babel's only sister, his wife, and his mother all left the Soviet Union—his sister and mother to settle in Belgium and his wife Evgenia to make a home in Paris. These separations, conceived of as temporary at first, were to prove permanent in the end and caused Babel and his family years of anguish. The departures gave Babel more immediate anxieties at the time: constant bother about passports, visas, residence permits; worries over health (his mother's and sister's) and financial affairs. His wife's departure was further clouded by the development of a serious crisis in their relationship, and matters between them were not settled when Evgenia left. Nevertheless, the appearance in 1926 of the first full edition of *Red Cavalry* and his confirmed sense of a vocation must have greatly buoyed Babel's faith in the future. Although trying to ensure that there would still be a family home, he had come to the decision that he himself would remain where his art and his deepest desires were grounded—in Russia. He undoubtedly hoped that the apparent dissolution of his family would in time be corrected, but at least for the foreseeable future he had taken upon himself the role of rootless wanderer. "In order to accomplish the things I must do," he wrote at the end of 1925 to his sister, already abroad, "I will have to travel a lot in the forthcoming years and face some other adventures. But that can't be helped. I have picked a hellish trade."[6]

And that trade, refusing to allow Babel any lasting pleasure in the success he had already attained, was now goading him on to search for new achievement. As Babel himself had to admit, his art by the beginning of 1926 was posing some unexpected problems and a serious challenge to his ability to continue.[7] In his earliest writing Babel had experimented with a variety of styles, but his major achievement through the first half of the

[6] *Isaac Babel: The Lonely Years*, 66.
[7] See Babel's letter to his sister dated Jan. 1, 1926, in *The Lonely Years*, 67.

twenties had unquestionably been the mastery of the techniques which he had employed in *The Odessa Tales* and *Red Cavalry*.[8] His very success, however, was now beginning to pall, and he was no longer completely satisfied with the artistic methods of his recent past. Writing to Gorky, he had already expressed, as early as June 1925, a growing sense of unease: "At the start of this year—after eighteen months of labor—my writings began to fill me with doubt. I have found them artificial and florid."[9]

Babel's new attitudes partly reflected the changes in the literary climate. With the arrival of the mid-twenties the theme of the civil war and the stylistic extravagance that had been employed in its literary expression were no longer in vogue. The energies of the nation were now being devoted to economic recovery, and, at least in the mind of the state, the new era demanded new themes and the development of different literary styles for the portrayal of the postwar activities of reconstruction and social reorganization. In the works appearing after 1925 many of the features characteristic of the poetic prose of the early twenties began to disappear. More traditional forms, such as the novel, once more established their sway, and the cult of realism reasserted its customary dominance of Russian letters. The Party became increasingly suspicious of stylistic innovation and of any writing that suggested an ironic or ambiguous attitude; what it demanded of art, with growing insistence, was the simplistic portrayal of the glories of the new state and of its own infallible leadership.

This transition to a new era proved difficult for almost all of the

8 Most of the individual stories of the early twenties share themes and stylistic features which have been discussed in connection with the two major cycles. Some stories (e.g., "Through the Fanlight," "With Old Man Makhno," "Answer to an Inquiry," and "Tale of a Woman") express with a greater intensity than elsewhere Babel's wonderment at the mysteries of sex, and a few (e.g., "The Sin of Jesus," "The End of St. Hypatius," and especially "Bagrat Ogli and the Eyes of His Bull") explore additional methods of stylistic imitation and parody. A few pieces, including the 1922 Tiflis newspaper writing and the short story "You Were Too Trusting, Captain!," reveal an effort to display a greater degree of the expected Revolutionary sentiment.

9 *Literaturnoe nasledstvo*, LXX, 38.

established writers, but for Babel the general sense of cultural dislocation was further exacerbated by his personal artistic crisis. In his *Odessa* and *Cavalry* cycles, as time would show, Babel had exhausted an irreplaceable reservoir of spiritual strength. Feeding upon the justifiable resentments of his youth and overindulging perhaps his anticipation of change, he had attempted a kind of radical self-transformation that he would find difficult to sustain. If in *The Odessa Tales* he had discovered the insights which had permitted his greater achievement in *Red Cavalry*, he had also overcommitted both himself and his art to a hope born of violence; his effort to accept, against his nature, a chaotic and unjust universe was to leave a bitter taste of regret. In the Soviet Union the end of the war was no end to horror, and the political and social developments there and elsewhere made a mockery of Babel's private hope of emancipation. The attempt to make "Cossack" primitives out of Odessa Jews, as well as the effort, depicted in *Red Cavalry*, to become himself something he was not, appeared to him increasingly suspect. In hindsight Babel was compelled to acknowledge the possibility of self-deception, to recognize that his hopes had been doomed at the start. In the works following these early successes Babel probed deeper, and with more compassion, into the sources, especially in the Jewish community, which had formed his nature. Returning in his art to the images of his past, he sought to attain a finer apprehension of reality and a more compelling and truthful perception of the limits imposed upon experience by fate.

More than once as the years passed, Babel returned to the characters and milieu of *The Odessa Tales* in works whose tones grew increasingly somber. Amid the austere and dogmatic atmosphere of Soviet Russia, his somewhat theatrical Odessa bandits came to seem even more unreal, and one by one in later works they leave the stage. First (in a still rather sanguine screenplay of 1926 entitled *Benja Krik*) Benja himself falls victim to a regime that has no use for individualistic heroes; then the irrepressible Arye-Leib moves off, along with the other decrepit relics who reside in the Jewish poorhouse, all of them driven from the site where the Soviet future is being mapped ("The End of the Old Folks' Home," 1932). Finally Froim Grach (in a 1933 story of that title), the last of the great Odessan bandits, succumbs to a Cheka purge. This denouement of the Jewish drama implicit in his early work is not unexpected; in a sense it is even a desired fulfillment. But Babel's attitude in these later stories is more ambiguous than might have been anticipated, and he bids a surprisingly nostalgic farewell to the legends of his youth.[10]

With regard to *Red Cavalry* as well Babel's attitudes were not long in changing. He had originally planned some fifty chapters for this book, but after publication of the first collected edition only one or two additional stories appeared. Speaking to a meeting of writers in 1930, Babel would remark, somewhat sadly, that he had come to dislike everything he had written, mentioning in particular his displeasure with *Red Cavalry*.[11] The truth is that Babel was no longer able to sustain the illusion of having attained his vision, and the figure of Ljutov no longer provided an acceptable, convincing persona. Even in "Argamak," the tale that was ultimately added as the book's finale, there are intimations of a sense of unease; in the figure of Baulin, who has an extremely pragmatic view of reality, there is a suggestion that Ljutov's dream will not long survive. The Soviet state of the future was to have little use for a romantic cavalry and no place at all for visionaries such as Babel. Ljutov's struggle to master his horse and his shame before its peasant owner are a matter of indifference to those like Baulin, for whom the claims of poetry and grace are always irrelevant. The tragedy for Babel personally lay in the unexpected irony that he had learned to ride precisely at the moment when he discovered that his newly won ability was of little consequence to the natural riders of this world. As a result, not only the quality but the very existence of his achievement is cast into doubt, and Babel finds life's unexpected in-

---

[10] The Odessan characters appear in still two other interrelated works, a story of 1924 and a play of 1928, both entitled *Sunset*. The theme of an era ending is common to these two pieces as well, but for reasons to be discussed later they deserve special consideration.

[11] See *Literaturnoe nasledstvo*, LXXIV, 482.

transigence still another cause for self-denigration. Significantly, after *Red Cavalry* Babel's settings are not often out of doors. His stories and plays take place for the most part now in cities— inside buildings, in apartments or rooms. Men of the Benja or Cossack type begin to fade from his works or remain only with a deep shading of sadness, as images of a now unattainable ideal. Martial themes give way to the portrayal of more common human pursuits; women and children, the transmitters of civilization, begin to appear in his fiction as major characters.

Urged on by his private longings and loneliness, Babel turns his eye homeward, and in his next group of stories he sets about writing tales of childhood. The autobiographical nature of Babel's art is beyond dispute, but of course not every event recorded in his stories reproduces an actual occurrence. Babel himself, writing to his mother in Belgium concerning his new cycle, acknowledges that although "the subjects of the stories are all taken from my childhood, . . . there is much that has been made up and changed." The important point, however, is that even such changes are motivated by the desire to capture reality more fully, and for Babel the inner essence of his experience of Jewishness is darker than external events would imply. He was aware that his altered construction of the past would give pain to his family, and he attempted to soften the hurt by assuring his mother that "when the book is finished, it will become clear why I had to do all that."[12] The childhood cycle might be said to have its beginning as far back as 1915 when Babel wrote his earliest surviving sketch, "Childhood at Grandmother's." Only in 1925, however, when his work on *Red Cavalry* was drawing to a close, did he give any evidence of intending to write a series of tales. In that year two additional stories of reminiscence appeared, "First Love" and "The Story of My Dovecote," the latter providing a general title for the cycle as a whole. In 1931 two further tales, "The Awakening" and "In the Basement," the only others to deal exclusively with Babel's childhood, made

12 *Isaac Babel: The Lonely Years*, 189.

the project complete—at least as far as the published evidence indicates.

In these new works Babel shifted his approach from *Bildungsroman* to confession, tracing in the stories crucial moments in the consciousness of childhood: the shame he feels in his family's poverty; his rejection of his parents' religion and refusal to become either rabbi or sage; the awakening of the body and of an attendant sense of guilt; the yearning for nature and for experience of life; the first sickening, sweet taste of the world's cruelty; and, finally, the discovery of a vocation—literary artist. The stories continue to exploit many of Babel's familiar themes of flight and initiation, but they also acknowledge now the ineradicable presence of fate, the insurmountability of heritage. Babel's new awareness of how difficult it is to repudiate the claims of background and family, of those forces unconsciously absorbed in the years of childhood, imparts a new touch of humility to his work. The desire for escape, which remains undeniably strong, is now accompanied by a greater sense of fellowship with those who share his bondage, and the bitterness with which Babel regards his fate does not extinguish the expression of love and compassion for his "crazy, unlucky" family. The stories are thus touched, albeit fitfully, with the glow of purifying acceptance.

Stylistically too, the childhood stories give evidence of a desire to break with his earlier work. Much of the richness of texture remains, but the lush profusion of metaphors, the discordant blending of stylistic variables, and the contrastive transitions are all significantly reduced. As he retreats from the tightly compressed form of the miniature Babel allows a greater sway to the purely narrative element in his fiction; conveying experience in less boldly impressionistic terms, he also makes room for a more psychological approach to the portrayal of character. He still refrains from probing the minds of his heroes directly and he maintains an eye for grotesque detail, but he now makes use in his stories of a more fully developed background of social and psychological motivation. These autobiographical tales are not so dazzling, do not have as stylistically brilliant a surface as the earlier stories, but they possess a greater dimensionality and are the product of a more thoughtful, if more melancholy, mind.

Upon completion of his first few childhood pieces, Babel embarked upon a new period of hectic, most solitary wandering. Writing was harder than ever for him and there were new personal problems as well. Babel's separation from his family was the cause of a constantly nagging sorrow, but he bore his troubles with fortitude and wit. His letters to his mother and sister, written over a span of some fourteen years, are an eloquent, moving record of his continuing solicitude and love—and of frequent exasperation as well at the "dear fools" who added so greatly to his own burdens with their constant report of worries and fears. Helping to support his relatives in Brussels and his wife in Paris and to maintain himself in his ceaseless wanderings in search of both the material and the solitude necessary to his writing, Babel had to expend enormous energy in securing an income. Nor was his immediate family the only beneficiary of his concern: there were innumerable aunts, uncles, cousins, and other relatives, in and outside of Russia, who received both financial and moral support from the harried writer. Through it all Babel maintained his commitment to art, pursuing with relentless devotion his struggle to be a writer. "I am prepared to give up all except one thing—my work,"[13] he wrote in November 1926, and all of the frustrations and deprivations, personal and artistic, which he had to endure are a testimony to the passion and fidelity with which he adhered to his goal.

In the latter part of 1927, after long and frequent postponements, Babel was able at last to travel abroad, where he spent about a year visiting with his family, satisfying his curiosity about Europe, and above all attempting to continue with his work. The unsettled, hectic circumstances of what was only a temporary, if prolonged, stay in foreign places made working extremely difficult and hardly contributed, as Babel put it, to flights of inspiration. Nonetheless, he thrust himself into his

13 *Ibid.*, 81.

labors with renewed vigor. "Again, as in the days of my youth," he informed a friend in Russia, "I am planning a *coup d'état* in my writing. We shall see if I succeed. I am a bit tired and then, too, this *coup* is proving more difficult than the first."[14] But he pushed on, buoyed by the excitement of a new challenge: "I have taken on the labor of Sisyphus, which is almost unbearable for me. My overburdened brain often betrays me and I have to call on all my will power to help me win out in this battle—and battle it is—that I'm waging. I'm at war with my nerves, with my mind, with fatigue, with my own lack of talent, with attacks of weakness, and with the conditions of life abroad."[15] Results were tortuously slow in coming, and Babel, struggling for his artistic life, refused as always to hurry his efforts or prematurely release work he considered in need of more polishing. He turned a deaf ear to the impatient entreaties of his editors in Russia. Writing in mid-1928 to Vyacheslav Polonsky, chief editor of *Novyj mir* (New World), Babel defended his protracted silence in the name of artistic honesty:

> Dear Vyacheslav Pavlovich! I have been forwarded from Paris your editorial board's letter, formally correct and monstrously unjust and tormenting in its essence. I'll answer it as sincerely as I can and I'll tell you precisely what I think—which is that in spite of my outrageous financial situation and in spite of my confused personal affairs, I don't intend to make the slightest change in my accepted manner of work. Not by a single hour will I forcibly or artificially hasten its course. I haven't been trying to turn my mind and soul inside out; I haven't withdrawn into solitude, kept silent, slaved, and attempted to purify myself both spiritually and as a writer just in order to betray myself for God knows what, for some sort of temporary advantage.[16]

14 "Iz pisem k druz'jam," *Znamja*, No. 8 (Aug. 1964), 150.
15 *I. Babel': Izbrannoe* (Moscow, 1966), 450.
16 *Ibid.*, 440–41. Babel had written to another friend, a few months before, that "it would be possible to accomplish more than I do, but it still seems to me that my slowness in working is in submission to the laws of art—and not of hack work, vanity, or greed." In still another letter of the same period he says that he will return "subdued, quieted, my presumptions curtailed; but a thousand times more obstinate than before. I believe that if one lacks wisdom, then obstinacy is a good replacement." *Znamja*, No. 8 (Aug. 1964), 151, 156.

Although he loved Paris, where most of his time abroad was spent, Babel seemed unable to work there. He saw himself, only half in jest, as a lyric poet growing old and bald, marking time while death drew nearer. "The trouble," he wrote a friend at home, "is not that death is approaching—that's a great thing after all—but that we just stand in place or even go backward. Well I for one intend to move on."[17] As the unproductive months abroad continued to lengthen, Babel's thoughts were irresistibly drawn back to Russia, to the sources of his language and his art. In his letters he expresses a growing desire to return; Paris is "beautiful, but foreign," he writes, "and it's time for me to settle down in my homeland."[18] Or again: "Everything is very interesting, but to tell the truth, there's no food for the soul. Spiritual life in Russia is nobler. I'm spoiled by Russia, miss it terribly, think only of Russia."[19]

By October 1928 he was finally back in the Soviet Union. Once again he found himself thwarted in his effort to work by the necessity for endless literary and financial negotiations, but just being back in Russia was a boon to his spirits. "Despite all this hustle and bustle," he writes his mother from Kiev, "I feel fine on my native soil. There is poverty here, much that is sad, but it's my material, my language, something that's of direct interest to me. I realize more and more with each passing day that I'm getting back to my normal state, whereas in Paris I felt as if there was something pasted on inside me that wasn't my own. I don't mind going abroad on vacation, but I must work here."[20]

Despite these protestations and assurances, directed as much to himself it would seem as to his worried relatives in Europe, Babel's work continued to give him trouble. Before going abroad in 1927 he had completed a play, *Sunset*, his first attempt at a piece for the stage, but since that time his labors had borne little fruit. Upon his return to Russia, Babel struggled desperately, but in vain, to set his affairs in order and to get back to work. Not only the crush of personal obligations, but political develop-

17 *Znamja*, No. 8 (Aug. 1964), 148.
18 *Ibid.*

19 *Ibid.*, 149.
20 *Isaac Babel: The Lonely Years*, 106.

ments in the Soviet Union were fast encroaching upon the artistic options available to him, and he realized only too well that his life was being pushed into a fateful race with time. In an effort to alleviate the financial pressures bearing down on him Babel began to take writing assignments from various Soviet film studios. He had already, back in 1925, turned his *Odessa Tales* into a screenplay, and now he began to spend considerable time and energy in editing and doctoring the scripts of others, a task for which he acquired a considerable reputation in film circles. Throughout his mature years as an artist he continued writing for films, adapting numerous works of literature to the screen and even completing a few original scenarios.[21] Although for the most part he accepted these assignments regretfully, he told himself that through films he was gaining the means to pursue his "true work." The years were crowding in upon him, however, and always in the background was the unsettled state of his family affairs.

In July 1929 Babel's daughter Nathalie was born in Paris, and he immediately made plans for another trip abroad. Only in late 1932, however, when his daughter was already three years old, was he finally able to get away. Again Babel spent about a year in Europe, becoming acquainted with his child, seeing old friends, and as always trying to work. On this trip he also visited his old friend Gorky, just then preparing to return to the Soviet Union for good.

During this second stay abroad, Babel must have given renewed and serious thought, especially now that he had a daughter as well as a wife to consider, to his plans for the future. According to the artist Yury Annenkov, with whom Babel formed a warm friendship during his days in Paris, the question of his place of residence had actually been more or less resolved in favor of Babel's staying in the West.[22] In many of their talks, says the

21 The Bibliography gives an idea of the extent of Babel's film work.
22 Jurij Annenkov, *Dnevnik moix vstreč* (New York, 1966), I, 306. Annenkov's remembrance of Babel, part of a series of such portraits of literary friends and acquaintances, must be viewed with caution, but it does give an interesting if brief glimpse of Babel during his Paris days. Annenkov remarks on Babel's keen

painter in his memoirs, Babel expressed a growing despair with the state of political and cultural affairs in Moscow and proclaimed his determination to become a "free citizen." At the same time, continues Annenkov, Babel bitterly rejected the idea of a life as one of Paris' "Russian taxi drivers." His dilemma was truly excruciating. If he were ever to share a home with his wife and child, it would have to be in Europe, and although Babel's sense of himself demanded freedom from the constraints of family life, certainly a part of him still felt the need and obligation of accepting his role as a husband and father. Furthermore, with the growing abridgment of intellectual and artistic freedom in the Soviet Union, Paris might have seemed to offer a climate more congenial to the artist in him.[23] But these were two strangely contradictory havens that Europe offered: one respectably middle-class, the fulfillment of a tradition he had long resisted, and the other a kind of super-Bohemia, in which aesthetic pursuits were an accepted style of life. Perhaps Babel fled from both. Despite his love for French art and literature, he was always at heart a sojourner in Paris. Exile, even voluntary, was not at all to Babel's taste, and one of the central themes in his life's work is precisely that refusal to become the wandering, exiled Jew, to follow the ancient pattern of countless merchants and bearers of culture. Furthermore, Babel had come to find France, the only country he even vaguely considered an alternative home, too small and confining, rather provincial after all, and lacking that "rush of great thoughts and passions" which attracted him to Russia.[24] Babel actually may never have made in his own mind a clear and final decision about his return, and the pressures of circumstances naturally played their part in the course of events. But ultimately he went back because he had

interest in painting, especially in the impressionists and in the sources of non-objective, abstract art.

23 One cannot help but recall the appeal that Paris also exerted upon American writers of Babel's generation; how they too sought a greater artistic freedom in France than could be found at home.

24 Cf. letter of Jan. 10, 1928, to his friend I. L. Livšic (quoted in *Znamja*, No. 8, Aug. 1964, 150).

to, because the sufferings and the hopes and the challenges of his life lay in Soviet Russia.

At the beginning of August 1933, abandoning an unsuccessful project with a French film studio for a scenario and with debts crushing his spirit, Babel prepared to depart for Moscow.[25] Except for one brief visit he would be permitted to make to Paris in the summer of 1935, it was a final farewell. With his future plans uncertain—indeed, with his whole literary and personal fate in the balance—he left. A letter received by Annenkov at the time reveals Babel's frame of mind:

> A strange summons to Moscow. I am leaving in the most dramatic circumstances, without money and in debt. It's possible that I won't be able to see you before my departure. I am more sorry about that than I can say.
> Live well without me. Don't forget Evgenia Borisovna [Babel's wife] in my absence.
> I kiss you. I am happy to be going to Moscow. All the rest is bitter and dark.[26]

Upon his return, Babel once again had to set about putting his literary and personal affairs in order. After an absence of almost a year "all sorts of absurd but sinister rumors" had begun to circulate, and official suspicions about his political reliability had grown alarmingly.[27] Impatient editors were still clamoring for Babel's stories, but as yet he had little he would release for publication. He had always put his hopes in the quality of his work rather than its quantity, but in the production-minded atmosphere then pervading Moscow even writers were expected to deliver regularly, on schedule, and Babel's silence was begin-

25 See Babel's letters of May 18, June 18, and July 10, 1933 (in *Isaac Babel: The Lonely Years*, 234, 236, 239) and the one of July 30, 1933 (in *Znamja*, No. 8, Aug. 1964, 163).
26 Jurij Annenkov, *Dnevnik moix vstreč*, 307. Annenkov states flatly that Babel had no desire for his wife and child to share the dangerous path that he himself had chosen to follow, but the numerous appeals that Babel made in his letters for his family to join him would seem to contradict this view. Of course Babel's words may have been prompted in part by the knowledge that the censor was sure to be reading his mail, but this does not necessarily invalidate their sincerity.
27 See Babel's letter of Sept. 1, 1933 (in *Isaac Babel: The Lonely Years*, 239).

ning to provoke ominous signs of hostility. He had been writing constantly, of course, but he had serious doubts about whether or not he dared publish his latest works. While still abroad he had taken advantage of his visit to Gorky in Sorrento to seek the older man's reaction to his most recent work and his counsel as to the course he should pursue. Gorky, as always, was full of encouragement and even, since he planned to precede Babel in returning to Russia, offered to take several stories with him and secure a suitable place for their quick publication.[28] The stories ("Froim Grach," "Dante Street," "My First Fee," and "Oil") found a chilly reception, however; only two of the four were published during Babel's lifetime, and the rejection of the others boded little good for his literary future.

Babel's continuing struggle, throughout the late twenties and early thirties, to find new material and a new style followed three fairly separate, distinct paths: he continued to write stories, though their manner was changing; he made a serious effort at composing longer works of fiction; and he turned with increasing excitement to a completely new field, the drama. In all these directions Babel found his work to be excruciatingly difficult. He was always ready to sacrifice everything to his unwavering goal to become a first-rate craftsman and professional writer; his letters from the late twenties on are an almost endless catalogue of the trials, agonies, and hopes which accompanied his dedication to that goal:

*February 24, 1928*
    Till February I was working in fine fettle; then I undertook to write an absolutely astounding piece, which yesterday at eleven-thirty in the evening I discovered to be a piece of absolute crap, and grandiloquent crap at that. A month and a half of my life wasted on nothing. Today I'm still grieving, but tomorrow I'll already begin to think that one learns from mistakes.

---

28 It is one of those curious coincidences that Babel's unexpectedly hasty departure for home should have occurred so close upon the heel of Gorky's. His fate was strangely linked at many crucial points in his career with the life of his older friend, and in this instance both men were no doubt responding to the growing insistence that Soviet luminaries come home to stay.

AFTER *Red Cavalry*

*March 20, 1928*
My transfer to new literary rails is giving me trouble. The professional pursuit of literature (and I am now for the first time pursuing it as a professional) is giving me trouble.

*August 31, 1928*
It is much more difficult for me to work than before. I have different demands and a desire to move on to another "class" of art—the class of quiet, clear, subtle, and not trivial, writing.

*May 29, 1933*
In my work—no success. I have written a play, but it didn't turn out.[29]

*April 17, 1935*
My stories haven't been coming off too well—certain mental and literary changes have taken place within me that are beyond my control. . . .[30]

*November 17, 1936*
All that I'm doing now is not finished work, but in any case it already resembles true writing and a professional approach.[31]

In the stories belonging to the thirties Babel pruned away much of his earlier exoticism; he was more careful in his expenditure of adjectives and metaphors and sought in general for a purer, more reflective, classical form.[32] The Gogol of "The Overcoat," he confessed to Ilya Ehrenburg, was closer to his heart now than the Gogol of the early tales.[33] He was drawn more and more to "eternal" themes, to pursuing the meanings of birth and sex, of death and fate. Among the relatively few stories from these years are some of the finest Babel ever wrote: "The Road," "Karl Yankel," "Guy de Maupassant," "My First Fee," "Dante

29 *I. Babel': Izbrannoe* (Moscow, 1966), 436, 454, 455–56, 452, respectively.
30 *Isaac Babel: The Lonely Years*, 280.
31 *Znamja*, No. 8 (Aug. 1964), 165.
32 Speaking in the late thirties to a group of young writers, Babel characteristically advised that his listeners take to heart Pushkin's "golden words": "Precision and brevity are the primary virtues of prose." Then he cautioned with a smile: "Only do not think that it's simple—to attain this precision and brevity. It's the most difficult thing of all, far more difficult than to write beautifully." Quoted by G. Munblit, in "Isaak Ėmmanuilovič Babel' (Iz vospominanij)," *Znamja*, No. 8 (Aug. 1964), 121.
33 *I. Babel': Izbrannoe* (Kemerovo, 1966), 11.

Street," "Di Grasso." But the inwardness of these stories, the intensity of their feeling, and the light of wisdom that they shed upon the unchanging human condition made their composition in Soviet Russia an act of treason. Refusing to produce hackneyed panegyrics to the state, Babel was fast becoming unpublishable.[34] Some of the stories, such as "The Road" and "My First Fee," were more complicated reworkings of earlier tales. As if obsessed, Babel kept returning to the images of his past work, forever reforming and rewriting certain basic themes, searching for their perfect expression. Victor Shklovsky, commenting in 1937 on Babel's by then protracted silence, felt that his problem lay in just this inability to discover new themes.[35] Babel, who might have agreed, was indeed seeking new content, but his search took the path of experimenting with new forms.

Babel's least productive experiment of the thirties was his attempt to write in a longer narrative form. He had always been attracted to the possibilities of a larger architectural frame, as his use of the connected cycle of tales indicates. But by the late twenties, when the short story was retreating before the advance in popularity of the novel, his inclination toward a larger scale became irresistible. Writing to Vyacheslav Polonsky in April 1929, Babel described, not without a certain ulterior hope that his words might help keep his impatient editor at bay, how this new impulse had taken possession of him:

> And now for my latest misfortune: in the past, when I was always casting about for novels, all I ever came up with were stories shorter than a sparrow's tail; but what a change God has wrought in me now. I try to polish off a little eight-page piece (because you'll die of starvation if you don't, you son of a bitch, I tell myself) and out of it, out of this tiny thing, comes a three-hundred-

34 One of the reasons for Babel's trouble was his frank interest in erotic situations and sexual relationships. This interest was nothing new, but with the greater development in his tales of psychological (as opposed to social) motivations, he was treading on ideologically dangerous ground. As a youth Babel had briefly been a student in a psychoneurological institute in Leningrad, and like most modern authors his writing reflects awareness of the discoveries and revelations of Freudian psychology. Certainly his work would repay study from this point of view.
35 Viktor Šklovskij, "O prošlom i nastojaščem," *Znamja*, No. 11 (1937), 278–88.

page novel. This is a major turnabout in a long-suffering life, my dear editor, but it's true—I have a thirst to write long! . . . And since I still compose not by the page, but word by word—you can imagine what my life is like. I'll send you the first draft in August, word of honor.[36]

There are numerous references in the literature on Babel to novels which he is said to have worked on or even to have completed. In the early twenties, for example, he had considered a book about the Cheka, and may actually have written sections of it. Another reported novel of the late twenties or early thirties, entitled *Kolya Topuz*, is supposed to have shown the remaking of a reprobate hero by means of the Soviet system of soul engineering. The stories "Gapa Guzhva" and "Kolyvushka," both dated 1930 and dealing with the upheavals of collectivization, also appear to be parts of a projected novel, but only the first of these was published during Babel's lifetime. He also completed at least part of still another long piece entitled *The Jewess*, but it too remained unpublished. Unfortunately almost nothing has survived from these several ambitious projects, and under the circumstances it is impossible even to know how much Babel completed, let alone to guess at the stylistic or thematic characteristics of his venture into longer forms.[37]

Babel's other major effort of the thirties, his playwriting, was a more successful attempt to discover a new path. Through the drama, as earlier through the epic, he found a means of subduing and rechanneling that deeply personal, lyric element which was a major component of his artistic temperament. There is a famous passage in which James Joyce, formulating a theory of aesthetics, discusses the lyric, epic, and dramatic modes of art:

Even in literature, the highest and most spiritual art, the forms are often confused. The lyrical form is in fact the simplest verbal

---

[36] Letter of April 8, 1929, in *I. Babel': Izbrannoe* (Moscow, 1966), 443.

[37] The unfinished manuscript of *The Jewess*, which has recently been published in the U.S. (see Bibliography), clearly demonstrates that Babel was seeking a new and more objective narrative style. Employing an impassionate and, for Babel, untypical third-person frame, the story shows a definite turn toward descriptive realism. It concerns the fate of a Jewish family, one much like Babel's, as it responds to the shock of great social changes.

vesture of an instant of emotion, a rhythmical cry such as ages ago cheered on the man who pulled at the oar or dragged stones up a slope. He who utters it is more conscious of the instant of emotion than of himself as feeling emotion. The simplest epical form is seen emerging out of lyrical literature when the artist prolongs and broods upon himself as the centre of an epical event and this form progresses till the centre of emotional gravity is equidistant from the artist himself and from others. The narrative is no longer purely personal. The personality of the artist passes into the narration itself, flowing round and round the persons and the actions like a vital sea. . . . The dramatic form is reached when the vitality which has flowed and eddied round each person fills every person with such vital force that he or she assumes a proper and intangible esthetic life. The personality of the artist, at first a cry or a cadence or a mood and then a fluid and lambient narrative, finally refines itself out of existence, impersonalizes itself, so to speak. The esthetic image in the dramatic form is life purified in and reprojected from the human imagination. The mystery of esthetic like that of material creation is accomplished. The artist, like the God of the creation, remains within or behind or beyond or above his handiwork, invisible, refined out of existence, indifferent, paring his fingernails.[38]

The progression that Joyce describes from lyric through epic to dramatic might almost be read as an exegesis of Babel's attempted creative path. In *Red Cavalry* he had reached that intermediate stage in which "the centre of emotional gravity" was equidistant from himself and from others. Many of his later narrative fictions were attempts to refine still more of the lyric intensity out of his writing, and his final effort—in a logical progression—was to essay the dramatic directly. Babel's first play, *Sunset*, which he worked on through much of 1926 and 1927, showed some departures from tradition as well as some new uses of it. First of all, the play has no acts, but is set in eight scenes. The action revolves around the five members of the Krik family, some of whom are familiar from *The Odessa Tales*, but in the play the lives of these Odessa carters and bandits is given a sordid rather than idealized coloring. It is the story of the decline

---

[38] James Joyce, *A Portrait of the Artist as a Young Man* (New York, 1964), 214–15.

and fall, the sunset, of the once mighty Mendel Krik. The old man, like a grotesque but not ignoble King Lear, rages against the passage of time and the loss of his youth and vigor. Resisting the succession of his sons and daughter, he seeks to recapture the past through an affair with a young girl, to flee to a mythical Bessarabia, to a garden of Eden where time and the generational law can be denied. But Mendel is brought low by his sons. Benja's rude entry into his father's bedroom at night announces the Oedipal theme and presages the fight for succession and mythic slaying to follow. The misrule and darkness that pervade the House of the Kriks (in Russian: "the House of Yells") come to stand for the decay of a world and for the end of its patriarchal way of life.

Through image and motif Mendel is linked, in Babel's usual manner, with symbolic figures of the past: Samson and Joshua and, mockingly, Christ.[39] These religious motifs find support in the play's language—in its proverbs, refrains, and biblical rhythms, which, as is frequently the case in Babel's Jewish settings, contrast with the comic effects of contemporary Odessa jargon. Mendel's tragedy is further defined through the use of a chorus—a bizarre and grotesque one, but a chorus nonetheless. Not only the choir of blind singers in the tavern scene but almost all of the minor characters serve a choral function; they sympathize with the hero, comment upon events, and follow the course of the family drama as if watching the fate of the gods (and thereby their own as well). The final banquet scene is a magnificent achievement. It is a celebration at once of Mendel's wake, Benja's accession, Dvoira's wedding, and Klasha Zubareva's pregnancy. It thus unites death, birth, and all that lies between in a

---

39 The play is full of obvious symbolic references. A few of the Christ images should suffice as an example: Mendel in his prime has stolen some telegraph poles and "carried them home on his shoulders" (the image suggests Samson as well as Christ); in the tavern scene he receives a "kiss of death"; in the graveyard his mistress, Marusya, and the priest, Father John, drink some wine that was Mendel's; the climactic battle with his sons takes place amid the apocalyptic setting of a crucifixion (one son is hard, one has pity, darkness fills the sky); in the final supper scene Mendel is robed and his pretensions to kingship are mocked.

hymn to life, to its pains and its joys. The old rabbi, speaking for the chorus at the close, gives a final explanation and benediction:

> Day is day, Jews, and evening is evening. Day drowns us in the sweat of our labors, but evening holds ready the fans of her divine coolness. Joshua, who stopped the sun, was only an impulsive fool. Jesus of Nazareth, who stole the sun, was an evil madman. And now Mendel Krik, a member of our synagogue, has proved to be no wiser than Joshua. He wanted to spend his whole life in the spot where noonday found him. But God has policemen on every street, and Mendel Krik had sons in his house. Policemen come and make order. Day is day, and evening is evening. All is in order, Jews. Let us drink a glass of vodka![40]

Despite the ecclesiastical rhetoric of the play's final speech, its philosophical import remains anticlerical. Babel's spirit in this work is still deeply Nietzschean. In the rabbi's last speech, both the Old and the New Testaments have been subtly rejected, and with them the dream of personal immortality, the hope of an end to time. Only the Dionysian, not the Hebraic-Christian, rebirth is at hand—the eternal recurrence, the cyclical rebirth not of persons, but of life itself. This is a concept, as Nietzsche perceived, which reinvests life with the tragic dimension that was lost with the Greeks, and thus Babel's comedy (as he called the play) was really an attempt to remind us once again that tragedy was born out of the worship of Dionysus, the god of wine who was hacked to death as a symbol of joy and life. The final stage directions of the play, like the sordid tale of the Kriks itself, bring the bacchic origins straight into view: "The tinkle of a flute, the ring of goblets, disconnected shouts, and thunderous laughter."

Babel was abroad when *Sunset* had its Moscow Art Theatre premiere in February 1928, and he expressed from a distance his misgivings about the play's reception. Foreseeing that the

---

[40] The text given here is quoted by G. A. Gukovskij in his article "Zakat," *I. E. Babel': Stat'i i materialy* (Leningrad, 1928), 90–91. Later editions of the play retain the reference to Joshua (Iisus Navin), but omit the one to Christ (Iisus iz Nazareta).

actors would find it difficult to tread his fine line between pathos and humor, and recognizing that the play had nothing in common with the political dramas then in fashion, he anticipated the failure that, indeed, came after sixteen performances.[41] Babel seems not to have been greatly upset, however, and his confidence in his powers did not desert him. To one of his friends in Moscow he wrote: "The 'event' has produced upon me, as it were, a favorable impression; first, because I was prepared for it and it therefore confirms my suspicion that I'm a sober and intelligent fellow; and secondly, because the fruits of this failure will be in the highest degree useful to me."[42] A few weeks later he was already talking of the future: "If I should ever again in my life write a play (and I believe that I shall), I'll make sure to be present during all the rehearsals."[43]

Several years were to pass, however, before Babel would again try a drama. The late twenties and early thirties were largely given over to his experiment with longer narrative forms, and only in the spring of 1933, while he was abroad, did Babel again make mention in his letters of a play. In May, while staying with Gorky, Babel suddenly announced to his friends the completion of a new drama, *Maria*. "As, of course, it does not fit in with the 'general party line,' " he wrote, "it can expect rough going, but everyone wholeheartedly acknowledges its artistic qualities. The settings and the characters are new ones, such as I've never used before, and if it comes off I shall be happy."[44] Gorky, to whom Babel read the manuscript in Sorrento, proved less than enthusiastic, however. He advised that the play in its current form not be submitted and even warned that people

41 An earlier production of the play in Babel's native Odessa, where both actors and audience had a keener appreciation for the characters and milieu, met with greater success. Recent years have witnessed a revival of interest in Babel's first drama, and productions have been mounted in Hungary, Czechoslovakia, East Germany, Israel, England, and elsewhere. In the Soviet Union, however, *Sunset* has yet to be restaged.

42 Letter of March 7, 1928, quoted in *Znamja*, No. 8 (Aug. 1964), 153.

43 Letter of March 20, 1928, quoted in *ibid.*, 154.

44 Letter of May 2, 1933, in *Isaac Babel: The Lonely Years*, 232.

would infer political attitudes from the text that would be harm-
ful for Babel.[45] Nonetheless, Babel was resolved to proceed with
his work and, after withholding the play until revisions could
be made, he submitted a new version. By February 1934, he was
writing from Russia that his play had been accepted and that
rehearsals were to begin almost at once with the Vakhtangov and
the Jewish theaters. But Babel's optimistic plans were soon cut
short. Both his own and Gorky's presentiments proved prophetic.
After an apparently stormy controversy and some considerable
suspense, performance of the play was abruptly forbidden. Babel
was able eventually to publish the text (which even then provoked a hostile reaction), but he was never to see *Maria* staged.[46]

*Maria* is a complex play, in form, style, and theme. As with
*Sunset*, Babel divides the action into eight brief scenes, and he
further, in a striking move, keeps his title character completely
offstage. The setting is Petrograd, 1920, a year that was crucial
for the war-ravaged Soviet state. In returning for his theme to
this early Revolutionary period, to the time of civil war, Babel
was evincing once again his fascination with that particular
moment when history seemed about to change course. Naturally
he knew that the subject had been treated in literature often
and that in the climate of the thirties it might well seem untopical
and long out of date, but for Babel the potent attraction of that
moment of upheaval had not yet been exhausted. In his new
work he would approach the theme from a different direction,
obliquely, through the microcosmic portrayal of the Revolution's effect on a single family and the people about them.

The Mukovnins are a new departure for Babel in character
portrayal. Members of the pre-Revolutionary intelligentsia, they
recall in their now degraded circumstances those decaying fami-

45 Gorky had reservations about the play's literary qualities as well. His final
verdict was that "the play is cold, its purpose is indefinite, the author's aim unclear." The letter in which Gorky expressed his views is of uncertain date, but
if one can judge from his reference to the manuscript, he was probably speaking
of an early draft. Gorky's full letter is in *Literaturnoe nasledstvo* (Moscow, 1963),
LXX, 43–44.

46 The play never has been produced in the Soviet Union, but it has in recent
years been performed in Czechoslovakia and, with particular success, in Italy.

lies of Chekhov's great plays, *The Cherry Orchard* and *Three Sisters*. Like them, the Mukovnins are an emasculated breed; the line has run to women. General Mukovnin, the father, immerses himself in the past to avoid confronting a present in which his daughter Ludmila sells her body for food. The old nurse Nefedovna, worn by toil and bewildered in her old age by an unexpected insecurity, calls to mind Firs, the old servant of the Ranevskys. The decay of the family spreads outward, embracing all who belong to their circle: it touches Golitsyn, the former prince who has retreated from life into religious quietism, and it falls upon the family's serving companion, Katya, who speaks for them all when she says, "People like us are unfortunate and we'll never be happy. We've been sacrificed, Nikolai Vasilyevich."[47]

Along with this Chekhovian strain there are more typically Babelian motifs and characters. The scenes at the Mukovnin home alternate with a series of scenes that take place inside sordid back rooms and even at a police station; the aristocratic Mukovnins depend for their existence on the Jewish fence Dymshits and his band of smugglers, a beastlike crew of decrepit, disabled former soldiers. There are several crudely naturalistic scenes in which sexual encounters, including a rape, take place either directly on stage or described in dialogue—rather as if the rotting world of the play were still struggling through its flesh to survive. Most of the sexual pairings, a sign of the social collapse and impending transformation, seem incongruous: Dymshits and a princess, Dymshits and Ludmila, Viskovsky and Ludmila, Katya and the Cheka agent Redko, the sailor Kravchenko and the French woman Dora, Maria and Golitsyn, Maria and the Red Army Commander.

The figure of Maria gives a symbolic dimension to the play. By her absence Maria is set apart from all of the other Mukovnins and is thus exempted from the decay and corruption which have become their lot. She is the strong one ("the only real woman among us," says Katya), the sister who has joined the political section of the army to work actively in the Revolutionary cause.

47 *I. Babel': Izbrannoe*, 339.

Her support of that cause is no small tribute in the eyes of Babel, for she is both Mary and Life, giving birth to the future. She has deserted her family (the name Mukovnin in Russian suggests "sufferers, the tormented," those passed by: old Russia and old world) not without pity and love, but through necessity—as a result of the inevitable renewal of life.[48] And if Maria is Mary as well as Life, she has also left her son, the ascetic former prince and impotent redeemer Golitsyn. There are several additional motifs and symbols which might be adduced to support and corroborate this interpretation, but one should suffice: the symbolic ring of the Mukovnins. Endowed with an extraordinary power, this ring exerts its spell on several of the characters: on Ludmila, who would steal it; on Dymshits, who would sell it; and on Viskovsky, who dreams of fleeing with it to Paris. But, significantly, the ring is identified with Maria; she and not her fallen sister has inherited the family treasure, which is not a jewel but a symbol of strength and continuity, of the eternal circular rhythm of life which moves upward through decay to a new creation. Such is the manifest meaning as well of the play's last scene, in which a new set of characters moves onto the stage and into the Mukovnins' vacated house. At the end the ring is invoked once more in the song of the cleaning girl Nyusha, who stands at the window like a caryatid supporting the firmaments, framed by the sunlight of spring.

For all its implied faith in the future, Babel's play, like most of his later writings, fixes its gaze upon the crumbling past. No doubt this, as well as the originality of his form and style, accounts for the ultimate banning of the play. The censor, true to form, proved unable to abide a philosophical independence from the narrow clichés of Soviet ideology. Babel, however, continued

---

48 This is the choice that Babel believed himself to have made as well. In the name of life and the future he was prepared both to give and to accept those private sufferings that his abandonment of family and past would bring. Perhaps in the character Dymshits, who is also separated from his family, there is a less favorable estimate of his decision and act; or perhaps in that figure Babel sought a symbol through which he might purge his beliefs of their personal stain and thus (in the figure of Maria) allow them the beauty of an ideal.

to hope that a change in official attitudes would eventually allow his drama to be performed, and in the meantime a flood of creative energy was pushing him forward.

He had barely completed *Maria* when he was writing to relatives that he had started another play, one to which he attached even greater importance. "A great change," he tells them, "has come over me—I don't feel like writing in prose. I want to use only the dramatic form."[49] *Maria* was apparently intended as only the first link of a planned trilogy which was to embrace the period from 1920 to 1935. Nothing of Babel's further labors in the drama is known to have survived, however, and what was perhaps the most promising of his later experiments thus came to a premature end. With his mastery of dialogue and his attempt at a wedding of the naturalistic and symbolist traditions, Babel had given promise of a large and original dramatic talent. The two plays he completed show the tragicomedy to have been his chosen form, but that future in which Babel had placed his faith was now taking the direction of pure tragedy.

The fate of *Maria* can be seen in retrospect as marking the end of Babel's career. In the years after 1935 very few of his writings could expect publication, and he himself, like the rest of his countrymen, had to contend with the pervasive fear and mistrust of that terrible time. His personal response to the danger was to maintain an almost unbroken silence. His editors continued to badger him for manuscripts, but Babel felt compelled to respond by playing a cautious game of hide-and-seek, to wheedle advances on the promise of new work and then beg for more time in an endless routine of delays and excuses. "As long as I don't publish I am merely accused of laziness. If, on the other hand, I publish, then a veritable avalanche of weighty and dangerous accusations will descend upon my head. I feel like a beautiful girl at a ball, with whom everyone wishes to dance. If I were to let myself be persuaded, however, the entire gathering, like a single person, would instantly turn against me. As soon as I had begun to

<hr>

[49] *Isaac Babel: The Lonely Years*, 275. See also his remarks in the letters given on pp. 246, 250, and 254 of this reference.

dance, it would become apparent that I was beautiful only so long as I stood on the side. . . . Among those who invite me to the dance . . . are many who do it only because they know that as soon as I accept the first waltz . . . *Addio mare.*"[50] Thus is Babel quoted by an acquaintance who shared his house for several months in 1936–37. Throughout these years, the writer occupied himself with the spiritually unrewarding but less dangerous work of rewriting ailing scenarios: "Daily I read idiotic screenplay manuscripts and revise them. I do anything—just in order not to write, let alone publish."[51]

What a terrifying confession for a man who had given everything for art, for whom writing was a kind of religious vocation. But Babel's art, like his dreams, had been crushed beneath the ruins of Utopia. By the late thirties no hope remained for a return to the untarnished idealism of the Revolution's earlier days. In service to that idealism Babel had tried to make himself a hard, rational realist, but he was to the end an inveterate romantic and humanist. A compassionate man, he was compelled to express his compassion, and for this—despite his deep, self-sacrificing commitment to Revolutionary ideals—Babel, like many others in Stalin's Russia, was found to be expendable. All of his life he had fought against the threatening power of an essentially tragic vision. Looking back one sees that the struggle against fate, in one form or another, is inherent in all that he wrote, and Babel's own life takes on the contours of a tragic tale—a tale of presumptuous longings, of noble impulses, of guilt and ultimate defeat. In his work, however, Babel never relinquished his belief that joy, not tragedy, was life's truest promise. The joyous vision in which he had a personal stake is increasingly removed in his later work toward an impersonal future, but it is never completely abandoned. All those pregnant women and newborn infants who inhabit his stories and plays become the

---

[50] E. Sinkó, *Roman eines Romans*, 314. Sinkó's account of his relationship with Babel makes for sad and oppressive reading, but it provides a revealing supplement to the picture given in Babel's evasive and politically uninformative letters to his relatives.

[51] *Ibid.,* 346.

final repository for his hopes and dreams. The story "Karl Yankel," in which the child's name evokes Babel's old Hebrew-
Marxist synthesis once more, expresses the import of them all:
"It's not possible, Karl Yankel, that you won't be happy. It's not
possible that you won't be happier than I."

Blasphemy, as T. S. Eliot remarked, is closer to belief than indifference, and Babel, a mocker who created myths of his own
in order to give some form to the anarchy of contemporary history, was never as far from the religious as he seemed. Still, in
his later stories, one does hear the awful confession of guilt, and
in their search for purgation the terrible note of doom. The story
"Guy de Maupassant," reverting again to the personal past,
acknowledges a returning sense of sin, and with it comes a new
alienation—not this time as a Jew, but as an artist, one whose
heart contracts "at the foreboding touch of some ominous truth."
In "Di Grasso," almost his last and certainly one of his finest tales,
Babel writes of his youth with a knowledge of all that has happened in the years of manhood. "A Tale of Odessa" is the story's
subtitle, and it evokes what for Babel was the heroic and hopeful beginning of his Odyssey. It takes place "the year the Italian
opera flopped in Odessa," when the narrator was a boy of fourteen, and supplies a final restatement of Babel's concept of art.

One of the story's most interesting features is its use of the
play within the tale, another instance of Babel's setting of mo-
tion within the static and a kind of structural metaphor for his
theme of art as controlled violence. In the play are represented,
one guesses, Babel's views of the possibilities of both life and
art. The drama itself is a pedestrian one, and its conventional
depiction of betrayal, injustice, and disillusion would seem to
reflect what Babel apprehends as the given texture of life. But
suddenly, in the play's one transcendent moment of passion, the
villain Giovanni is brought down by his victim's soaring, mur-
derous leap of revenge. The wronged peasant who is "swung
aloft by an incomprehensible power" is played by the tragedian
Di Grasso, and his performance provides an incontrovertible
proof that "there is more justice and hope in an outburst of

noble passion than in all the joyless rules of this world." The leap of the hero then becomes a metaphor for Babel's continuing belief in the heroic; in redeeming aesthetically the mediocrity of the play in which it is mired, the act also suggests the possibility of shattering the bondage to which man is condemned, and in its violent enactment it proposes once again the renunciation of that passivity which Babel abhorred. That the violence takes place not only in the name of justice, but within the framework of art, lends it a kind of moral purity that Babel seldom achieved, and this moral dimension is furthermore carried beyond the limits of art and is seen to have consequences in the lives of those who were witness to its power.

The young boy, whose profound experience of art has become the mature writer's theme, is himself in bondage to the oppressive reality of life outside the theater. He has taken without permission and pawned with the unscrupulous ticketseller for whom he works a watch which belongs to his father and which at any moment may be missed. Although the boy has repaid his loan, the ticketseller refuses to part with his trophy, and the youth is thus caught between the claims of two unjust, constraining figures of authority. Preparing to run away, he decides to make a farewell visit to the theater, where Di Grasso is playing the role of the noble shepherd for the last time. The audience on this final night includes Kolya Schwartz, his tormentor, and his fat, ungainly wife. It is this grotesque and unlikely creature who, moved by Di Grasso's performance to the recollection of noble sentiments, demands that her husband give back the watch. An aesthetic experience has given rise to a generous act, and although it is only the impulsive gesture of a moment, for the youth it means nothing less than the renewal of life's possibilities. Through the power of art, time itself has been redeemed, freed from its bondage to meanness and fear. The effect on the young narrator of this coming together of life and art is a sublime catharsis; poised between boyhood and manhood, he is granted in the story's closing paragraph a vision of eternal peace, an intimation of immortality. As he gazes around him he sees for the first time things as they really are, "frozen in silence and ineffably beautiful." The current Soviet regime, however, allowed of no such beauty, and with the death of Gorky in June 1936 the cloud of fear and isolation enveloping Babel wrapped itself closer around him. During August of 1936, as the first of the great purge trials began, Babel retreated—in life as in art—to Odessa, away from the dangers and disillusions of the present to the place where he had hoped, as he remarked in his remembrance of the poet Bagritsky, to grow old in the sun, sitting by the sea and gazing at the women as they passed. But the dream of an Odessan future, like that of a return to an Odessan past, was not fated to be. Babel had to go back for the playing out of the final act to the north, to the despised Moscow. From there he still writes to his family abroad, but the thought of their eventual reunion is expressed no more, and his letters studiously avoid any indication of the true nature of his existence.[52] When he can he escapes to his country house, situated not in Odessa where he wished, but in Peredelkino, the writers' colony not far from the capital.

There, in his dacha, on the morning of May 15, 1939, Babel was arrested. "They didn't allow me to finish," he is reported to have said as he was taken away.[53] But among those things that he did finish are some of the finest short stories of our time. "At least ... you will read the stories," he had once comforted his bereaved family,[54] and these exist for others as well. The precise manner and date of Babel's death are unknown. The rest was silence.

[52] Babel eventually remarried, and in Jan. 1937, his second child, another daughter, was born.
[53] *Isaac Babel: The Lonely Years*, xxvi.
[54] *Ibid.*, 187.

# X

# EPILOGUE

When Isaac Babel declared himself the master of a new genre of silence at the first Soviet Writers' Congress in 1934, he gave what has since seemed a tragically accurate characterization of his creative activity during the last decade of his life. To some it has appeared that if Babel, unlike many of his contemporaries, retained his artistic integrity, he did so at the cost of ignoring publicly some of the great moral issues of his time and place.

Having survived the worst of the purges physically unharmed, Babel was still free as late as 1939, at a time when the wheels of terror and violence were at last grinding to a halt. Then, suddenly and unexpectedly, he was arrested. All work in progress as well as the unpublished manuscripts that Babel still held were seized by the secret police and have since disappeared. Subsequently, Babel's very name was expunged from the official histories of Soviet literature, and for some twenty years not one of his works was republished. Then in December 1954 following a reexamination of his case by a military tribunal, Babel was partially and posthumously "rehabilitated," and during the so-called "thaw" that accompanied official de-Stalinization the way was opened for republication of at least some of his works. In 1957 and again in 1966 collected editions of Babel's writings were at last reissued, but in severely edited form and to the accompaniment of new attacks against him in the Soviet press.

The actual circumstances of Babel's fate have remained shrouded in mystery and surrounded by rumor. The military tribunal that reviewed his case announced the revocation of his sentence, but failed to indicate what that sentence had been. An official death certificate, also issued in 1954, gives the date of Babel's death as March 17, 1941, but whether this information is accurate and whether he was ever actually accorded a trial remain uncertain. We shall probably never know the complete details of what actually happened to Isaac Babel, and if we were to uncover them it would do nothing to mitigate his personal tragedy or our sense of shameful waste. With regard to the mystery of Babel's arrest, however, the situation is different, and any discovery in this area might cast a significant light on Babel both as artist and as man. In 1963 a recently unearthed and previously unknown original screenplay by Babel was published in a Soviet film journal. Very likely the last work that the writer completed, it offers a convincing explanation for his arrest and a demonstration that silence was not the only answer that Babel gave to his country's anguish.

The scenario, entitled *Old Square, No. 4*, is one of the few original works Babel did for the screen and was written in twenty days during April of 1939.[1] Such a burst of creative energy is unusual in a writer who often took years to polish a single story, and it may point to a special sense of urgency prompting his labor. That Babel actually submitted the script to the studio is apparent from notes made on the manuscript by some editor or director, but it was never filmed and indeed fell into that limbo of "lost works" which seems to hold so large a part of Babel's writing.

[1] The scenario is found in *Iskusstvo kino*, XXXIII, No. 5 (Moscow, 1963), 54–78. In his introductory article, L. Livšic, the text's editor, describes and discusses the manuscript, the authenticity of which he considers to be beyond question. Apart from this brief and rather careful discussion, the screenplay has been ignored by both Soviet and Western critics.

At first glance the scenario is a disappointment. Loosely structured and constantly dissolving into apparently unconnected digressions, it hardly seems the work of so conscious a craftsman and stylist as Babel. A number of poorly realized secondary characters obscure the plot lines, and the theme itself is far from promising. On the eve of war, the Soviet Union has need of a greater development of its military-scientific resources. The script tells of the efforts to speed construction of an advanced type of dirigible. Several mutually hostile scientists seem to be competing for control of the project, and one, the villain of the piece, comes close to wrecking the entire operation. On the whole the scenario would seem to belong to that all too familiar and depressing genre, the Soviet construction melodrama. On closer analysis, however, the screenplay takes on a quite different shape. Some of its surface coloring begins to recede; other elements, at first unnoticed, fall into bolder relief and acquire a deeper significance. The more one examines the script, the more it assumes the proportions of a far-reaching political allegory.[2]

The conflicts that form the basis of the plot involve disputes about the type of guidance system to be used in the new airship and about who shall be chief designer for the project. But there is a hidden, more significant theme. The name of the tradition-shattering airship is "USSR-1," and the script's rather incongruous title, *Old Square, No. 4,* is a fictional address for the headquarters of the Party's Central Committee. Taken together these are crucial indicators of the play's central political theme and of the fact that the conflicts being allegorized concern the destiny of the ship of state itself and that they raged at the highest level of political power. As the issues, personalities, and essential lines of the conflict take shape, they begin to resemble events of the first two decades after the Revolution.

Zhukov, a wild, black-maned, bearded inventor, has been appointed chief designer, and his controversial guidance system

---

2 Allegory, as we have seen, is not foreign to Babel's earlier work either, and in some of the later stories (e.g., "Di Grasso" and "Oil") there are allegorized hints of a specifically political nature.

has been selected for the experimental model of the dirigible. For him the present project, visionary as it is, is only the first step in a grand scheme to reach the moon, to conquer the cosmos itself. His opponents consider him eccentric and dangerous, a mad, impractical dreamer whose wild ideas will jeopardize the immediate goal of launching the new airship. The highly respected academician and theoretician Tolmazov, for twenty years a critic and rival of Zhukov's, is unable to conceal his indignation over Zhukov's selection as chief designer. The grounds of his opposition go beyond personal antagonism to fundamental theoretical differences: he believes the airship as Zhukov has designed it will not leave the ground. Others, for less principled reasons, join the attack in an attempt to block Zhukov's appointment. The charges leveled against him have the same ring: he is a fantasist, a madman, an autodidact. Zhukov is not, however, entirely without backing. His position is buttressed by unwavering support from rank-and-file members of the Party, and he strikes back by labeling Tolmazov a "high priest of science" and a "Nikonite." (Nikon was the seventeenth-century patriarch who precipitated the schism in the Russian church with his corrections and revisions in church texts and rituals.) When one places these charges and countercharges (fantasist, madman, self-taught vs. scholasticism, nikonism-revisionism) within a political context, they strikingly resemble those that swirled about the heads of prominent Revolutionary figures. "Perpetuum mobile," another of the critical remarks against Zhukov, sounds more than faintly reminiscent of a theory of permanent revolution, and the two rival scientists come to look like leaders of the so-called left and right opposition groups. Finally, and with a kind of shock, the features of Trotsky and Bukharin unavoidably come to mind.

But the most intriguing character in the play is a personage who does not occupy center stage at all—Professor Polibin, the scientist who eventually emerges as the villain. Polibin is a rather shadowy being on the periphery of the action whose appearances are almost invariably announced by his honeyed tenor voice. His arrival at the construction site, where he wishes to discuss possible candidates for the post of chief designer, is the cause of general alarm. It was he who, in secret, tried to block Zhukov's appointment with the charges of "madman" and "perpetuum mobile." Tolmazov, Zhukov's rival, he damns with faint praise, calling him "an academician and theoretician of the purest water." When the project director inquires whether Polibin himself might be persuaded to take on the job of chief designer, he is obviously pleased, but the project director decides on further consultation. Polibin, although he is always addressed with great respect as "professor" or even "esteemed professor," seems to possess no particular scientific abilities, and it is Zhukov who finally receives the appointment. Polibin, however, is extremely adroit in using the mutual hostility of his two colleagues to his own advantage; he aligns himself tentatively with Tolmazov, he is gently (at first) critical of Zhukov's design. His cautious political maneuvering is strikingly underscored by his peculiar voice and his almost obsessive use of the conditional mood. It is quite clear that Polibin has no attachment to either of the opposing schools and no alternative theory of his own; his only real concern is to improve his position, to outwit others in a bid for power. In pursuit of this goal Polibin enlists the aid of others, who are made his dupes. The younger scientist Vasiliev is a case in point. An opponent of Zhukov and ostensibly a follower of Tolmazov, he seems to have surreptitious links with Polibin. When his name is first brought up in connection with the dirigible project, it is Polibin who introduces it. When he is actually appointed to the design committee, it is not at the request of his superior, Tolmazov, but through unspecified and rather mysterious channels. There is an echo of Polibin's charge of "dilletantism" when Vasiliev accuses Zhukov of "amateurism and recklessness"; sometimes his opposition sounds even more ominous, as when he threatens to call either a psychiatric hospital or the NKVD concerning Zhukov.

Vasiliev's wife, an engineer on the project, is staunchly committed to Zhukov and considers her husband's activity shameful and stupid, worse than treason. But Vasiliev is enmeshed in

his ties with Polibin. When the first flight ends in a crash land-
ing, discrediting both Zhukov and Tolmazov, it is to the confused
Vasiliev that Polibin explains the delights of such a "combination shot." But the master is less than pleased with the help he
has received from his protégé Vasiliev; he tells him that if he
had been more energetic in the handling of his assignment,
Zhukov and company would never have budged, and he suggests
that as his deputy when he himself becomes chief designer he will
need someone who can handle an assignment with greater
assurance.

The near disaster of the flight is Polibin's cue to emerge from
the sidelines, and in his new, contemptuously aggressive de-
meanor there is no resemblance to the former self-effacing "professor." He is exultant in anticipation of the revenge his triumph
will bring, and to Tolmazov, who has belatedly decided to join
forces with Zhukov, Polibin is cuttingly malicious. "For an
academician," he hisses, "such energy is laudable, but just a little
late." For all the principal figures, the situation has become
threatening: the director is to await the results of an investigation before continuing the project; Zhukov is to be removed from
his post at once; and the dirigible, the Revolutionary ship itself,
is to be tossed on the dump heap or carted off to the pawnshop.
Nor is this all. Materials have been turned over to the public
prosecutor, and the chairman of the newly appointed investigat-
ing commission is none other than Polibin himself, whose first
official act is to order the hangar sealed and work stopped.

In all of this there is, it seems clear, more than a hint at the
powerful figure whose ambitions knew neither limits nor scruples
and whose bloody purges decimated the ranks of the Communist
Party. The more one ponders the structure of this screenplay, the
more irresistibly the impression grows that the figure of Polibin
is a portrait of Joseph Stalin. There is an almost exact parallel
between Polibin's methods and the shrewd, deceitful political tac-
tics which Stalin employed to oust his potential rivals—Trotsky,
Bukharin, and others. There is even a reflection of Stalin's well-
known technique of avoiding a personal commitment on issues,

of biding his time. There are hints at his method of using other people to do the more disagreeable tasks and of his notorious ingratitude for services performed. Polibin's whole personality is suggestive: the false modesty, the contempt for men of superior intellectual abilities, the vindictiveness and utter lack of conscience—all of these bring Stalin vividly to mind. Is all of this to be taken as an accident, a coincidence? That seems improbable. And if these impressions are correct, they are only the beginning. Babel not only analyzes his shadowy villain; he condemns his power as the end of everything that talented, idealistic, decent people have struggled for, and he suggests a way to combat the apparent victory of a Polibin.

With the order to seal the hangar and stop all work the dirigible project appears doomed. Zhukov, who was wounded in the test flight, is disheartened and no longer provides effective leadership to those who believe in his ideas. But there are some who will not simply stand by and watch the scrapping of the "USSR-1." Babel makes a point of emphasizing that it is the younger Communists who rebel; even Vasiliev at last joins their ranks as they stage a false fire alarm so that the dirigible will have to be sent into the air to avoid destruction. In this illegal, second flight (a sort of second Revolution), the ship and its adherents are completely vindicated. As it soars into the sky it is seen by Polibin, whose car is racing along the highway below; its path is followed by the older workers on the ground, by Zhukov and Tolmazov; and it is admired by the pilots, correspondents, and others who have hurried from Moscow at the good news. With the "USSR-1" safe and in flight, the ship of state would seem to be back on its course.

The careful reader of this scenario will come to the inescapable conclusion that Babel, the master of silence, found, near the end of the thirties, a voice. It may be that Babel spoke more from a sense of public and moral duty than in answer to the call of his muse, but the firmness of his decision is unmistakable. Writing to relatives abroad on April 20, 1939, just after completing the script, Babel expressed both relief and satisfaction at the end of his labors:

Oof! . . . A mountain has fallen from my shoulders. I've just completed my job—I wrote a scenario in twenty days! Now, I suppose, I'll be able to lead an "honest life." Am leaving for Moscow on the 22nd in the evening. The completion of my labors has coincided with the first Spring day—the sun is shining. I'll go and have a walk now after my righteous efforts.[3]

Like one of the characters in his screenplay (the Jewish pilot Friedman, who exclaims, "I'll burn the dirigible before the grave diggers will ever see it! . . . You don't know me, Petrenko . . ."), Babel had come to a point where moral indignation demanded expression. After a decade of near silence he came forth with a bitingly sharp analysis of Stalinism and a denunciation of its pervasive evils. But although he attacks the disease, he believes the organism will survive. With his incomparable trust in the future, Babel expresses his enduring faith in the true Revolution and a firm hope that a younger generation will rise up in its defense. As a consequence of his own courage in speaking out, Babel himself was very shortly to pay: within a few weeks of his submitting the manuscript, he was arrested.[4]

The question remains as to why Babel chose to speak out when he did. Perhaps it was simply the unbearable weight of all the suffering and fear accumulated through those years of purges, or perhaps particular circumstances combined to prompt his decision.[5] Babel's thoughts at this time must have returned more

3 *Isaac Babel: The Lonely Years*, 377.
4 Certain aspects of this scenario may offer an explanation for the persistent rumors linking Babel's arrest with a charge of "Trotskyism." That bespectacled Jewish intellectual and activist, war leader and literateur, whose Judaic passion for the Revolution he shared, may indeed have been one of Babel's heroes. Trotsky's concept of permanent revolution, in particular, would surely have appealed to the writer who (in *Sunset*) called Jesus and Joshua, those slayers of the sun, madmen. The theme of eternal recurrence, of life as an unending cycle of transference, has been suggested several times as one of Babel's basic motifs.
5 Because of Babel's habitual reticence concerning work in progress, it is impossible to state with certainty when he first conceived the idea of writing this screenplay. It may well be that the work is the result of a sudden decision, and

than once to his former mentor, Maxim Gorky, who had died on the eve of the great purge and who may himself have been one of its victims. During the days when Babel decided, quite suddenly it seems, to write this amazing scenario, he was already at work on a film of Gorky's life, and through most of April 1939 he was in Leningrad, revisting places connected with his early association with Gorky and with the beginnings of his own career. It may well have seemed to Babel that his life had run full circle and that he stood at a crossroad of decision. But whatever the immediate cause of his action it defines him as a figure whose moral courage assumes the quality of grandeur, bearing witness to the dignity and the hope of man.

---

if such is the case it may suggest (together with Babel's uncharacteristic hurry to complete and turn in the scenario) that he had a premonition of impending disaster. Ervin Sinkó, in his memoirs, states unequivocally that in the late thirties Babel found a new protector in none other than the NKVD chief himself, Nikolai Yezhov. With Yezhov's fall from power in Nov. 1938 and his subsequent disappearance (he was last seen publicly in March 1939), Babel may indeed have felt the breath of terror. According to Sinkó, Babel was an old friend of Yezhov's wife, which makes it not unlikely that she and her husband are the persons represented in the screenplay by Vasiliev and his wife.

# BIBLIOGRAPHY

I. The Works of Isaac Babel
(with first known publication where available)

There is no definitive, scholarly edition of Babel's works. Practically all Soviet editions bear at least some marks of censorship, and Babel himself made various changes in his works as new editions presented him the opportunity. Furthermore, no single edition contains all of the author's corpus, relatively small as it appears to be. The most recent Soviet editions, while in scope more comprehensive than earlier collections, have been both selective and edited.

Some of Babel's writing, appearing in relatively obscure and short-lived provincial magazines or newspapers, has never been republished and is practically unobtainable, and there is reason to believe as well that he may have finished a number of works that have never been published at all. Over the years an occasional new piece does appear, either newly discovered or unearthed in some long-forgotten journal of the early Soviet period. There may be other material of this kind available in the Soviet Union; if so, it most likely belongs either to Babel's earliest creative period or to late work that was confiscated at the time of his arrest. We may expect to see such things trickle into print in an unsatisfactory piecemeal fashion until Soviet scholars undertake to give us a good complete edition—soon we hope.

A word should be said about the author's dating which accompanies several of the stories listed below. Due to Babel's method of revising his material over long periods of time, these dates frequently are not accurate indications of when a story was written. Furthermore, with regard to the *Red Cavalry* stories, the dates given refer not to the time of composition, but to the time of the events related in the stories.

This bibliographical information has been compiled from a number of sometimes contradictory sources. Since it has proved impossible to check all of these references, more than one entry is sometimes given for a single piece—as, for example, when there are indications that publication took place in two or three journals almost simultaneously. The bibliography also includes such information as is available, again from widely scattered sources, on Babel's newspaper and film work, and there is a listing as well of such unpublished works as may yet be forthcoming. The result is the most comprehensive bibliography of Babel's writings to be found either in the Soviet Union or abroad.

### Konarmija

"Perexod čerez Zbruč." First published in *Pravda*, No. 175 (Aug. 3, 1924), under the heading "Iz dnevnika." Published again in *Krasnaja nov'*, No. 3 (April 1925). Dated by the author "Novograd-Volynsk, July, 1920."

"Kostel v Novograde." First published in the newspaper *Izvestija Odesskogo gubispolkoma KP(b)U i gubprofsoveta*, No. 963 (Feb. 18, 1923), under the heading "Iz knigi 'Konarmija'." Again in *Krasnaja niva*, No. 39 (Sept. 1924).

"Pis'mo." First published in the newspaper *Izvestija Odesskogo gubispolkoma*, No. 957 (Feb. 11, 1923), under the heading "Iz knigi 'Konarmija' " and again in the magazine *Lef*, No. 4 (Aug.–Dec. 1923). Dated by the author "Novograd-Volynsk, June, 1920."

"Načal'nik konzapasa." In *Lef*, No. 4 (Aug.–Dec. 1923), under the original title "D'jakov." Under its present title in the first book edition of *Konarmija* (Moscow, 1926). Dated by the author "Belev, July, 1920."

"Pan Apolek." In *Krasnaja nov'*, No. 7 (Dec. 1923), under the heading "Miniatjury."

"Solnce Italii." In *Krasnaja nov'*, No. 3 (April–May 1924), under the title "Sidorov" and with author's dating "Novograd, July, 1920." Under its present title in the first book edition of *Konarmija* (Moscow, 1926).

"Gedali." In *Krasnaja nov'*, No. 4 (June–July 1924), with the subtitle "Iz knigi 'Konarmija'." Dated by the author "Žitomir, June, 1920."

"Moj pervyj gus'." In *Lef*, No. 1 (1924), with the subtitle "Iz knigi 'Konarmija'." Dated by the author "July, 1920."

"Rabbi." In *Krasnaja nov'*, No. 1 (Jan.–Feb. 1924).

"Put' v Brody." First published in the literary supplement to *Izvestija Odesskogo gubispolkoma*, No. 1060 (June 17, 1923), under the heading "Iz knigi 'Konarmija'." Again in the journal *Prožektor*, No. 21 (Dec. 1923). Dated by the author "Brody, August, 1920."

"Učenie o tačanke." In *Izvestija Odesskogo gubispolkoma*, No. 967 (Feb. 23, 1923), under the heading "Iz knigi 'Konarmija'." Again in *Prožektor*, No. 21 (Dec. 1923).

"Smert' Dolgušova." In *Izvestija Odesskogo gubispolkoma*, No. 1022 (May 1, 1923), under the heading "Iz knigi 'Konarmija'." Again in the magazine *Ogonek*, No. 9 (May 1923) and also in *Lef*, No. 4 (Aug.–Dec. 1923). Dated by the author "Brody, August, 1920."

"Kombrig dva." In *Lef*, No. 4 (Aug.–Dec. 1923), under the title "Kolesnikov." Under its present title in the first book edition of *Konarmija* (Moscow, 1926). Dated by the author "Brody, August, 1920."

"Saška Xristos." In *Krasnaja nov'*, No. 1 (Jan.–Feb. 1924).

"Žizneopisanie Pavličenki, Matveja Rodionyča." In the Odessa magazine *Škval*, No. 8 (Dec. 1924). Again in the journal *30 dnej*, No. 1 (April 1925).

"Kladbišče v Kozine." In *Izvestija Odesskogo gubispolkoma*, No. 967 (Feb. 23, 1923), under the heading "Iz knigi 'Konarmija'." Again in *Prožektor*, No. 21 (Dec. 1923).

"Priščepa." In the literary-scientific supplement to the newspaper *Izvestija Odesskogo gubispolkoma*, No. 1060 (June 17, 1923), under the heading "Iz knigi 'Konarmija'." Again in *Lef*, No. 4 (Aug.–Dec. 1923). Dated by the author "Demidovka, July, 1920."

"Istorija odnoj lošadi." In *Krasnaja nov'*, No. 3 (April–May 1924), under the title "Timošenko i Mel'nikov." Under its present title in the first book edition of *Konarmija* (Moscow, 1926). Dated by the author "Radzivillov, July, 1920."

"Konkin." In *Krasnaja nov'*, No. 3 (April–May 1924). Dated by the author "Dubno, August, 1920."

"Berestečko." In *Krasnaja nov'*, No. 3 (April–May 1924). Dated by the author "Berestečko, August, 1920."

"Sol'." In the literary supplement to the newspaper *Izvestija Odesskogo gubispolkoma*, No. 1195 (Nov. 25, 1923), under the heading "Iz knigi 'Konarmija'." Again in *Lef*, No. 4 (Aug.–Dec. 1923).

"Večer." In *Krasnaja nov'*, No. 3 (April 1925), under the title "Galin" and with the heading "Iz dnevnika." Also in the Odessa magazine *Škval*, No. 15 (1925). Under its present title in the first book edition of *Konarmija* (Moscow, 1926). Dated by the author "Kovel', 1920."

"Afon'ka Bida." In *Krasnaja nov'*, No. 1 (Jan.–Feb. 1924).

"U svjatogo Valenta." In *Krasnaja nov'*, No. 3 (April–May 1924). Dated by the author "Berestečko, August, 1920."

"Èskadronnyj Trunov." In *Krasnaja nov'*, No. 2 (Feb. 1925), with the subtitle "Iz knigi 'Konarmija'." Again in the Odessa magazine *Škval*, No. 13 (1925).

"Ivany." In the magazine *Russkij sovremennik*, No. 1 (1924), with the subtitle "Iz knigi 'Konarmija'."

"Prodolženie istorii odnoj lošadi." In *Krasnaja nov'*, No. 3 (1924). Originally published together with first part under the single title "Timošenko i Mel'nikov." Under the present title in the first book edition of *Konarmija* (Moscow, 1926). Dated by the author "Galicija, September, 1920."

"Vdova." In the literary supplement to the newspaper *Izvestija Odesskogo gubispolkoma*, No. 1084 (July 15, 1923), under the title "Ševelev" and with the heading "Iz knigi 'Konarmija'." Again under the same title in *Krasnaja nov'*, No. 3 (April–May 1924). Under its present title in the first book edition of *Konarmija* (Moscow, 1926). Dated by the author "Galicija, August, 1920."

"Zamost'e." In *Krasnaja nov'*, No. 3 (April–May 1924). Dated by the author "Sokal', September, 1920."

"Izmena." In the literary anthology *Proletarij* (Kharkov, 1926) with the subtitle "Nenapečatennaja glava iz 'Konarmij'."

"Česniki." In *Krasnaja nov'*, No. 3 (April–May 1924).

"Posle boja." In *Prožektor*, No. 20 (Oct. 1924), with the subtitle "Iz knigi 'Konarmija'." Dated by the author "Galicija, September, 1920."

"Pesnja." In *Krasnaja nov'*, No. 3 (April 1925), under the title "Večer" and with the heading "Iz dnevnika." Under its present title in the first edition of *Konarmija* (Moscow, 1926). Dated by the author "Sokal', August, 1920."

"Syn rabbi." In *Krasnaja nov'*, No. 1 (Jan.–Feb. 1924).

"Argamak." In *Novyj mir*, No. 3 (March 1932), with the subtitle "Nenapečatennaja glava iz 'Konarmii'." Beginning with the fifth edition of *Konarmija* (Moscow–Leningrad, 1931) this story closes the book. Dated by the author "1924–1930."

### Odesskie rasskazy

"Korol'." First published in the Odessa newspaper *Morjak*, No. 100 (June 23, 1921). Again in *Izvestija Odesskogo gubispolkoma*, No. 1–3 (May 14–16, 1923) and in *Lef*, No. 4 (Aug.–Dec. 1923). Dated by the author "1923."

"Kak èto delalos' v Odesse." In the literary supplement to the paper *Izvestija Odesskogo gubispolkoma*, No. 1025 (May 5, 1923) and in *Lef*, No. 4 (Aug.–Dec. 1923). Dated by the author "1923."

"Otec." In *Krasnaja nov'*, No. 5 (Aug.–Sept. 1924), with the subtitle "Iz Odesskix rasskazov." Dated by the author "1924."

"Ljubka Kazak." In *Krasnaja nov'*, No. 5 (Aug.–Sept. 1924) with the subtitle "Iz Odesskix rasskazov." Again in the Odessa magazine *Škval*, No. 1 (Sept. 1924). Dated by the author "1924."

### Independent Stories

(Listed alphabetically, following the Russian alphabet; those entries followed by an asterisk indicate stories long out of print and difficult to obtain.)

"Bagrat-Ogly i glaza ego byka." In the Odessa magazine *Siluèty*, No. 12 (1923), under the heading "Iz knigi 'Oforty'." Again in *Krasnaja nov'*, No. 4 (1924). Recently republished in the Tashkent magazine *Zvezda vostoka* (March 1967).*

"Vdoxnovenie." In the magazine *Žurnal žurnalov*, No. 7 (1917), under the heading "Moi listki." Again recently in *Znamja*, No. 8 (Aug. 1964), 122–24.

"Večer u imperatricy." In the Odessa magazine *Siluèty*, No. 1 (1922), under the heading "Iz Petersburgskogo dnevnika." Again in *Znamja*, No. 8 (Aug. 1964), 135–37. Dated by the author "1922." A considerably reworked version of this story is found as part of the later story "Doroga."

"V podvale." In *Novyj mir*, No. 10 (Oct. 1931), with the subtitle "Iz knigi 'Istorija moej golubjatni'." Dated by the author "1930."

"V ščeločku." In the Odessa magazine *Siluèty*, No. 12 (1923), and again in the anthology *Pereval*, No. 6 (Moscow–Leningrad, 1928). Also in the Russian-language magazine *Opyty*, No. 3 (New York, 1954).

"Gapa Gužva." In *Novyj mir*, No. 10 (1931). Recently republished in *Znamja*, No. 8 (Aug. 1964), 137–41, under the heading "Pervaja glava iz knigi 'Velikaja krinica'." Dated by the author "Spring, 1930." This story was intended as part of a projected novel or connected cycle of stories about collectivization upon which Babel worked in the thirties. Another story, "Kolyvuška," shares several characters with this story and is apparently a part of the same planned work.

"Griščuk." In *Izvestija Odesskogo gubispolkoma* (Feb. 23, 1923). Dated by the author "16 July, 1920." Recently republished in the Tashkent magazine *Zvezda vostoka* (March 1967). Thematically related to the *Red Cavalry* stories, this story was never included in the completed collection.

"Gjui de Mopassan." In the magazine *30 dnej*, No. 6 (June 1932).

"Dezertir." In the Odessa magazine *Lava*, No. 1 (June 1920).*

"Detstvo u babuški." First published in *Literaturnoe nasledstvo*, (Moscow, 1965), LXXIV, 483–88. Dated by the author "Saratov, 12.11.15."

"Di Grasso." In *Ogonek*, No. 23 (Aug. 1937).

"Doroga." In *30 dnej*, No. 3 (March 1932). Dated by the author "1920–1930." The story represents a greatly reworked version of the earlier "Večer u imperatricy."

"Zakat." First published in the magazine *Literaturnaja Rossija*, No. 47 (Nov. 1964) and also, in truncated form, in the New York Russian-language newspaper *Novoe russkoe slovo* (Dec. 10, 1964), under the heading "Neizvestnyj rasskaz I. Babelja." This story, belonging probably to the period 1924–25, is closely related to the cycle of Odessa stories and served as the basis for Babel's later play of the same title.

"Ivan-da-Mar'ja." In *30 dnej*, No. 4 (1932). Dated by the author "1920–1928."

"Iisusov grex." In the anthology *Krug*, No. 3 (Moscow, 1924). Dated by the author "1922." For another variant of the same tale see the story entitled "Skazka pro babu."

"Il'ja Isaakovič i Margarita Prokof'evna." In *Letopis'*, No. 11 (Nov. 1916). Again in *Znamja*, No. 8 (Aug. 1964), 124–26.

"Istorija moej golubjatni." In *Krasnaja nov'*, No. 4 (May 1925). Dated by the author "1925." This was the first story of Babel's autobiographical cycle to appear and was meant to provide a title for the cycle as a whole. Three other tales were to be added in time: "Pervaja ljubov'," "V podvale," and "Probuždenie." The much earlier story "Detstvo u babuški" is also thematically related to the autobiographical cycle.

"Ix bylo devjat'." This story has never been published in the Soviet Union, but an English translation, "And Then There Were None," by Max Hayward appeared in *Dissent* (Nov.–Dec. 1966). A note provided by Nathalie Babel says that the story was written in 1923. It belongs to the *Red Cavalry* group, but was never included in the completed cycle, no doubt because Babel reworked the same material for the story "Èskadronnyj Trunov." Recently the story has been published in Russian, in the New York magazine *Novyj žurnal*, No. 95 (June 1969), 16–20.

"Karl-Jankel'." In the magazine *Zvezda*, No. 7 (July 1931).

"Kvaker." In the Odessa magazine *Lava*, No. 1 (June 1920).*

"Kolyvuška." This story remained unpublished in the Soviet Union until it appeared in the March 1967 issue of the magazine *Zvezda vostoka*. It appeared in Russian earlier in the émigré magazine *Vozdušnye puti*, No. 3 (New York, 1963), 45–51. Dated by the author "Spring, 1930," and subtitled "Iz knigi 'Velikaja Starica'." It is evidently a part of the same planned work to which the story "Gapa Gužva" belongs, although the title of the projected book is slightly different in each case. The two stories are apparently the only segments of the projected book to have survived.

"Konec bogadel'ni." In *30 dnej*, No. 1 (Jan. 1932), with the subtitle

"Iz 'Odesskix rasskazov'." Dated by the author "1920–1929."
"Konec sv. Ipatija." In the newspaper *Pravda*, No. 175 (Aug. 3, 1924), under the heading "Iz dnevnika." Again in *30 dnej*, No. 5 (May 1925). Dated by the author "1925."
"Linija i cvet." In *Krasnaja nov'*, No. 7 (Dec. 1923), with the subtitle "Istinnoe proisšestvie," under the heading "Miniatjury."
"Mama, Rimma i Alla." In *Letopis'*, No. 11 (1916). Again in *Znamja*, No. 8 (Aug. 1964), 126–31.
"Moj pervyj gonorar." This story was published for the first time in the Soviet Union in *Zvezda vostoka* (March 1967), but it appeared in Russian earlier in the émigré journal *Vozdušnye puti*, No. 3 (New York, 1963), 35–44. Dated by the author "1922–1928." The story represents a reworked version of the earlier story "Spravka."
"Na pole česti." In the Odessa magazine *Lava*, No. 1 (June 1920). Again in the émigré magazine *Vozušnye puti*, No. 3 (New York, 1963), 52–53.
"Neft'." In the newspaper *Večernjaja Moskva*, No. 37 (3066) (Feb. 14, 1934).
"Pervaja ljubov'." In the anthology *Krasnaja nov'*, No. 1 (Moscow–Leningrad, 1925). Dated by the author "1925."
"Poceluj." In *Krasnaja nov'*, No. 7 (July 1937). Although connected with the *Red Cavalry* cycle in theme, the story was never included in the completed version of the book.
"Probuždenie." In the magazine *Molodaja gvardija*, No. 17–18 (Sept. 1931), with the subtitle "Iz knigi 'Istorija moej golubjatni'." Dated by the author "1930."
"Semejstvo papaši Maresko." In the Odessa magazine *Lava*, No. 1 (June 1920).*
"Skazka pro babu." In the Odessa magazine *Siluèty*, No. 8–9 (1923). Again in *Krasnaja nov'*, No. 4 (1924). For another variant of the same tale see the story entitled "Iisusov grex."
"Spravka." This story was first published in the Soviet Union in *I. Babel': Izbrannoe* (Kemerovo, 1966). At least two earlier English translations exist: "A Reply to an Inquiry," published in *International Literature*, Moscow, 1937 (and the same translation in *The Noble Savage*, No. 3, New York, 1961), and also Max Hayward's translation, "Answer to an Inquiry" (in *Isaac Babel: The Lonely*

*Years*, New York, 1964.) The story represents an early version of "Moj pervyj gonorar."

"Staratel'naja ženščina." In the anthology *Pereval*, No. 6 (Moscow–Leningrad, 1928).

"Sud." In the magazine *Ogonek*, No. 23 (Aug. 1938), under the heading "Iz zapisnoj knižki."

"Sulak." In the magazine *Molodoj kolxoznik*, No. 6 (June 1937). Again in *Znamja*, No. 8 (Aug. 1964), 144–45.

"Ty promorgal, kapitan!" In the magazine *Krasnaja niva*, No. 39 (Sept. 1924). Again in *Krasnaja nov'*, No. 3 (April 1925), under the heading "Iz dnevnika." Dated by the author "1924."

"U bat'ki našego Maxno." In *Krasnaja nov'*, No. 4 (1924). Dated by the author "1923."

"Ulica Dante." In *30 dnej*, No. 3 (March 1934).

"Froim Grač." First published in the Russian-language magazine *Vozdušnye puti*, No. 3 (New York, 1963), 29–34. In the Soviet Union it was first published in *Znamja*, No. 8 (Aug. 1964), 141–45. The story was most likely completed in 1933.

"Xodja." In the Odessa magazine *Siluèty*, No. 6–7 (1923), with the subtitle "Iz knigi 'Peterburg 1918g.' " Again in the anthology *Pereval*, No. 6 (Moscow-Leningrad, 1928).*

"Šabos-naxmu." In the Petrograd newspaper *Večernjaja Moskva* (March 16, 1918) with the subtitle "Rasskaz iz cikla 'Geršele'." Again in *Znamja*, No. 8 (Aug. 1964), 132–35.

### Reminiscences

"Bagrickij." In the anthology *Èduard Bagrickij* (Moscow, 1936).

"Načalo." First published under this title in *Literaturnaja gazeta*, No. 33 (June 18, 1937). Under the title "Iz vospominanij" in *Pravda*, No. 213 (June 18, 1937). Retitled "Načalo," it was published in the book *God XXI, al'manax 13* (Moscow, 1938). The basis for the piece was an interview Babel gave to *Komsomol'skaja pravda*. A transcript of the interview was published in that paper, No. 172 (July 27, 1936), under the title "Učitel'." This first variant differs slightly from the others.

## Plays

"Zakat." In *Novyj mir*, No. 2 (Feb. 1928). Again, with differences, in a separate edition (Moscow–Leningrad, 1928).

"Marija." Published in full for the first time in the magazine *Teatr i dramaturgija*, No. 3 (March 1935). Excerpts had appeared earlier in the newspapers *Literaturnyj Leningrad*, No. 19 (April 26, 1935), and *Literaturnaja gazeta*, No. 14 (March 10, 1935). The play was published in a separate edition (Moscow, 1935).

## Screenplays

Over a period of some fourteen years, from about 1925 to the very end of his career in 1939, Babel spent a great deal of time and effort working on screenplays. Although at times he complained of being distracted thereby from his "true work," he evinced a genuine and lasting interest in the film form. In addition to writing several original scenarios, he adapted for the screen a number of works by other writers. The quality of his film work was considered so high that he acquired the reputation of a film "doctor" and was frequently called upon to rewrite the scripts of films that were in trouble.

The list below makes no claim to completeness, but it may give some idea of just how great Babel's involvement in film work was. Unfortunately, very little of it has been published (only the first three entries represent published material), and those pieces that have been printed are for the most part difficult to obtain.

A. PUBLISHED SCREEN WRITING (arranged chronologically):

"Bluždajuščie zvezdy." Excerpts from this screenplay based upon a Sholom Aleichem story were published in the Odessa magazine *Škval*, No. 3 (1925) and in *30 dnej*, No. 4 (1926). The full scenario (with a preface by the author) was published in Moscow in 1926.

"Benja Krik." First published in *Krasnaja nov'*, No. 6 (1926). Again, in a separate edition, Moscow, 1926. Babel's stories "Korol' " and "Kak èto delalos' v Odesse" served as a basis for the film which was made in Odessa in 1926 and shown the following year.

"Staraja ploščad', 4." Published in *Iskusstvo kino*, XXXIII, No. 5 (1963). This very interesting original screenplay, which Babel completed shortly before his arrest, is probably the last thing he wrote.

Lost since 1939, the typewritten manuscript was rediscovered after some 20 years and published for the first time in 1963.

B. UNPUBLISHED SCREEN WRITING (arranged as far as possible chronologically):

"Sol'." In 1925 Babel wrote a scenario based on his story of the same name, and the film was apparently made in Odessa at that time.

"Evrejskoe sčast'e." A film adapted from Sholom Aleichem. For Babel's contribution see N. Nikitin, "O nadpisjax," *Sovetskij èkran*, No. 6 (1926), 7, and A. Sobol', "Evrejskoe sčast'e," *Sovetskij èkran*, No. 1 (1926), 12–14.

"Kitajskaja mel'nica." This original film comedy was written by Babel in 1927 and actually made in 1928.

"Džimmi Xiggins." Sometime in the twenties Babel worked on this scenario, based on a novel by Upton Sinclair.

Babel also participated in the making of a documentary film about his native city, Odessa.

"Azef." According to his second wife, Babel actually completed a scenario in the early thirties on the socialist revolutionary, terrorist leader, and infamous double agent, Y. F. Azev.

"Konarmija." It is possible that Babel worked on a screenplay based upon his stories some time in the early thirties; the evidence is inconclusive, and the work, if actually undertaken, in any case remained unfinished. If he did work on such a screenplay it was probably while he was abroad and under contract with a French film company.

"Duma pro Opanasa." In 1934 Babel spent considerable time working on a scenario based on this narrative poem by his friend, the poet E. Bagritsky.

"Letčiki." In 1934–35, Babel participated in the creation of this film, considered one of the finest of that era.

"Bežin lug." In 1936 Babel rewrote another writer's scenario for this film based on a Turgenev story. The film's director was Sergei Eisenstein, and both he and Babel were subjected to some severe criticism for the film's ideological errors. Ultimately the film was banned.

"V tjur'me u Petljury." A segment from the scenario based upon the novel *Kak zakaljalas' stal'* by N. Ostrovsky. For some comment on Babel's contribution see "Nemcy na Ukraine," *Literaturnaja gazeta* (Oct. 30, 1938).

Shortly before his arrest in 1939, Babel was working on a film devoted to the life of his literary mentor and protector Maxim Gorky. The film was apparently never completed.

## Newspaper Articles

Babel's journalistic writings, while not of great quantity, are extremely interesting, and to a degree helpful in understanding his other work. He began his writing career, it should be remembered, as a reporter, and more than once in the years that followed was a regular contributor to newspapers. Indeed, it was while serving as a war correspondent attached to the First Cavalry Army that he collected the material for *Red Cavalry*. But it is not only as a source of subject matter that Babel found his reportorial activity fruitful; his very style and form—terse, impressionistic, detached, often displaying qualities characteristic of documentary writing—owe something to his experience as a reporter. Furthermore, it is in some of his newspaper pieces (and interviews) that Babel gives expression to the ideas and attitudes that underlie his aesthetic practice.

In addition to essays, feuilletons, speeches, and articles, this section includes such things as published transcripts of the author's remarks on literary matters made in appearances before writers' groups. It should be noted that the list given here does not pretend to be exhaustive or bibliographically complete. The sources for this information are varied and sometimes contain only references to the titles of essays, with little or no bibliographical documentation. The order of this listing is chronological, based upon dates of publication.

At the very beginning of his career Babel published a number of essays and feuilletons in a weekly magazine called *Žurnal žurnalov*. Under the heading "Moi listki" and signed "Bab-Èl'," these pieces appeared in the winter of 1916–17. They include:

"Publičnaja biblioteka." *Žurnal žurnalov*, No. 48 (1916), 11–12. Reprinted in *Literaturnaja Rossija* (March 13, 1964) and in the New York émigré newspaper, *Novoe russkoe slovo* (March 29, 1964).

"Devjat'." *Žurnal žurnalov*, No. 49 (1916), 7. Reprinted in *Literaturnaja Rossija* (March 13, 1964) and in the New York émigré newspaper, *Novoe russkoe slovo* (March 29, 1964).

"Vdoxnovenie." *Žurnal žurnalov*, No. 7 (1917), 8–9. Again in *Znamja*, No. 8 (Aug. 1964). This piece, included in several recent collections of Babel's work, has also been listed in the stories section of this bibliography.

"Odessa." *Žurnal žurnalov*, No. 51 (1917), 4–5. This piece still has not been republished in the Soviet Union.

In the period from March to July 1918, Babel published a number of essays in the Petrograd Social-Democratic newspaper *Novaja žizn'* in which Gorky played a leading role as contributor and guiding spirit. Babel's pieces appeared under the general heading "Dnevnik" and were signed "Bab-Èl'." They include:

"Pervaja pomošč." *Novaja žizn'* (March 9, 1918).

"Bitye." *Novaja žizn'* (March 29, 1918).

"Nedonoski." *Novaja žizn'*, No. 51.

"Dvorec materinstva." *Novaja žizn'*, No. 56 (271) (March 31/18, 1918).

"Èvakuirovannye." *Novaja žizn'*, No. 66 (April 13, 1918).

"Mozaika." *Novaja žizn'*, No. 73.

"Zaveden'ice." *Novaja žizn'*, No. 76.

"Slepye." *Novaja žizn'*, No. 94.

"Večer." *Novaja žizn'* (May 21, 1918).

"Listki ob Odesse." In the Petrograd newspaper *Večernjaja zvezda*, No. 38 (March 21, 1918).

"Ee den'." In the military newspaper *Krasnyj kavalerist*, No. 235 (Sept. 19, 1920). Again in *Literaturnoe nasledstvo* (Moscow, 1965), LXXIV, 488. This appears to be the only extant piece of journalism dating from Babel's cavalry days. The essay was written under the pseudonym of "Ljutov," which is the same name that Babel gives to his narrator in *Red Cavalry*.

In 1922, again under the pseudonym "Ljutov," Babel published a number of essays in the Tiflis newspaper *Zarja vostoka*. Precise bibliographical information is unavailable, but the essays published at that time (and now unavailable) include: "V dome otdyxa"; "Bez rodiny"; "Pis'ma iz Adžarii"; "Abxazskie pis'ma"; "Pis'mo iz Batuma" (this, with the additional title " 'Kamo' i 'Šaumjan'," was republished in *I. Babel': Izbrannoe*, Kemerovo, 1966); and "V čakve" (this piece was published again in the Odessa *Izvestija*, March 25, 1923).

"Pisatel' I. Babel' v 'Smene'." In the magazine *Smena*, No. 17–18 (1932). A report of the writer's discussion with the journal's writing staff. Babel talked about his story "Guy de Maupassant."

"Ja rad zakrepit' našu družbu—Babel' u komsomol'cev." In *Literaturnaja gazeta*, No. 40 (Sept. 5, 1932). Another account of Babel's meeting with the Smena staff.

"I. Babel', Na Zapade." In the newspaper *Večernjaja Moskva*, No. 213 (Sept. 6, 1933).

"Glazami pisatelja. I.È. Babel' o zagraničnoj poezdke." In *Literaturnyj Leningrad* (Sept. 26, 1933). Babel writing on his trip to France, on French and Soviet literature.

"Rabota nad rasskazom." In *Smena*, No. 6 (June 1934), with the subtitle "Iz besedy s načinajuščimi pisateljami" and under the heading "Laboratorija tvorčestva." Again in *I. Babel': Izbrannoe* (Moscow, 1966).

"Reč na Pervom Vsesojuznom c"ezde sovetskix pisatelej." With the title "Sodejstvovat' pobede bol'ševistskogo vkusa." In *Literaturnaja gazeta*, No. 110 (Aug. 24, 1934). Under the title "Pošlost'— vot naš vrag," in *Pravda*, No. 234 (Aug. 25, 1934). The *Pravda* text differs significantly from the other version. The version from *Literaturnaja gazeta* has been republished in *I. Babel': Izbrannoe* (Moscow, 1966).

"Pisateli—Kirovu." A collection (Moscow, 1934). Babel, with other writers, is said to have contributed to the article "V ljuboj moment my gotovy smenit' pero na vintovku."

"Vstreča s I. Babelem." *Literaturnaja gazeta* (May 5, 1935). On Babel's appearance before the editorial board of *Dve pjatiletki* on April 26, 1935, in the Moscow House of Writers.

"Širokim frontom protiv fašizma. Tt. I. Babel', V. Kiršon i I. Luppol o Kongresse zaščity kul'tury." In *Literaturnaja gazeta*, No. 45 (Aug. 15, 1935), the author of the article: Del'man.

"O rabotnikax novoj kul'tury." Published in *Literaturnaja gazeta*, No. 19 (March 31, 1936), with the subtitle "Iz reči tov. I. Babelja." On Babel's appearance at an All-Moscow gathering of writers held on March 21, 1936, in connection with the *Pravda* articles attacking formalism and naturalism. Republished in *I. Babel': Izbrannoe* (Moscow, 1966).

"Vystuplenie Babelja na večere, posvjaščennom 10-letiju so dnja smerti D. Furmanova." In *Moskva*, No. 4 (1936).

"Putešestvie vo Franciju." In the magazine *Pioner*, No. 3 (March 1937). Again in *I. Babel': Izbrannoe* (Moscow, 1966).

"M. Gor'kij." In the magazine *SSSR na strojke*, No. 4 (April 1937). A brief literary portrait in a special number of the magazine. Babel was also responsible for the plan and layout of the issue. Republished in *I. Babel': Izbrannoe* (Moscow, 1966).

"Literaturnye mečtanija." In *Literaturnaja gazeta* (Dec. 31, 1938). About the necessity for a complete edition of the works of Tolstoy and about his interest in the works of that writer.

"V Odesse každyj junoša." The article was written in 1923 (as an introduction for a planned miscellany), but was first published only in *Literaturnaja gazeta* (Jan. 1, 1962). Again in *I. Babel': Izbrannoe* (Moscow, 1966).

"O tvorčeskom puti pisatelja." In the magazine *Naš sovremennik*, No. 4 (1964), 96–100. On Sept. 28, 1937, at the building of the Union of Soviet Writers, an evening was devoted to the works of Babel. The author read two of his stories ("Di Grasso" and "Answer to an Inquiry") and then answered questions. The text published here is an edited transcript of Babel's remarks.

## Miscellaneous Writings

"Avtobiografija." First published in the collection *Pisateli. Avtobiografii i portrety sovremennyx russkix prozaikov*, ed. Vl. Lidin (Moscow, 1926). Again in *I. È. Babel': Stat'i i materialy* (Leningrad, 1928). Dated by the author "Sergiev Posad. November, 1924."

"Dnevnik." During the 1920 Polish campaign Babel kept a diary, the material of which, reworked and transformed, played a large part in the construction of *Konarmija*. Unfortunately, not all of the diary has survived. The entries begin with June 3, 1920, and end with Sept. 15, 1920, but a large section in the middle (notebook pp. 69–89, covering the period from June 6 to July 11) is missing. The surviving portions, in the possession of the writer's widow, A. N. Pirožkova, have not been published in full, but they are discussed and extensively quoted in several recent articles by Soviet scholars: I. A. Smirin: "Na puti k 'Konarmii'," *Literaturnoe nasledstvo* (Moscow, 1965), LXXIV, 474–82. Diary excerpts are also quoted in the notes accompanying Babel's plans and drafts, printed in the same number of *Literaturnoe nasledstvo*, 497–99. Also see L. Livšic, "Materialy k tvorčeskoj biografii I. Babelja," *Voprosy literatury*, No. 4 (1964), 110–35.

"Iz planov i nabroskov k 'Konarmii'." In *Literaturnoe nasledstvo* (Moscow, 1965), LXXIV, LXXIV, 490–99.

"Na biržu truda!" In *Ogonek*, No. 9 (1927). This is the ninth chapter of a novel by 25 writers, entitled *Bol'šie požary*.

*Kolja Topuz.* Over a number of years (in the late twenties and early thirties) Babel worked on (and is said to have completed) this novel about the adventures of a Benja Krik-like bandit. He is supposed to have shown the gradual remaking, under Soviet conditions, of his hero, who becomes successively a worker on a kolkhoz and a Donbass miner.

"Evrejka." This unfinished prose work (novel?), written apparently in the late twenties or early thirties, remains unpublished in the Soviet Union. Both a Russian text and an English translation have recently appeared in the United States: the former in the New York Russian-language magazine *Novyj žurnal*, No. 95 (June 1969), 5–16, and the latter in *Isaac Babel: You Must Know Everything, Stories 1915–1937*, trans. by Max Hayward, ed. and with notes by Nathalie Babel (New York, 1969), 163–84.

A novel on the Cheka (Soviet secret police). There is frequent reference in the literature on Babel to novels he is said to have worked on or completed. Mention has been made of two of these projects (see the two entries immediately above, and for information on a projected novel about collectivization see entries for the stories "Gapa Gužva" and "Kolyvuška"). Babel also is supposed to have worked on a novel about the Cheka. That he was fascinated with the subject there can be no doubt; early in his career he may have worked for the Cheka and his interest in that organization is reflected in several stories (e.g., "Večer u imperatricy," "Doroga," "Sulak," and "Froim Grač"). Dm. Furmanov, in his diary (entry of Jan. 24, 1926), tells of Babel's intention to write a book on the subject. According to Furmanov, Babel considered this a major work. How much of such a novel he may have completed it is impossible to say, since apparently no trace of it remains. Babel himself speaks of his efforts in the long form as unproductive, and it may be that his work never progressed much beyond the stage of preliminary notes and plans.

Letters. There is no good edition of Babel's letters and little likelihood of one soon since they are scattered in various hands both in and outside of the Soviet Union. Babel's first wife is said by her daughter Nathalie to have destroyed all of the letters she received from her husband shortly before she died, but Babel's correspondence with other members of his family living outside of the Soviet Union has been published, albeit in English translation. Only a small sampling of letters has been published in the Soviet Union, and these mostly in the form of edited excerpts. The most significant collections published to date are:

*Isaac Babel: The Lonely Years 1925–1939.* Unpublished stories and private correspondence, ed. and with an introduction by Nathalie Babel, trans. into English by Andrew R. MacAndrew (New York, 1964). Excerpts (in the original Russian) from some of the same letters may be found in the entry below.

"Vyderžki iz pisem I.È. Babelja k materi i sestre." In the New York magazine *Vozdušnye puti,* No. 3 (1963), 101–15.

"Iz pisem k druz'jam." In *Znamja,* No. 8 (Aug. 1964), 146–65.

The section "Pis'ma" in the recent edition *I. Babel': Izbrannoe* (Moscow, 1966).

Babel also worked as editor and translator of works of French and Jewish literature (see *Isaac Babel: The Lonely Years,* letter of March 1, 1936, p. 302, where Babel speaks of editing the works of Sholom Aleichem; and also biographical note in *Russkie Sovetskie*

*Pisateli–Prozaiki,* bibliografičeskij ukazatel' [Leningrad, 1959], I, 104).

## II. Major Editions and Collections of Babel's Works

Between 1925, the year his first book appeared, and 1966 there have been some 30 separate Soviet editions of Babel's works. Most of these were issued during the author's lifetime, and they give eloquent testimony to his lasting popularity. It will be noted, however, that this popularity came to an abrupt, if artificially induced, end in the late thirties when Babel's name was quietly removed from the official history of Soviet literature. Some 20 years separate the last edition published during the author's lifetime and the next; in fact, only three editions have appeared since the author's death: one in 1957 after the so-called "thaw," which permitted Babel's partial and posthumous "rehabilitation," and two in 1966. All three of these recent editions, as well as some of the earlier ones, were edited in accordance with the vagaries of Soviet censorship: sometimes for reasons of a political nature, sometimes as a result of the Soviet anti-pornography syndrome.

*Rasskazy* (Moscow, 1925). This is the first separately issued Babel collection and the first appearance in book form of any of the *Red Cavalry* stories. It contains: "Pan Apolek," "Put' v Brody," "Učenie o tačanke," "Kladbišče v Kozine," and "Žizneopisanie Pavičenki, Matveja Rodionyča."

*Ljubka Kazak–Rasskazy* (Moscow, 1925). Contents: "Ljubka Kazak," "Otec," and "Èskadronny Trunov."

*Rasskazy* (Moscow–Leningrad, 1925). Contents: "Korol'," "Kak èto delalos' v Odesse," "Otec," "Iisusov grex," "Linija i cvet," "Pis'mo," "Smert' Dolgušova," "Saška Xristos," "Sol'," and "Zamost'e."

*Istorija moej golubjatni–Rasskazy* (Moscow–Leningrad, 1926). Contents: "Istorija moej golubjatni," "Pervaja ljubov'," "Ljubka Kazak," "Ševelev" (a *Konarmija* story; its title was later changed to "Vdova"), "Konec sv. Ipatija," "U bat'ki našego Maxno," and "Ty promorgal, kapitan!"

*Konarmija* (Moscow–Leningrad, 1926). This is the first full edition, containing 34 stories. There were eight separate editions of *Kon-*

*armija*, the eighth and last (illustrated) in 1933; it was also published in later editions of collected works. The first edition contained all of the stories now found in the cycle except "Argamak," and in the traditional sequence established by Babel himself.

*Rasskazy* (second edition; Moscow–Leningrad, 1927). Contents: "Korol'," "Kak èto delalos' v Odesse," "Otec," "Ljubka Kazak," "Iisusov grex," "Linija i cvet," "Istorija moej golubjatni," "Pervaja ljubov'," "Konec sv. Ipatija," "U bat'ki našego Maxno," and "Ty promorgal, kapitan!"

*Konarmija* (fifth and sixth edition; Moscow–Leningrad, 1931). This edition contains the same 34 stories as above, but also adds the important story "Argamak," which brought the cycle to its final form.

*Odesskie rasskazy* (Moscow–Leningrad, 1931). Contents: "Korol'," "Kak èto delalos' v Odesse," "Otec," "Ljubka Kazak," "Zakat (p'esa)," "Iisusov grex," "Istorija moej golubjatni," "Pervaja ljubov'," "Konec sv. Ipatija," "U bat'ki našego Maxno," and "Ty promorgal, kapitan!"

*Rasskazy* (Moscow, 1932). Contents same as above, with the addition of: "Probuždenie," "V podvale," "Karl Jankel'," and "Konec bogadel'ni."

*Rasskazy* (Moscow, 1934). This edition bears the marks of political censorship; in particular, references to Trotsky were expunged from the text. Contents: "Konarmija" (all 35 stories); "Odesskie rasskazy: "Korol'," "Kak èto delalos' v Odesse," "Otec," "Ljubka Kazak," *Zakat* (p'esa); Rasskazy: "Iisusuv grex," "Istorija moej golubjatni," "Pervaja ljubov'," "Konec sv. Ipatija," "U bat'ki našego Maxno," "Ty promorgal, kapitan!," "Karl Jankel'," "V podvale," "Probuždenie," " 'Ivan-da-Mar'ja,' " "Gjui de Mopassan," "Neft'," "Ulica Dante."

*Rasskazy* (Moscow, 1936). Contents same as above, with variations in texts.

*Izbrannye rasskazy* (Moscow, 1936). This 1936 edition of Babel stories was the last during the author's lifetime and the last until the recent editions of 1957 and 1966. Contents: "Smert' Dolgušova," "V podvale," "Gjui de Mopassan," and "Neft'."

*I. Babel': Izbrannoe*, Intro. by I. Èrenburg (Moscow, 1957). This edition, based according to the editors on the 1936 collection, contains: *Avtobiografija; Konarmija* (all 35 stories); *Odesskie rasskazy:*

"Korol'," "Kak èto delalos' v Odesse," "Otec," "Ljubka Kazak"; *Rasskazy* (16 stories in all), same as 1934 and 1936 editions above except that "U bat'ki našego Maxno" and " 'Ivan-da-Mar'ja' " are omitted and the following stories added: "Konec bogadel'ni," "Doroga," "Sud," "Di Grasso," "Poceluj." Several stories in this edition are severely edited. *Iz vospominanij*: "Bagrickij," "Načalo"; P'esy: *Zakat, Marija*.

*I. Babel': Izbrannoe* (Kemerovo, 1966). This edition is based on the 1957 edition and is similarly expurgated. It eliminates the two plays and the reminiscences of Gorky and Bagritsky that were included in the 1957 edition, but adds 12 stories that were not included in that edition. These are: "Froim Grač," "Il'ja Isaakovič i Margarita Prokof'evna," "Mama, Rimma i Alla," "Vdoxnovenie," "Šabos-naxmu," " 'Kamo' i 'Šaumjan,' " "Večer u imperatricy," "Linija i cvet," "Spravka," "Ivan-da-Mar'ja," "Gapa Gužva," "Sulak"; the edition also contains Babel's "Avtobiografija" and an introduction by I. Èrenburg that differs from the introduction he wrote for the 1957 edition.

*I. Babel': Izbrannoe* (Moscow, 1966). This latest edition is based according to the editors on the 1957 edition, and like it is an expurgated one. The edition is equipped with a good introduction by L. Poljak and with fairly extensive notes. Contents: *Avtobiografija, Konarmija* (35 stories), *Odesskie rasskazy, Rasskazy*—same as 1957 edition with the following stories added: "Il'ja Isaakovič i Margarita Prokof'evna," "Šabos-naxmu," "Linija i cvet," "Froim Grač," "Sulak," Vospominanija: "Bagrickij" and "Načalo"; P'esy: *Zakat* and *Marija*; Stat'i, Vystuplenija (six selections, including the 1934 speech at the Soviet Writers' Congress); Pis'ma (a selection of 32 letters to friends and professional associates). Though this is in most respects the fullest edition to date, it lacks some seven stories that were included in the edition that appeared in Kemerovo the same year (see above).

## III. TRANSLATIONS OF BABEL'S WORKS INTO ENGLISH

### Stories

*Isaac Babel—The Collected Stories*, ed. and trans. by Walter Morison with an introduction by Lionel Trilling (New York, 1955). This is the best and fullest edition of Babel's stories available in English.

It contains the *Red Cavalry* stories, the *Odessa Tales*, and a good selection of other stories.

*Isaac Babel—Lyubka the Cossack and Other Stories.* A New Translation with an Afterword by Andrew R. MacAndrew (New York, 1963). This collection contains different translations of most of the same stories available above, but has in addition three pieces not included in the other volume: "The Beginning" (Načalo), "The Road There" (Doroga), and "The Trial" (Sud). The translator ignores the sequence established by Babel for the *Red Cavalry* stories and with no explanation has omitted several stories and inserted another which Babel never made a part of the final book.

*Isaac Babel: The Lonely Years 1925–1939, Unpublished Stories and Private Correspondence*, ed. with an introduction by Nathalie Babel, and trans. by Andrew R. MacAndrew (New York, 1964). In addition to Babel's correspondence with relatives living outside the Soviet Union, this volume contains a translation of Babel's short autobiographical statement dated 1924, as well as the following eight stories not available in other collections: "Kolyvushka" (Kolyvuška), "Froim Grach" (Froim Grač), "Answer to an Inquiry" (Spravka), "My First Fee" (Moj pervyj gonorar), "Gapa Guzhva" (Gapa Gužva), "Mamma, Rimma and Alla" (Mama, Rimma i Alla), "Ilya Isaako-vich and Margarita Prokofievna" (Il'ja Isaakovič i Margarita Prokof'-evna), and "A Tale of a Woman" (Skazka pro babu). An appendix contains some journalistic pieces pertaining to and by Babel, including the author's 1934 Writers' Congress speech and a 1936 talk that he gave on Dm. Furmanov.

*Isaac Babel—Benya Krik, the Gangster and Other Stories*, ed. by Avraham Yarmolinsky (New York, 1948). This is a collection of 10 stories, all available in different translations in the two entries above.

*Isaac Babel: You Must Know Everything, Stories 1915–1937*, trans. by Max Hayward and ed. by Nathalie Babel (New York, 1969). This recent collection contains a number of stories and sketches (covering more than 20 years of Babel's career) that are otherwise unavailable, neither in the original Russian nor in translation. The book contains: "You Must Know Everything" (Detstvo u babuški); the 1916–17 pieces which appeared in *Žurnal žurnalov*: "The Public Library," "The Nine," "Odessa," "Inspiration"; "Shabos Nahamu"; six of the pieces published in 1918 in *Novaja žizn'*: "Mosaic," "A Fine Institution," "The Blind Men," "Evacuees," "Premature Babies," "The

Palace of Motherhood"; "On the Field of Honor"; "The Deserter"; "Old Maresco's Family"; "The Quaker"; "An Evening at the Empress's"; "The Chinaman" (Xodja); "Bagrat-Ogly and the Eyes of his Bull"; "Grishchuk"; "And Then There Were None" (Ix bylo devjat'); "Sunset" (the story, not the play); "A Hard-Working Woman"; "The Jewess"; and "Sulak." In addition to the stories, an appendix contains a translation of Babel's 1937 interview published in *Naš sovremennik* (No. 4, 1964) and reminiscences of Babel by Ehrenburg, Nikulin, Munblit, and Paustovsky.

### Plays

*Sunset* (Zakat), trans. by Raymond Rosenthal and Mirra Ginsburg. In *Noonday 3* (New York, 1960), 99–146.

*Maria*, trans. by Denis Caslon in *Tri-Quarterly*, No. 5 (1966), 7–36. Another translation by Michael Glenny and Harold Shukman has been published in *Three Soviet Plays*, ed. by Michael Glenny (Baltimore, 1966), 79–134.

*Benja Krik: A Film Novel*, trans. by I. Montagu and S. S. Nalbandov (London, 1935).

### IV. SECONDARY SOURCES

Alexandrova, V. *A History of Soviet Literature: 1917–1964 From Gorky to Solzhenitsyn* (New York, 1963).

Annenkov, Jurij. *Dnevnik moix vstreč*, I (New York, 1966).

Arnold, Matthew. "Hebraism and Hellenism," *The Portable Matthew Arnold*, ed. and with introductory notes by Lionel Trilling (New York, 1949), 557–73.

Arxipov, V. "Uroki," *Neva*, No. 6 (June 1958), 187–99.

Babel, Nathalie, ed. *Isaac Babel: The Lonely Years 1925–1939, Unpublished Stories and Private Correspondence*. Trans. from the Russian by Andrew R. MacAndrew and Max Hayward, ed. and with an Introduction by Nathalie Babel (New York, 1964).

Benni, Jak. "I. Babel'," *Pečat' i revoljucija*, No. 3 (1924), 135–39.

Blake, Patricia, and Max Hayward, eds. *Dissonant Voices in Soviet Literature* (New York, 1962).

Boguslavskij, A. O., and L. I. Timofeev, eds. *Russkaja sovetskaja literatura* (Moscow, 1963).

Bondarin, S. A. *Grozd' vinograda* (Moscow, 1964).

―――. "Razgovor so sverstnikom," *Naš sovremennik*, No. 5 (1962), 175–92.

Brewster, D. *East-West Passage: A Study in Literary Relationships* (London, 1954).

Brown, E. J. "Isaac Babel: Horror in a Minor Key," *Russian Literature Since the Revolution* (New York, 1963), 115–24.

Budennyj, S. "Babizm Babelja iz *Krasnoj Novi*," *Oktjabr'*, No. 3 (1924), 196–97.

―――. "Pis'mo Gor'komu," *Krasnaja gazeta* (Oct. 26, 1928).

―――. *Projdennyj put': Voennye memuary*, II (Moscow, 1965).

Burke, K. *The Rhetoric of Religion: Studies in Logology* (Boston, 1961).

Čalmaev, V. "Po povodu nekotoryx statej i predislovij," *Voprosy literatury*, No. 1 (Jan. 1958), 201.

Carlisle, O. A. *Voices in the Snow* (New York, 1962).

Choseed, B. "Jews in Soviet Literature," *Through the Glass of Soviet Literature: Views of Russian Society*, ed. by Ernest J. Simmons (New York, 1953), 110–58.

Čužak, N. "Udivljajsja, no ne podražaj," *Al'manax Proletkul'ta* (Moscow, 1925), 170–76.

Dymšic, A. "Publicističnost' i masterstvo kritiki," *Literaturnaja gazeta* (July 12, 1958).

Eisenstein, S. "A Course in Treatment," *Film Form: Essays in Film Theory*, ed. and trans. by Jay Leyda (New York, 1949), 84–107.

Eliade, M. *Cosmos and History* (New York, 1959).

―――. *The Sacred and The Profane* (New York, 1961).

Èrenburg, I. "Predislovie," *I. Babel': Izbrannoe* (Moscow, 1957), 5–10.

―――. "Predislovie," *I. Babel': Izbrannoe* (Kemerovo, 1966), 5–14.

―――. *Memoirs 1921–1941*, trans. by Tatania Shebunina and Yvonne Kapp (Cleveland, 1964).

―――. *People and Life 1891–1921*, trans. by Anna Bostock and Yvonne Kapp (New York, 1962).

Evgen'ev-Maksimov, V. "I. Babel'," *Očerk istorii novejšej literatury*, third ed. (Moscow–Leningrad, 1927), 290–95.

Falen, J. "A Note on the Fate of Isaak Babel'," *The Slavic and East European Journal*, XI, No. 4 (1967), 398–404.

Fanger, Donald. *Dostoevsky and Romantic Realism* (Cambridge, Mass., 1965).

Frolov, V. *Žanry sovetskoj dramaturgii* (Moscow, 1957).

Furmanov, Dmitri. *Sobranie sočinenij v četyrex tomax*, IV (Moscow, 1961).

Gext, S. "Povidat' by sprosit," *Naš sovremennik*, No. 4 (1959).

———. "U steny strastnogo monastyrja," *Naš sovremennik*, No. 4 (1959), 229–33.

Gorbačev, G. *Dva goda literaturnoj revoljucii* (Leningrad, 1926).

———. "O tvorčestve Babelja i po povodu nego," *Zvezda*, No. 4 (1925), 270–86.

Gor'kij, M. *O literature*, third ed. (Moscow, 1937).

———. "O tom, kak ja učilsja pisat'," *Gor'kij-Sobranie sočinenij* (Moscow, 1953), XXIV, 466–99.

Gukovskij, G. A. "Zakat," *Stat'i i materialy*, serija—Mastera sovremennoj literatury (Leningrad, 1928), 73–99.

Hayward, Max, and Leopold Labedz, eds. *Literature and Revolution in Soviet Russia 1917–1962* (London, 1963).

Howe, I. "The Right to Write Badly," *New Republic*, No. 133 (July 4, 1955), 16–18.

———. "The Genius of Isaac Babel," *The New York Review of Books* (Aug. 20, 1964), 14–15.

Hyman, S. E. "Identities of Isaac Babel," *The Hudson Review*, VIII, No. 4 (1956), 620–27.

Il'inskij, I. "Pravovye motivy v tvorčestve Babelja," *Krasnaja nov'*, No. 7 (July 27), 231–40.

Jakubovskij, G. "Iskusstvo Babelja," *Pisateli i kritika* (Moscow, 1926), 51–57.

———. "Iskusstvo Babelja," *Prožektor*, No. 19(65) (1925), 22–23.

Joyce, James. *A Portrait of the Artist as a Young Man* (New York, 1964).

Kaufmann, W., ed. and trans. *Basic Writings of Nietzsche* (New York, 1968).

———. *The Portable Nietzsche* (New York, 1954).

Kogan, P. *Literatura velikogo desjatiletija* (Moscow, 1927).

Kondjurina, E. "Ob osobennostjax tvorčeskogo metoda I. Babelja,"

*Naučnye trudy vyšego učebnogo zavedenija Litovskoj SSR,* No. 3 (Vilnius, 1962), 35–45.

Kruti, I. "Babel' i ego kritiki," *Škval,* No. 9 (Odessa, 1925), 13.

Kručenyx, A. *Zaumnyi jazyk u: Sejfullinoj, Vs. Ivanova, Leonova, Babelja, I. Sel'vinskogo, A. Veselogo i dr.* (Moscow, 1925).

Kunitz, J. *Russian Literature and the Jew* (New York, 1929).

Kuvanova, L. K. "Furmanov i Babel'," *Literaturnoe nasledstvo* (Moscow, 1965), LXXIV, 500–12.

Leiter, L. H. "A Reading of Isaac Babel's 'Crossing Into Poland'," *Studies in Short Fiction,* III (1965/66), 199–206.

Lelevič, S. *Na literaturnom postu* (Tver, 1924).

Levidov, M. Ju. "Bez gneva i pristrastija," *Prostye istiny.* (Moscow, 1927), 90–102.

Levin, D. *Stormy Petrel: The Life and Work of Maxim Gorky* (London, 1967).

Levin L. "Čelovečeskij materijal," *Zvezda,* No. 5 (1936), 236–38.

Lewisohn, L. "Russian Grotesques," *Saturday Review,* No. 38 (July 9, 1955), 11.

Ležnev, A. "I. Babel'," *Krasnaja niva,* No. 8 (1927), 22.

_____. "I. Babel' Zametki k vyxodu 'Konarmija'," *Pečat' i revoljucija,* No. 6 (1926), 82–86.

_____. "Literaturnye zametki," *Pečat' i revoljucija,* No. 4 (1925), 149–51.

Ležnev, I. "Novaja p'esa I. Babelja," *Teatr i dramaturgija,* No. 3 (1935), 46–51.

Lidin, V., ed. *Pisateli: avtobiografii i portrety sovremennyx russkix prozaikov* (Moscow, 1926).

*Literaturnoe nasledstvo. Gor'kij i sovetskie pisateli; neizdannaja perepiska,* LXX (Moscow, 1963).

*Literaturnoe nasledstvo. Iz tvorčeskogo nasledija sovetskix pisatelej,* LXXIV (Moscow, 1965).

Livšic, L. "I. Babel'. 'Staraja Ploščad' 4'," *Iskusstvo kino,* XXXIII, No. 5 (1963), 54–58.

_____. "Materialy k tvorčeskoj biografii I. Babelja," *Voprosy literatury,* VIII, No. 4 (1964), 110–35.

_____. "Vy, po suti, romantik . . ." (Gor'kij i Babel'), *Prapor* (Kharkov), No. 8 (1964), 95–98.

MacAndrew, A. "Afterword," *Ljubka the Cossack and Other Stories* (New York, 163), 271–85.
Mackail, J. W., trans. *Virgil's Works* (New York, 1950).
Maguire, R. A. *Red Virgin Soil: Soviet Literature in the 1920's* (Princeton, 1968).
Majzel', M. "Dragocennye oskolki," *Literaturnyj Leningrad* (Nov. 1, 1935).
Makarov, A. "Razgovor po povodu," *Znamja*, No. 4 (1958), 187–218.
Mallori, D. "Krik 'Beni Krika'," *Sovetskij èkran*, No. 7 (1927), 7.
Mandelstam, N. *Hope Against Hope: A Memoir* (New York, 1970).
Marcus, S. "The Stories of Isaac Babel," *Partisan Review*, XXII, No. 3 (Summer 1955), 400–11.
Matthewson, R. W., Jr. *The Positive Hero in Russian Literature* (New York, 1958).
Men'šoj, A. "O Babelje," *Žizn' iskusstva*, No. 1 (1925), 8–9.
Mirsky, D. S. *A History of Russian Literature*, ed. by Francis J. Whitfield (New York, 1960).
Moračevskij, N. Ja., ed. *Russkie sovetskie pisateli—bibliografičeskij ukazatel'*, I (Leningrad, 1959).
Munblit, G. "I. È. Babel'—iz vospominanij," *Znamja*, No. 8 (Aug. 1964), 166–74.
Murphy, A. B. "The Style of Isaac Babel," *Slavonic and East European Review*, XLIV, No. 103 (July 1966), 361–80.
Nikulin, L. V. "Gody našej žizni. I. Babel'," *Moskva*, No. 7 (1964), 182–87.
Novickij, P. I. "Babel'," *Stat'i i materialy*, serija—Mastera sovremennoj literatury (Leningrad, 1928), 45–69.
Paustovskij, K. "Neskol'ko slov o Babele: Memuary," *Nedelja*, No. 11–17 (Sept. 1966).
———. *Povest' o žizni* (Moscow, 1966).
———. *Vremja bol'šix ožidanij* (Odessa, 1961).
Percov, B. "Kakaja byla pogoda v èpoxu graždanskoj vojny?" *Novyj lef*, No. 7 (1927), 36–45.
———. *Pisatel' i novaja dejstvitel'nost'* (Moscow, 1958).
Piksanov, N. K. *Oblastnye kul'turnye gnezda* (Moscow–Leningrad, 1928).
Plotkin, L. "Tvorčestvo Babelja," *Oktjabr'*, No. 3 (1933), 174–84.
Poggioli, R. "Isaac Babel in Retrospect," *The Phoenix and the Spider* (Cambridge, Mass., 1957), 229–38.

Poljak, L. "Babel'—Novellist," *Izvestija akademii nauk SSSR*, serija —Literatury i jazyka, No. XXV (Moscow, 1966), 313–28.

————. "I. Babel'," in *I. Babel': Izbrannoe* (Moscow, 1966), 3–22.

————. "I. È. Babel'," *Istorija russkoj sovetskoj literatury v četyrex tomax* (Moscow, 1967), I, 343–69.

Poljanskij, V. "I. Babel'," *Voprosy sovremennoj kritiki* (Moscow–Leningrad, 1927), 278–96.

Polonskij, V. "Kritičeskie zametki o Babele," *Novyj mir*, No. 1 (1927), 197–216.

Popkin, H. "Stories for the Spirit of this Age," *Commonweal*, No. 62 (Aug. 26, 1955), 523–24.

Puškin, A. S. *Polnoe sobranie sočinenij*, VI (Moscow–Leningrad, 1937–49).

Rajsner, L. "Protiv literaturnogo banditizma," *Izbrannoe* (Moscow, 1965), 503–10.

Rosenthal, R. "The Fate of Isaac Babel, A Child of the Russian Emancipation," *Commentary*, No. 3 (Feb. 1947), 126–31.

Rževskij, L. "Babel'—stilist," *Vozdušnye puti*, No. 3 (New York, 1963), 217–41.

Sejfullina, L. *O literature* (Moscow, 1958).

————. *Izbrannye proizvedenija* (Moscow, 1958).

Sinkó, E. *Roman eines Romans: Moskauer Tagebuch* (Cologne, 1962).

Shestov, Lev. *Athens and Jerusalem*, trans. and with an introduction by Bernard Martin (New York, 1968).

Šklovskij, V. "Babel'—K vyxodu knig 'Konarmija', 'Istorija moej golubjatni' i drugix," *Naša gazeta* (June 12, 1926).

————. "I. Babel', kritičeskij romans," *Lef*, No. 5, kn. 2 (1924), 152–55.

————. "Jugo-Zapad," *Literaturnaja gazeta* (Jan. 14, 1933).

————. "O Babele," ˇZili—byli (Moscow, 1964), 390–93.

————. "O ljudjax, kotorye idut po odnoj i toj že doroge i ob ètom ne znajut. Konec barokko," *Literaturnaja gazeta* (July 17, 1932).

————. "O prošlom i nastojaščem," *Znamja*, No. 11 (1937), 278–88.

————. *Xudožestvennaja proza* (Moscow, 1959).

Slonim, Marc, *Modern Russian Literature. From Chekhov to the Present* (New York, 1953).

————. *Soviet Russian Literature—Writers and Problems* (New York, 1964).

Smirin, I. A. "Na puti k 'Konarmii', literaturnye iskanija Babelja," *Literaturnoe nasledstvo* (Moscow, 1965), LXXIV, 467–82.

*Sovetskie pisateli, Avtobiografii v dvux tomax*, I (Moscow, 1959).

Stepanov, N. "Novella Babelja," *I. È. Babel'—Stat'i i materialy*, serija—Mastera sovremennoj literatury (Leningrad, 1928), 11–41.

Strelec (M. Stoljarov). "Pis'ma o sovremennoj literature: Dvulikij Janus (Babel' i Seifullina)," *Rossija*, No. 5 (1925), 290–95.

Terras, V. "Line and Color: The Structure of I. Babel's Short Stories in *Red Cavalry*," *Studies in Short Fiction*, III (1965/66), 141–56.

Tertz, A. *On Socialist Realism* (New York, 1960).

Timofeev, L. *Sovetskaja literatura* (Moscow, 1964).

Trilling, L. Introduction, *Isaac Babel, The Collected Stories*, ed. and trans. by Walter Morison (New York, 1955), 9–37.

Txorževskij, I. *Russkaja literatura* (Paris, 1946).

Utechin, S. V. *Concise Encyclopedia of Russia* (London, 1961).

Van der Eng, J. "La description poetique chez Babel," *Dutch Contributions to the Fifth International Congress of Slavicists* (The Hague, 1963), 79–92.

Vešnev, V. "Poèzija banditizma," *Molodaja gvardija*, No. 7–8 (1924), 274–80.

Vinogradov, I. *Bor'ba za stil'* (Leningrad, 1937).

Voronskij, A. *Literaturno-kritičeskie stat'i* (Moscow, 1963).

Zavalishin, V. *Early Soviet Writers* (New York, 1958).

# INDEX